KEEPING THE FAITH

*Reflections on Politics & Christianity
in the Era of Trump & Beyond*

Edited by Jonathan P. Walton,
Suzie Lahoud, & Sy Hoekstra

KTF Press LLC
Middletown, DE

Grateful acknowledgement is made to the following for permission to reprint previously published material:

Christianity Today: "Speak Truth to Trump" by Andy Crouch, copyright © 2016 by Andy Crouch. Reprinted by permission of Christianity Today Magazine.

The Dispatch: "Do Pro-Lifers Who Reject Trump Have 'Blood on their Hands'?" by David French, copyright © 2020 by David French. Reprinted by permission of The Dispatch Magazine.

Politico LLC: "The Real Origins of the Religious Right" by Randall Balmer, copyright © 2014 by Randall Balmer. Reprinted by permission of Politico LLC.

Sojourners: "The Fullness Thereof" by Randy Woodley, copyright © 2019 by Randy Woodley. Reprinted by permission of Sojourners Magazine.

ISBN 978-1-7358337-0-5
ebook ISBN 978-1-7358337-1-2

Cover design concept by Elizabeth Hampson; Cover photo printed with permission from Associated Press.

"I am the LORD your God,
who brought you out of Egypt, out of the land of slavery.
You shall have no other gods before me."
Exodus 20: 2, 3 NIV

Table of Contents

Acknowledgments

It takes a village, and executing this project was truly a communal act. We, as editors, know there are many faithful Christians who are coming forward to take a stand against Trumpism and its antecedents; a group that we hope will grow and build momentum in the weeks leading up to the election; and continue regardless of the outcome on November 3.

The journey of this book coming into existence is itself a powerful testament to that movement. In less than three months, this entire project went from vision to fruition including drafts of proposals, emails, invitations, submissions, contracts, cover art, and more. Thirty-six contributions later, this volume is the fruit of leaders steeping in these thoughts for four years, or, for some, several decades.

So many thanks are due. To our respective spouses – Priscilla, Marvin, and Gabrielle – who stood with us, even when we had to forgo our daily routines and responsibilities. To our daughters – Maia, Everest, and Nora – may this be the part of our legacy of faithfulness that we proudly hand to you. May it help you steward the resistance long after we are gone. To our extended families who supported us – particularly Rosette Mansour and Sally Lahoud – for your help with childcare, housekeeping, moral and emotional support; thank you. To those who offered their time and talents; thank you. To faithful friends who guided this project with their wisdom and support; thank you.

Chris and Cecilia Hampson- thank you to Chris for serving as the official hype man and unofficial consigliere. This project would never have happened without your friendship.

Elizabeth Hampson– an early adopter, a major contributor to the cover design, and our Co-Director of Outreach for our marketing campaign: thank you for your boundless enthusiasm, admirable professionalism, and kind and sincere spirit.

Kristy Garza Robinson– thank you for feeding the dream and, moreover, for helping to make that dream become a reality.

Charles Samuel, our digital marketer– it's one thing to publish a book. It's quite another to get it into the hands of enthusiastic readers. Thank you for lending your brilliance to help make that happen.

Christophe Bourlon– thank you for working with Charles to create the website of our dreams! We don't know how you all made the magic happen, but we are truly grateful.

Benjamin Krapohl, a.k.a. Copywriter Ben – thank you for nailing it every. Single. Time. Your giftedness truly elevated our work.

Alisse Goldsmith-Wissman– thank you for believing in our team and this project enough to offer your time, expertise and resources.

Jesse Wheeler, our second Co-Director of Outreach– thank you for not only contributing a brilliant piece to this anthology, but moreover, for going above and beyond in helping us to contact potential contributors and get the word out to potential readers. The amount of enthusiasm and energy that you have poured into this project has been remarkable.

To Emily Craig and Kristal Calkins– thank you for exercising your administrative and editing gifts to move this work forward.

To our proofreader, Margaret Vincent–thank you for putting up with our queries, unconventional work hours, and mistakes. Materially-speaking, this book would not have happened without you.

To all of our contributors– thank you for your generosity and courage in sharing your wisdom, insight, and hearts for the Kingdom of Heaven to be made more palpable here on earth.

To you, our reader. Thank you for taking the time to read and wrestle. Our prayer is that we all might experience God as we engage with the words on these pages and be refined to reflect a little more of Christ in this world. May it be so.

Introduction

Pollsters and pundits continue to highlight that white evangelical Christians helped bring Donald Trump to victory in 2016 and continue to buoy him to this day. Less widely known are the perspectives of Christian leaders and lay people who stand faithfully in opposition to this narrative. This anthology of dissent offers a collection of articles and essays that are cross-generational, multiethnic, and located at different places on the political spectrum from a range of well-known and emerging voices. Yet despite the array of views and experiences this work presents, the two attributes that all of the contributors have in common are first, their firm commitment to their faith in Jesus Christ; and second, that they have determined that they will not be casting their vote for Donald Trump in November 2020.

Keeping the Faith draws on that opposing perspective through moving individual stories buttressed by biblical and incisive critique, to provide fresh lenses and frameworks that Christians can use to navigate the deep and often murky waters of faith and politics. This book offers rich theological reflection, profound grappling, solidarity, and much-needed clarity for these complex times.

If you are a Christian who is struggling to discern how to use your vote, this book is for you. If you are a Christian searching for a sense of political belonging within the church, this book is for you. If you are a Christian who is looking for brothers and sisters who will stand with you as allies in the fight for justice, this book is for you. And more pointedly, if you are a Christian who has been in mourning and lament since 2016, then this book is for you.

Our desire, ultimately, is that the perspectives provided in these pages serve to expand the political and moral imagination of our readers. Our longing is to tell a story not just of what we, as Christians, are against, but what we are for; a story not of embracing cynicism, but of striving together in and toward a hope that does not disappoint.

There remain many voices and perspectives that are not adequately represented in these pages. This is a shortcoming that we openly acknowledge. We regret that many we invited to contribute were unable to do so because of the demands on them during this tumultuous season.

We seek to combat the white American church's overwhelming embrace of the bigotry and fear propagated by the Trump administration. Four of the authors in this book felt the need to contribute anonymously due to the personal and professional backlash they could receive for openly expressing their views. Others considered doing so as well. This is indicative of just how far we, as the church, have strayed from the call to mutual acceptance and reciprocal love. Shouldn't the church, rather than being the strongest of cancel cultures, reclaim its prophetic call to Christian charity? Shouldn't the people of God possess the ability to disagree in love?

In that spirit, this anthology does not, and never intended to, present a single theory of political engagement. The editors do not agree with all of the positions presented in these pages, nor do the contributors all agree with each other. Thus, regardless of your theological leanings or your political affiliation, we anticipate that you will find something in this collection that disrupts, disorients, or challenges you.

May we enter collectively into the layered tension of this cultural moment with the courage and grace necessary to speak and live as though Jesus is King. Every election is a point of inflection and an opportunity for change. But in 2020, we find ourselves at a particularly critical juncture in our nation's history in the midst of COVID-19, a global reckoning on race, economic uncertainty, and heightened political discord. May we choose together to seek justice, love mercy, and walk humbly with our God.

Jonathan P. Walton
Suzie Lahoud
Sy Hoekstra

The Fierce Urgency of Now

Scenes of Political Blasphemy
By Gregory Coles

Scene One

In my first memory of American politics, George W. Bush has just beaten Al Gore in the 2000 presidential election, and I am pleased.

I'm not sure, even at the time, exactly why ten-year-old Greg is happy about Bush's victory. I don't have a clue about Bush's policies or Gore's, about the differences that separate them or the similarities that unite them. American politics are mostly a mystery to me. The politics I know best are the politics of the country I grew up in, Indonesia, which held its first democratic election just one year prior in 1999. But I know at least enough of American politics—I *think* I know enough—to know that Christians are supposed to be pleased when Democrats are routed and Republicans are triumphant. Even from ten thousand miles away, I've managed to learn that Jesus wears an elephant suit in America.

As far as ten-year-old Greg is concerned, every political ad supporting George Bush is probably concluded by the voice of God himself, booming down from the clouds: "I approve this message."

It's comforting, thinking the lines of political good and evil can be so tidily drawn.

Scene Two

Two decades later, the president at the helm of the Republican party is a serial liar known for his bluster, his reprehensible dealings, his sexual misdeeds, and his callous disdain toward those on the margins. His life reads like a cautionary tale of the moral decay that so often accompanies extravagant wealth. I'd like to think that even ten-year-old Greg would have known better than to confuse this man's political victory with a divine triumph.

And yet, somehow, the perceived alliance between Christian faith and the GOP persists in 2020. White evangelical Christian support for Donald Trump remains high, with Pew Research reporting that 72% of white evangelical Protestants approve of Trump's administration as of June 2020, and 82% anticipate voting for him.[1] One prominent evangelical figure goes so far as to describe opposition to Trump's presidency as "almost a demonic power;" another describes the battle over Trump as "a spiritual battle."[2]

I want to be surprised at the way these Christians festoon the name of Jesus onto politicians and policies that have nothing to do with him. But I am not surprised. America has a gift for baptizing evil in the language of religious goodness. We look at land stolen from Indigenous people, at wealth earned by the exploitation and murder of African slaves, and call them God's blessings to us. We look at discrimination against LGBTQ+ people and celebrate our religious freedom. We look at families torn apart by brutal immigration policies and thank God for keeping us safe from foreign intruders.

We pray for America to be first in the world, to be favored, to be comfortable at every other nation's expense. And when it is, we say the kingdom of heaven has come near.

We forget that heaven makes its home in slums and empty stomachs, not in the overfed belly of Babylon.

Scene Three
At a campaign rally in Greenville, North Carolina, in July of 2019, Trump describes plans to bomb ISIS: "They'll be hit so goddamn hard." Later, he warns his listeners, "If you don't

support me, you're going to be so goddamn poor." Some of Trump's supporters complain that he is alienating his evangelical voter base by "using the Lord's name in vain."[3]

I find myself wondering if the same evangelical voters are concerned with Trump's cavalier attitude toward wreaking vengeance against America's enemies. I wonder if they are concerned with his idolization of wealth. Many of the same self-styled Christians who balk at Trump's profanities seem perfectly pleased to accept his political agenda. They call it God's work—Christian government par excellence—when food stamp programs to feed the hungry are cut, when incarceration increases, when borders are closed to migrants in search of homes. Jesus himself may be among the hungry and imprisoned and alienated, but his brand name and trademark are given to the satisfied and comfortable.

"To take the name of God in vain," says John Piper, "is to take up some expression of God's reality into our thoughts or emotions or words or actions when the truth of God has gone out of them, and true affections for God are missing."[4] The related word *blasphemy* comes from the Greek *blasphemia*, from roots meaning "to speak falsely about." When we take the sacred name of Jesus and smear it with the very kinds of selfishness and cruelty and power-mongering that Jesus himself decried, we become guilty of blasphemy. We wear our savior's name in vain, wanting it for its power and status but not for its bold disruption of our lives.

On December 6, 2019, Trump hosts a crowd of celebrity evangelical worship leaders at the White House. Vice President Mike Pence gives the visitors an hour-long "faith briefing" before they gather in the Oval Office to take a photo with and pray for President Trump. Attendees post videos praising God's work through the Trump administration.[5] Their tenor matches the words of another evangelical leader two years earlier, who celebrates Trump's attacks against ISIS and his anti-immigrant policies by declaring that "evangelicals have found their dream president."[6]

Scene Four

I am told that perhaps the white evangelical vote for Trump is all about abortion. As long as Trump declares his intention to restrict access to abortion, and the Democrat candidate who will surely otherwise win the presidency plans to increase abortion access, my ethical duty as a Christian is clear. I must hold my nose against Trump's various odious odors and cast my vote for him as a vote to save the lives of unborn children.

I remember the words of Alabama pastor Dave Barnhart:

> "The unborn" are a convenient group of people to advocate for. They never make demands of you; they are morally uncomplicated, unlike the incarcerated, addicted, or the chronically poor; they don't resent your condescension or complain that you are not politically correct; unlike widows, they don't ask you to question patriarchy; unlike orphans, they don't need money, education, or childcare; unlike aliens, they don't bring all that racial, cultural, and religious baggage that you dislike; they allow you to feel good about yourself without any work at creating or maintaining relationships; and when they are born, you can forget about them, because they cease to be unborn. It's almost as if, by being born, they have died to you. You can love the unborn and advocate for them without substantially challenging your own wealth, power, or privilege, without re-imagining social structures, apologizing, or making reparations to anyone. They are, in short, the perfect people to love if you want to claim you love Jesus but actually dislike people who breathe.[7]

It strikes me how easily a would-be blasphemer could earn white evangelicals' affection by claiming to care for unborn children. Such a person could perhaps gain all the political perks of ostensible "Christianity," with none of the pesky inconvenience of actually following Jesus.

I try to picture Jesus holding his nose and voting for Donald Trump. I can picture White Jesus doing it. But not Real Jesus.

Scene Five

Someone will tell me they wish I hadn't talked about politics. I should have let faith be faith and politics be politics, and kept the two entirely separate. But not talking about things doesn't inoculate us against their dangers. White evangelicals have scrupulously avoided discussing our own whiteness, and it hasn't saved us from blasphemously plastering Jesus' name onto patterns of systemic racism and injustice.

Quite the opposite.

If I tell you I am evangelical in my theological convictions, and you see my white skin, the polling numbers give you an 82% chance that I'll be voting for Donald Trump this November. If I say nothing political in this moment, I risk participating in the same pernicious narrative I inherited from across the Pacific Ocean at the age of ten: that Jesus and his American followers are lifelong Republicans, no matter how reprehensible our presidential candidate may be.

I shall not take the name of the Lord my God in vain.

Gregory Coles (PhD, Penn State University) is a writer, speaker, and worship leader. His first book, <u>Single, Gay, Christian</u>, was a 2017 Foreword INDIES Award Finalist. A second book, <u>No Longer Strangers</u>, is forthcoming in 2021.

Speak Truth to Trump
By Andy Crouch

*A version of this article first appeared in "Christianity Today" on October 10, 2016. The text is included here for its enduring relevance."

As a non-profit journalistic organization, *Christianity Today* is doubly committed to staying neutral regarding political campaigns—the law requires it, and we serve our readers best when we give them the information and analysis they need to make their own judgments.

Just because we are neutral, however, does not mean we are indifferent. We are especially not indifferent when the gospel is at stake. The gospel is of infinitely greater importance than any campaign, and one good summary of the gospel is, "Jesus is Lord."

The true Lord of the world reigns even now, far above any earthly ruler. His kingdom is not of this world, but glimpses of its power and grace can be found all over the world. One day his kingdom, and his only, will be the standard by which all earthly kingdoms are judged, and following that judgment day, every knee will bow, in heaven, on earth, and under the earth, as his reign is fully realized in the renewal of all things.

The lordship of Christ places constraints on the way his followers involve themselves, or entangle themselves, with earthly rulers.

On the one hand, we pray for all rulers—and judging from the example of Old Testament exiles like Daniel and New Testament prisoners like Paul, we can even wholeheartedly pray for rulers who directly oppose our welfare. On the other hand, we recognize that all earthly governments partake, to a greater or lesser extent, in what the Bible calls idolatry: substituting the creation for the Creator and the earthly ruler for the true God.

No human being, including even the best rulers, is free of this temptation. But some rulers and regimes are especially outrageous in their God-substitution. After Augustus Caesar, the emperors of Rome became more and more elaborate in their claims of divinity with each generation—and more and more ineffective in their governance. Communism aimed not just to replace faith in anything that transcended the state, but to crush it. Such systems do not just dishonor God, they dishonor his image in persons, and in doing so they set themselves up for dramatic destruction. We can never collude when such idolatry becomes manifest, especially when it demands our public allegiance. Christians in every place and time must pray for the courage to stay standing when the alleged "voice of a god, not a man" commands us to kneel.

This year's presidential election in the United States presents Christian voters with an especially difficult choice.

The Democratic nominee has pursued unaccountable power through secrecy—most evidently in the form of an email server designed to shield her communications while in public service, but also in lavishly compensated speeches, whose transcripts she refuses to release, to some of the most powerful representatives of the world system. She exemplifies the path to power preferred by the global technocratic elite—rooted in a rigorous control of one's image and calculated disregard for norms that restrain less powerful actors. Such concentration of power, which is meant to shield the powerful from the vulnerability of accountability, actually creates far greater vulnerabilities, putting both the leader and the community in greater danger.

But because several of the Democratic candidate's policy positions are so manifestly incompatible with Christian reverence for the lives of the most vulnerable, and because her party is so demonstrably hostile to expressions of traditional

Christian faith, there is plenty of critique and criticism of the Democratic candidate from Christians, including evangelical Christians.

But not all evangelical Christians—in fact, alas, *most* evangelical Christians, judging by the polls—have shown the same critical judgment when it comes to the Republican nominee. True, when given a choice, primary voters who claimed evangelical faith largely chose other candidates. But since his nomination, Donald Trump has been able to count on "the evangelicals" (in his words) for a great deal of support.

This past week, the latest (though surely not last) revelations from Trump's past have caused many evangelical leaders to reconsider. This is heartening, but it comes awfully late. What Trump is, everyone has known and has been able to see for decades, let alone the last few months. The revelations of the past week of his vile and crude boasting about sexual conquest—indeed, sexual assault—might have been shocking, but they should have surprised no one.

Indeed, there is hardly any public person in America today who has more exemplified the "earthly nature" ("flesh" in the King James and the literal Greek) that Paul urges the Colossians to shed: "sexual immorality, impurity, lust, evil desires, and greed, which is idolatry" (3:5, NIV). This is an incredibly apt summary of Trump's life to date. Idolatry, greed, and sexual immorality are intertwined in individual lives and whole societies. Sexuality is designed to be properly ordered within marriage, a relationship marked by covenant faithfulness and profound self-giving and sacrifice. To indulge in sexual immorality is to make oneself and one's desires an idol. That Trump has been, his whole adult life, an idolater of this sort, and a singularly unrepentant one, should have been clear to everyone.

And therefore it is completely consistent that Trump is an idolater in many other ways. He has given no evidence of humility or dependence on others, let alone on God his Maker and Judge. He wantonly celebrates strongmen and takes every opportunity to humiliate and demean the vulnerable. He shows no curiosity or capacity to learn. He is, in short, the very embodiment of what the Bible calls a fool.

Some have compared Trump to King David, who himself committed adultery and murder. But David's story began with a profound reliance on God who called him from the sheepfold to the kingship, and by the grace of God it did not end with his exploitation of Bathsheba and Uriah. There is no parallel in Trump's much more protracted career of exploitation. The Lord sent his word by the prophet Nathan to denounce David's actions—alas, many Christian leaders who could have spoken such prophetic confrontation to him personally have failed to do so. David quickly and deeply repented, leaving behind the astonishing and universally applicable lament of his own sin in Psalm 51—we have no sign that Trump ever in his life has expressed such humility. And the biblical narrative leaves no doubt that David's sin had vast and terrible consequences for his own family dynasty and for his nation. The equivalent legacy of a Trump presidency is grievous to imagine.

Most Christians who support Trump have done so with reluctant strategic calculation, largely based on the president's power to appoint members of the Supreme Court. Important issues are indeed at stake, including the right of Christians and adherents of other religions to uphold their vision of sexual integrity and marriage even if they are in the cultural minority.

But there is a point at which strategy becomes its own form of idolatry—an attempt to manipulate the levers of history in favor of the causes we support. Strategy becomes idolatry, for ancient Israel and for us today, when we make alliances with those who seem to offer strength—the chariots of Egypt, the vassal kings of Rome—at the expense of our dependence on God who judges all nations, and in defiance of God's manifest concern for the stranger, the widow, the orphan, and the oppressed. Strategy becomes idolatry when we betray our deepest values in pursuit of earthly influence. And because such strategy requires capitulating to idols and princes and denying the true God, it ultimately always fails.

Enthusiasm for a candidate like Trump gives our neighbors ample reason to doubt that we believe Jesus is Lord. They see that some of us are so self-interested, and so self-protective, that we will ally ourselves with someone who violates all that is sacred to us—in hope, almost certainly a vain hope given his mendacity and record of betrayal, that his rule will save us.

The U.S. political system has never been free of idolatry, and politics always requires compromise. Our country is flawed, but it is also resilient. And God is not only just, but also merciful, as he judges the nations. In these closing weeks before the election, all American Christians should repent, fast, and pray—no matter how we vote. And we should hold on to hope—not in a candidate, but in our Lord Jesus. We do not serve idols. We serve the living God. Even now he is ready to have mercy, on us and on all who are afraid. May his name be hallowed, his kingdom come, and his will be done on earth, as it is in heaven.

Andy Crouch is the former executive editor of "Christianity Today." A version of this article first appeared in "Christianity Today" on October 10, 2016 and can be found at: https://www.christianity-today.com/ct/2016/october-web-only/speak-truth-to-trump.html. It is reprinted here with permission.

Lost Homeland
By Dawn Sonntag

On a warm, breezy day in July 2009, as I sat with my husband's parents in their dining nook in their home in a small northern German village and looked at the macramé murals of the East Prussian and Pomeranian coats of arms that hung on the wall, I asked my mother-in-law, Christa Neuber Kuske, "Why did you leave East Prussia?"

"Mama," as I affectionately call her, had shown me photos of her childhood homeland, reminiscing about how her parents had taken her to the beaches of the Baltic Sea in the summer and how she and her brother had gone sledding and ice skating in the winters. Little did I know then how her answer to my simple question that day would inform both my perception of the danger Donald Trump poses to this country and my understanding of how the path leading to his rise in power began with a toxic synergism of religion and propaganda that has roots deep in this country's history.

"We had to, of course," she said, recounting her harrowing childhood experience as an East Prussian refugee during the final years of World War II. Her father, August, was a farmer and mayor of their small East Prussian farming village, Schoenberg, in northeastern East Prussia. Separated from the rest of Germany after World War I, the East Prussians had high hopes that Hitler would bring economic relief and reunite them with the rest of Germany. But after August was sent to Ukraine to survey farm land the Nazis had confiscated from Ukrainian farmers, he realized that Hitler was a dangerous con-man.

August and Elise began to distance themselves from the rest of the villagers, refusing to participate in Nazi social activities and guarding their children from Nazi propaganda. When the local Nazi party leader confronted August because he refused to wear his Nazi uniform to a local rally, August replied flippantly that it was "too drafty." At age 43, he was sent to the Russian front – normally a death sentence. Elise narrowly escaped a concentration camp. In December 1944, August returned home for a three-day furlough in order to warn her about the impending Russian invasion. To avoid arrest by the Nazis, who had forbidden East Prussians from even packing to leave, Elise prepared secretly while the children slept. After August's deployment, the Nazis sent her a young Ukrainian girl, the daughter of a wealthy baker, to do the heavy farm work. Ignoring Nazi directions to treat the Slavic forced laborers like slaves, Elise did the farm work herself while the girl helped with the childcare. The girl confided to Elise that she was half-Jewish; Elise kept this a secret. When the evacuation orders came in late January 1945, the East Prussians had hours to prepare for the 1000 km trek to western Germany. Elise drove the loaded horse wagon while the children walked behind. Upon their arrival in West Germany, Elise and her children were met with hostility and resentment. While her father survived and miraculously found her mother in western Germany a few months after the war's end, the Jewish-Ukrainian girl disappeared during the journey. After the war, August and Elise searched for the girl, but they never saw her again.

"We were fortunate. Others suffered much more than we did," Christa always said at the end of her stories, looking away sadly. She was dismayed by recent Neo-Nazi activity in Germany. "They have no idea," she said. "One must never forget." More than 300,000 East Prussian civilians perished in the evacuations during the winter of 1945. In turning their faces away from Hitler's cruelty while hoping he would bring them prosperity; millions of eastern European Germans died or forever lost their homeland and unique culture.

A native of Wisconsin, I moved to Germany from Texas in 1991 with my then-husband, who was an army nurse anesthetist, and our two small children. Soon after our arrival, we separated. My ex-husband planned to remain in the military, moving frequently. The realization that my sons and I would have more stability, support, opportunity, and freedom in Germany with only my student visa than as citizens in our home country was eye-opening. The educational system was excellent; my graduate school tuition was $25 a semester. My health care cost about $120 a year. We had safe, affordable housing through the university, and food was cheaper than in the U.S. As a music student, I was allowed to work at music-related jobs, and I received six weeks paid time off during the school breaks. In addition, I worked part-time as a chapel musician for the U.S. Army Protestant and Lutheran chapels and as an assistant conductor of a German chamber choir. This is where I met my husband, a doctoral theology student at the University of Heidelberg. He was raised in the Lutheran church in his hometown in northern Germany and obtained his undergraduate degree in Lutheran theology at the University in Bückeburg. We married in 1998 and I began the application process for German citizenship, but early in 2000, we decided to move to the U.S. and allow my sons to spend more time with their grandparents and cousins. I planned to pursue doctoral studies in music, and my spouse looked forward to being ordained in the Lutheran Church in America.

In order for my husband to accompany me to the U.S., I had to secure full-time employment that provided health insurance for us both. Luckily, I managed to secure a position as a full-time church musician at a large Methodist church in Westerville, Ohio. The church generously assisted us with our move, finding an apartment and used car for us, and donating furniture, as we had to leave behind many of our belongings.

But when we arrived, I learned that our insurance did not take effect until I had been employed for 90 days and covered no preexisting conditions. For three months, I lived in fear of an accident or serious injury. As for the preexisting conditions, I simply did not see a doctor for a year. We both had to pursue second masters degrees because our German educational credentials were not recognized. I was reminded of my former East German ESL students whose education and career experience were not recognized in western Germany.

On September 11, 2001, just before my husband began his studies at the LCMS seminary (Lutheran Church-Missouri Synod) in Fort Wayne, I stopped at the Ohio State recreation center before going to the music building. A crowd had gathered around a television in the lobby. They were watching replays of the large passenger jet flying directly into the first Twin Tower. Minutes later, the second tower was hit. After that, the Pentagon was struck and a plane crashed in Pennsylvania just a couple of hours east of Columbus. A student from Pakistan said, "It was already difficult for us here. Now they will blame us." When President Bush began talking about the "Axis of Evil" and "weapons of mass destruction," I was skeptical and strongly opposed the idea of war with Iraq, but my husband shared that most of his colleagues at the Fort Wayne Seminary supported Bush.

In 2003, when my husband and I both finished our studies, we relocated to Minneapolis, where I pursued a doctorate at the University of Minnesota while working as organist and choir director at Norwegian Memorial Lutheran Church and my husband began his LCMS internship. The wife of his supervising pastor was an intelligent, talented teacher who wanted to help us feel at home. "Fox News is the only objective news station," she told me. I started to laugh but caught myself when I realized she was serious. I learned that being a member of the LCMS assumed membership in the Republican Party. Journalist and LCMS member Mollie Ziegler Hemingway was emerging as a conservative voice, and was invited to speak at a local LCMS conference on liturgy. She began her presentation with, "I bet I know how everyone in this room voted." What this had to do with Lutheran liturgy was unclear to me. What was clear was that virtually everyone in the room agreed that voting Republican was necessary as a "good Lutheran."

When I was growing up in the Wisconsin Evangelical Lutheran Synod (WELS), a historical and theological cousin to the LCMS, politics were not discussed in church. Abortion and homosexuality were never mentioned. There was no mention of political parties or candidates at church, although my first-grade teacher held a class election while holding up a copy of *Time* magazine with Nixon's smiling face on the front. She never mentioned his opponent, Hubert Humphrey. Nixon won our election in a landslide. Our teacher seemed delighted. And every 4th of July, the entire school marched in the large city parade. We each carried a small flag, and church members decorated a large float. In the early 1980s, politics began to creep into church activities, if not the services. The pastor at my home church in Milwaukee presented a "recruiting" evangelism video produced by a non-Lutheran evangelical. It reminded me of an Amway sales training seminar. Then, in the late 1980s, I moved to Texas, where I became familiar with Rush Limbaugh and James Dobson, whose programs were scheduled back to back. While their styles were radically different, their view of women was eerily similar; Dobson condemned mothers who worked outside the home, and Limbaugh called career women "feminazis." Ironically, I listened to their shows while driving my children to daycare before my classes at the university. Although Dobson was not Lutheran, the pastor of the WELS church I attended in El Paso strongly supported his teachings on women, stressing that all women be subservient to all men at all times in a legalistic way that I had not experienced in Wisconsin. When I left Texas and moved to Germany, I left the WELS. For several years, I considered myself simply

"Christian," only re-embracing Lutheranism when I began working as organist for the Lutheran chapel, where an ELCA pastor served as chaplain. He became a close friend, performing our wedding, and was a mentor to my husband as he prepared for the U.S. seminary.

After my husband concluded his internship in Minneapolis, he received a call to a small rural church about an hour southwest of Minneapolis. Many members of the congregation were descendants of the German immigrants who had founded the church and a few still spoke German. Yet several members seemed to have a list of suspicions that included our education, the fact that my husband was not a U.S. citizen, and that I had been divorced and was pursuing a career. By this time, the U.S. was at war with Iraq, and when my husband heard members expressing fears and stereotypes about Muslims, he decided to lead a Bible study on Islam. When he explained that not all Muslims were violent and that the Old Testament included many examples of gruesome violence, their distrust in him increased. We both were increasingly criticized without reason. I knew that this situation was not sustainable.

Early in 2008, my husband revealed to me he had been researching joining the U.S. Army. He had a deep interest in Middle Eastern culture and history and a desire to support both the U.S. and the Afghan people. I grew increasingly disturbed by the realization that soldiers with young children shouldered the burden of the war, and I supported his interest. He was offered a position as an avionics specialist with the 10th Mountain Division in Fort Drum, New York. Meanwhile, I accepted a tenure-track position at Hiram College in Northeastern Ohio. I spent my school breaks with my husband in New York, and he drove to Ohio one weekend a month when he was not deployed.

When not deployed, my husband continued to translate and annotate Luther's works and was frequently invited as a guest pastor and lecturer. We joined a historical LCMS congregation near downtown Cleveland. A few members had immigrated to the U.S. after World War II, and I enjoyed conversing with them in German and hearing stories about their lives. There were a few older members who had grown up in the church and recalled how friends of the Rockefellers lived in a mansion across the street. But now the neighborhood was among the poorest in Cleveland. The beautiful domed sanctuary, which seated 1000, seemed hauntingly empty with the fifteen or so members who attended regularly, plus or minus a few homeless individuals or addicts who occasionally wandered in. One new member who said he had been looking for a church with "good family values" expressed concern that Muslims might purchase the vacant building next door. The church was struggling financially and the building was in need of major repairs. When a developer made the church an excellent offer for the building, members were concerned that it might be turned into a mosque and declined the offer.

In 2009, a friend of my husband invited me to perform a recital at the Bückeburg Castle. My husband could not accompany me, so I spent ten days alone with my in-laws. In addition to telling me her story, my mother-in-law shared with me her library of biographies of other refugees and books about East Prussian history, and I became engrossed in the history and lives of the Eastern European refugees who had been caught between the Nazis and the Russians. While doing further research for my opera, which I titled *Verlorene Heimat (Lost Homeland)*, I combed the internet for documentary films on the Third Reich and found several videos of Hitler speaking at rallies. "The intellectuals are weak," he shouted. "It is we, the farmers and laborers who made this land with our own works and hands. We must make Germany great again." But more shocking was what I discovered from recent times in the U.S. — photos of smiling American men in business suits standing in front of swastikas in Holiday Inn conference rooms; white nationalist conferences on the superiority of the white race;

diagrams demonstrating how First Lady Michelle Obama's skeletal features proved she was an ape-like man; and photos of President Obama dressed in Arab clothing. The rhetoric on social media sites of Republican politicians, especially those of the South, decried the danger of the so-called "socialist" college and university professors. Gun-rights were also a prominent theme on these sites. "There is a cultural civil war brewing in this country," I told my husband.

My discoveries not only shocked but also embarrassed me. Like many white Americans of European descent, I was not aware of the continued prevalence of racism in my own country. My father, who was my eighth-grade teacher, showed our class several films on the Holocaust. Most of my classmates were descendants of German immigrants; this was part of our heritage. We needed to know. But we viewed the Nazis as an evil entity separate from the "real" German people; only a few "bad Germans" knew what was happening at the time. I was ignorant about the undercurrent of antisemitism that was alive and well in my own country. The same was true of my knowledge of anti-Black racism. When I was very young, my mother had given me books on the Underground Railroad and I saw Father Groppi march with protestors down the street between my home and school in Milwaukee. But I did not understand what the protests were about and was unaware of the deep, systemic racism that affected all non-whites in our country.

The racism I uncovered in my research on my opera changed my perspective, and when support for Trump continued to grow despite the KKK's endorsement, I knew that the undercurrent of racism I discovered in 2012 was now erupting in plain sight. As Trump gained momentum, I predicted that he would choose an evangelical running mate to ensure the support of conservative Christians. And I feared that if he did so, many members and some pastors of the LCMS would declare him a suitable presidential candidate despite his braggadocious self-promotion, obsession with money, complete lack of knowledge of American government, and his brazenly immoral, offensive rhetoric about women and immigrants.

Since 2008, many sermons and prayers at LCMS services I attended in northeast Ohio and Washington State were tinged with political innuendo criticizing President Obama and objections to "big government" and "government handouts," and abortion and homosexuality made their way into every church service, although there were virtually no homosexual members and at many services, few women that attended were of childbearing age. The sins that were pointed out were always the sins of "the world." But during the Trump campaign, political commentary in church services increased. The government was socialist and trying to abolish Christianity; the Muslims were taking over the country; and the Democrats supported full-term abortions for any reason. Forcing myself to listen to broadcasts by Rush Limbaugh, who had gained exponential exposure since I had first heard him in the 1980s, confirmed my suspicion that such beliefs were being strongly propagated by right-wing media on "Christian" radio.

As the Republican Convention in Cleveland approached, one of the church officers suggested holding a special service at the church during the convention. just a mile away from the church. She proposed that a pro-gun Lutheran senator be invited to speak. My husband, who was studying law at Case Western Reserve Law School after completing six years of active duty service, wrote a letter to the pastor explaining that this was illegal and furthermore was theologically highly questionable. The idea was rejected not because of theological or legal implications but because of "safety concerns."

My husband and I later wrote to the pastor addressing our concern about the immoral, aggressive, unchristian rhetoric and political views of Donald Trump. The pastor did not reply. I decided to contact Jon Vieker, the executive assistant to the president of the LCMS. Rev. Vieker told me that most LCMS members and pastors were Republicans. It was simply a fact that I had to accept. When I asked what the poor should do when all tax-funded social safety nets were cut under Trump, he told me that people should turn to God, not the government. Finally, my husband and I travelled to Toledo to visit our District President. After we presented our concerns to him, he said, to our utter shock, "They are afraid of losing their white majority." We were surprised and relieved to hear him acknowledge what no one else in the LCMS would say. But he was a lone voice and was nearing retirement.

As I had predicted, Donald Trump won the election. Just weeks after the election, I was scheduled to teach a study abroad course in Germany with my colleague, Megan Altman, PhD., assistant professor of philosophy at Hiram College. Megan is Jewish, and several of her family members perished in the Holocaust. Entitled "Music and Philosophy in Germany," the course focused on music and philosophy in the Third Reich. Several students in the group had never travelled outside of Ohio and came from Trump-supporting families. While in Leipzig, we inadvertently happened upon a Neo-Nazi protest. At the Holocaust Museum in Berlin, Trump was portrayed as an evil "golem," a creature of Jewish mythology that sometimes destroys its creator. The analogy was fitting; the students were shocked.

While in Berlin, I attended an Independent Evangelical Lutheran Church (SELK) church service with members primarily from Iraq, Iran, and Afghanistan. When I arrived, there were no more hymnals and it was difficult to find a place to sit. I was one of perhaps four non-Middle Eastern individuals in the entire congregation. A woman seated towards the back gestured for me to join her and eagerly shared her hymnal. The service was bilingual, in Farsi and German, and the members sang and chanted the creeds and prayers with a conviction that was moving. The church was so full that communion took more than an hour. After the service, the woman, who was from Afghanistan, shared with me some of her experiences and invited me to join the choir. Later, I learned from the pastor that the German government was denying permanent residency to many of these members, claiming that they were only feigning Christianity to obtain German residency. Those who were sent back to the Middle East faced severe poverty, torture, or death.

Meanwhile, the president of the LCMS, Rev. Matthew Harrison, established the *Lutheran Center for Religious Liberty* in Washington, DC in response to perceived persecution of conservative Christians. A federal judge's complaint about having to sign a gay marriage certificate when no Christian church in the United States is forced to accept gays as members, much less perform homosexual weddings, compared to the martyring of Middle Eastern Christians seems ludicrous. Nevertheless, Rev. Harrison refused to sign the letter drafted by clergy across the U.S. protesting Donald Trump's January 2017 executive order on immigration that strongly targeted immigrants from the Middle East. This led to heated debate on the LCMS Facebook page. The comments by pro-Trump members included statements supporting Hamite ideology – the belief that the those of African heritage descended from Ham, who was cursed by God – and that "God loves all races but wants them to remain separate, in their own countries." The post was deleted a few days later, along with all of the contentious comments.

But the LCMS Facebook page continued to post articles that were clearly political, criticizing any anti-Trump protests, including the Women's March, claiming that the protests were dominated by pro-abortion rhetoric and were violent. Having attended the march in Cleveland and heard eye-witness accounts from friends at Women's Marches across the U.S., I commented that these assumptions were false. A subsequent post on domestic violence was accompanied by a photo of a white-blond women with a dark-haired, bearded man who clearly looked Middle Eastern. Trump had recently made comments about Mexicans and terrorists "raping American women." I pointed out that the photo supported racial profiling. My comments evoked aggressive responses. I was eventually banned from commenting on the LCMS Facebook page, "excommunicated," as it were, because "I politicized everything."

This was not the first time LCMS pastors or members reacted strongly to my criticism or questioning of Republican politics. In 2007, after President Obama introduced the Affordable Care Act, many LCMS pastors and members called the ACA "socialism" and "government overreach." If one needed to accept a certain job for health care benefits, it must be God's will that one accepts that job, regardless of whether it was a good fit for one's talents and interests. If one could not find a job with benefits, one must be "lazy." Furthermore, the ACA covered birth control pills, which can prevent a fertilized egg from implantation and was therefore an "abortifacient." Yet, when I asked LCMS clergy and members whether they would support the ACA if the pill was not covered, they objected that the ACA was "socialist" and that taxing the wealthy to support it was "stealing." But the Old Testament mandate "Thou shalt not steal" applied equally to the wealthy, who were to leave enough crops for the poor to gather. Many LCMS pastors and members who opposed the ACA had no objections to the reality that many jobs do not pay a living wage or provide health care benefits; or that without financial support for health care costs, education, housing, and food, very low-income pregnant women might be forced to choose between giving up a child they wanted and facing daunting levels of poverty. Any level of governmental support was "socialism," and "socialism" was inherently evil. Meanwhile the difference in incomes between CEOs and the average American had grown exponentially; yet requiring more tax from the wealthy was "stealing." Four of the highest paid radio personalities in the country – Limbaugh,

Stern, Savage, and Beck – convinced religious conservatives that it was more important to protect the wealth of the mega-rich than provide support for pregnant women and single parents.

Finally, when at our church's celebration service for the 500th anniversary of the Reformation; the list of condemnable sins by "others" – abortion, homosexuality, laziness – and the danger of the "Others" – non-Republicans – was the focus of the sermon and prayers, my spouse and I determined it was time to dust off our shoes. We no longer could belong to a church that filtered both the teachings of Martin Luther and Scriptures through the lens of Republican political propaganda, disregarding some of Luther's most important teachings on treatment of immigrants, the poor, and the role of government in protecting citizens from exploitation by the wealthy. But while we have left the LCMS; we are still Lutheran. In fact, it is because we treasure Luther's teachings that we could no longer ally ourselves with the LCMS.

Sadly, since our departure, many members of the WELS and LCMS, including former schoolmates of mine, seem to have slid even more into the grip of political propaganda and conspiracy theories such as QAnon. Publications like *The Federalist*, for which Mollie Hemingway is a senior editor, continue to garner strong support from many LMCS members. Hemingway, who is a frequently-invited guest of the LCMS *Issues* radio show, expressed doubts about Trump's conservatism during his campaign, but she has become one of his most enduring supporters. She claims that Democrats were unethical in their investigations of his alleged collusion with the Russians. Several *Federalist* articles support accusations that Democratic governors have purposely suppressed religious freedom and exaggerated the threat of COVID-19 to influence the election.

Just as Hitler's rise to power was preceded by decades of propaganda that placed the blame for Germany's ills on "the other," Trump's election was preceded by decades of right-wing media fear-mongering about "socialism," homosexuality, the "entitled" poor, immigrants, and peaceful protestors, all while promoting gun rights even in the face of horrific gun violence. Many Christians unwaveringly trust Trump's competence, dedication to Democracy, and sincere concern for citizens of all races and socioeconomic levels, despite overwhelming evidence to the contrary. And when all else fails, Roe v. Wade, originally passed by Republicans, is the "Trump" card to bring voters back to the Republican table. As we face this crisis of faith and nation, we recall Luther's words in his hymn, *Ein feste Burg*:

> Did we in our own strength confide,
> Our striving would be losing,
> Were not the right Man on our side,
> The Man of God's own choosing.
> You ask who that may be?
> Christ Jesus, it is he;
> Lord Sabaoth his name,
> From age to age the same,
> And he must win the battle.

Dawn Sonntag, DMA, is a classical music composer and performer, college and university educator, and church musician. Her works, which include opera and chamber, choral, and orchestral music, have been performed across the U.S. and in Germany, France, and Norway. A life-long Lutheran and Wisconsin native, Sonntag completed her BM in music at the University of Texas El Paso before relocating to Germany, where she resided for nine years, earning a graduate artist's diploma at the Hochschule für Kirchenmusik, Heidelberg. She holds a Master of Arts from Antioch University's McGregor School of the Arts in Tübingen, Germany; a Master of Music from the Ohio State University; and a Doctor of Musical Arts from the University of Minnesota. She has served as a church musician in Lutheran and Protestant denominations across the U.S. and in Germany. Sonntag is currently a lecturer in music composition at Pacific Lutheran University in Washington State and was previously Associate Professor of Music at Hiram College in northeast Ohio. She resides in Olympia, Washington.

No Trump Vote

By JR. Forasteros

Leading up to the 2016 election, my friend Julianna Baggott created a website that shared essays from people "dedicating their No Trump votes." I wrote the following essay for her, and when she shared it, she made sure to note that I'm a white evangelical pastor in Texas.

A Donald Trump presidency will cost me nothing. In fact, as a straight, white, male, evangelical Christian pastor, my position will become more secure than at any point in the last two decades.

As a man, I've never had to worry about sexual assault dismissed as "locker room talk."

As a white person, my culture and perspective have always been normalized. Everyone around me is defined by how they relate to me. My history is just "history" - not Black History or Native History. My experiences are just "how things are," while my friends are asked to elaborate on the "Asian-American experience" or the "Hispanic perspective."

As a Christian, I've never been barred from participating in City Council meetings (as atheists in the town I pastor have). I've never been lumped in with extremists so different from me it's pretty obvious we're not part of the same faith. I've never been in danger of being banned from the country of which I'm a citizen. Trump promised us Evangelicals power if we would support him (language that is lifted straight out of Satan's offer to Jesus in Matthew 4, if you're interested in religious parallels). But we already have power. We are the cultural majority. That might change in another decade or so. But the Christian faith sits uneasy on a throne. The Church has always flourished on the margins. I can't seek power and be a faithful messenger of Jesus' good news.

My #notrumpvote won't affect me one way or the other. So I dedicate my #notrumpvote to those it will affect.

I dedicate my #notrumpvote to my strong female friends who have to talk on the phone as they walk to their car at night. To my brilliant female friends who learned from the time they were small to apologize for their opinions and diminish the quality of their contributions. To my female friends who have been assaulted and not believed, or were too afraid to come forward, or were told it was your fault. To every woman who has ever been told to take responsibility for a man's wicked behavior. I vote for you.

I dedicate my #notrumpvote to all my friends who have had to answer, "Where are you really from?" with, "I was born here." To all my friends who have been called rapists, dangers to society. To my friends who have been ignored and overlooked.

To all those who find their path to the ballot box blocked by unjust laws and bureaucratic red tape. To all those who have been made to feel not "normal" because you don't look like me. I vote for you.

I dedicate my #notrumpvote to my Muslim friends. I dedicate my vote to each of you who thinks twice about going out in public every time another terror strike breaks news. To each of you who receives glares, hears whispers, and lives with fear of retaliation for acts that couldn't have less to do with you. I dedicate my vote to every friend I have who isn't a Christian, who wonders how much longer you would be welcomed under a Trump presidency. I vote for you.

This election will cost me nothing. I dedicate my #notrumpvote to those who do have something on the line.

Rereading this essay four years later, I marvel at my naivety. I was profoundly wrong in my essay – Trump's victory has cost me (though not nearly as much as those who lack my privilege). Because I pastor an evangelical church, I've seen people leave the congregation because they don't like the political views I share on my personal social media.

Worse, I have seen many, many friends of color leave evangelicalism betrayed and heartbroken at the overwhelming majority of white evangelicals who pledge blind allegiance to Trump even as he desecrates our sacred symbols and stokes the fires of white supremacy. These faith-filled friends led an exodus from not just our congregations, but Christianity itself because of the naked hypocrisy of evangelical support for a president who so openly disdains everything for which Jesus stands.

But perhaps most painful has been my friends who are outside the faith expressing deep disillusionment. They're not anti-Christian. Far from it – they express urgent hunger for a faith that is tangible; a faith that welcomes the stranger rather than barring them at the border; a faith that looks for the Spirit at work so they can follow her, rather than a faith that predetermines who's in and who's out; a faith that seeks out injustice to pull it up by the root; a faith that doesn't make excuses for the profane, but practices what it preaches.

White Evangelicals took the devil's bargain – we traded faithfulness for power. And God is giving us what we wanted – brief moments in the spotlight. We've received our reward – at the cost of our very selves.

But God always preserves a remnant, and this is no different. Even when Elijah felt abandoned, God reminded him there were yet thousands who had not bent the knee to Ba'al. So too, in the face of overwhelming capitulation to Donald Trump, a remnant remains who has not embraced him. Whatever grows out of the corpse of evangelicalism will grow from that remnant.

It will be a faith that is far less structured, unmoored from the framework of institution, and more free to follow where the Spirit blows. It will be a faith that looks to the margins because we know that's where our Lord walks. And it will be a faith that truly embraces Jesus' call to give up whatever privileges we have for the sake of our neighbors.

This is the only faith that lasts forever, because it is the only faith that grows up from love. So when I go to the ballot box in November, I will yet again cast my vote not for myself, but for my neighbor.

JR. Forasteros is a pastor in Dallas, Texas. He is the author of Empathy for the Devil *and co-hosts The Fascinating Podcast and In All Things Charity. Otherwise, he's likely breaking in a new board game, perfecting smoked brisket or announcing roller derby while his wife, Amanda, skates for Assassination City Roller Derby.*

The Storm Before the Calm
By Scott Hall

I believe white American Christians need to sail into the storm, rather than fleeing to calmer seas.

I'm speaking to myself here. I am a white American Christian and I love Jesus.

In eighth grade, after being caught red-handed in a phase of rebellion and deceit, Jesus spoke to me in a dream that shapes me to this day. I experienced divine love that changed everything for me, and learned that those of us touched by God's love are released to bring that love into the world.

Yet over the years, I haven't seen what I learned reflected in the white American church. Back in 2007, the Barna Group conducted research on tens of thousands of Americans, ages 16 to 29 years old.[8] The primary descriptors this demographic associated with Christians were: hypocritical, "get saved," anti-homosexual, sheltered, too political, and judgmental. In the summary of their research, the study's authors Kinneman and Lyons wrote, "Christianity has an image problem."[9]

But is it an image problem? Or is it something deeper?

As a college minister, I still hear students associate the above list with Christians, only today they add "misogynist," "colonial," and "white supremacist" as well.

Until this presidential term, I'd never seen a religious demographic—in this case, white American Christians—so shamelessly couple themselves with a partisan identity. I thought Christians were citizens of heaven whose faith transcends political divisions with the love of Jesus. Instead, it seems we have collectively placed ourselves, or been placed, on one side of a culture war which no one seems to be winning, but where all sides are becoming increasingly suspicious, cynical, and self-righteous.

Are these associations and descriptors undeserved? Caricatures sketched by liberal critics? Possibly, especially in today's political climate, but I don't think it's that simple. Are we under spiritual attack, needing to reach back to an earlier time of more Christian expression of faith in our nation? If that is the case, what time are we reaching back to, exactly? Reagan's 1980s, when our nation thrived economically, but our Black brothers and sisters suffered under "trickle-down economics?" Or the Leave it to Beaver 1950s, when white suburbia was born as people of color were "put in their place" as second-class citizens? Or to World War II when American heroes fought Hitler while we simultaneously interned Japanese Americans?

Our critics may be on to something.

Remember the story after Jesus fed the five thousand? It's the one where, after participating in a glorious miracle, Jesus sends his disciples in a boat across the sea without him, and then a massive storm picks up that has them fearing for their lives. If you look closely at that passage you see that Jesus KNOWS that the disciples are struggling against the wind ... and yet he WAITS until "shortly before dawn" to join them by walking across the water. That means that Jesus intentionally allowed them to struggle through the storm for most of the night, even when he could have helped them. Why would he do that? The Scripture says he did so because their hearts were hardened. They had some deep work to do. They needed to take a pause, to check themselves, to look in the mirror, and to reexamine their posture toward Jesus and the things of God.

I believe this is the very invitation from Jesus to those of us who are white American Christians: to take a look in the mirror, to check our hearts, and to adjust the posture we've had toward what it means to love God and to love our neighbor.

Rather than attempting to list our collective blind spots and faults, I'll keep it simple: we need to put 1 Corinthians 12:26 into practice. When one part of the body suffers, every part suffers with it. Our history is one of unequal levels of suffering. It's time for us who are white to listen to our brothers and sisters of color about how it feels to not be white in this country, and when they tell us the truth—especially when their answers implicate us—to believe them, to take responsibility, and to change. This is what it means to let Jesus lead us into the storm.

And would that really be such a horrible thing? Learning to listen, taking responsibility for our faults, choosing to change, and embracing humility? Doesn't that actually sound ... Christian?

Scott holds a BA from UCLA in African American Studies, and an MA in Intercultural Studies from Fuller Theological Seminary. Raised in Oakland, California, Scott grew up as a white kid who lived on the wealthy side of town, but was always aware of racial divisions. As a result of the racial unrest in Los Angles in 1992, he changed his major to Black Studies and launched himself on a journey of learning from peers of color, and finding his place in the restoration of the shalom of God's kingdom. Scott is married to Jenny, and has thirteen-year-old twin children.

A Practical View of White American Folk Religion Contrasted with Real Christianity

By Jonathan P. Walton

81% of White Evangelicals voted for Donald Trump[10] to Make America Great Again. But it was not Christianity that got him elected. White American Folk Religion (WAFR) did. This ideology, not Christianity, is the oxygen burned in the spiritual fire of the United States. That heretical flame is not the Holy Spirit. WAFR is a race, class, gender-based hierarchy that hijacks the Christian label to sanction abuse, greed, and violence, and then absolve leaders who live lives contrary to the teachings of Jesus and wield power in opposition to God's plan for the world. This is not limited to the White House.

It was not faithful Jesus followers that rejoiced as Kavanaugh was belligerent and unrepentant during his confirmation hearings.[11] The cheering was from those who believe Jesus to be a White, straight, American Protestant male of *pure* Anglo-Saxon descent. And it is not disciples of Christ that are rallying to defend Jerry Falwell Jr.'s shady real estate deals, toxic campus culture, [12] and whatever happened in night clubs or with pool boys in Miami. [13] The people lined up behind Falwell Jr. exchanged the Kingdom of God for America and are lined up to defend their prophets, their pockets and their positions.

And though the pundits and pollsters will say it was the cocktail of neglect and dismissal toward the "flyover" states, urban elitism, the toxicity of Hillary Clinton, and the grievances of those on the losing side of globalization that ushered in the result of the 2016 election, an honest look at history reveals a different, more potent force at work. This power will fight for Jerry Falwell Jr. to keep his million-dollar salary even after he resigns, for Kavanaugh to stay on the Supreme Court, and for Trump to get four more years. Those devoted to WAFR align themselves with and pledge allegiance to the protected class of white, well-connected, well-resourced, straight men, the heresy of Christian Empire, and America as the New Jerusalem. This unchristian faith heralded at the 2020 Republican National Convention by Vice President Mike Pence and Housing Secretary, Ben Carson, aligns itself with political power for profit and protection and then absolves its prophets and people of sexual abuse, violence, and exploitation of people and the planet. This is not new. In fact, it is older than the constitution, the first thirteen colonies, or Columbus getting lost at sea.

In the time after Jesus' crucifixion, His followers experienced terrible persecution. This is especially true during the early life of Eusebius. He was a theologian and historian who chronicled much of this violence in a work called Church History.[14] He seems faithful at first, but after Constantine's conversion, Eusebius' work took a turn away from taking up his cross to raising the cup of empire. Instead of continuing to write about the wonders of Christ and the martyrs of the church, he began to record the marvelousness of the emperor and his empire.[15] His recordings stand in stark contrast to Jesus' Great Commission in Matthew 28 to "go and **make disciples of all nations**, baptizing them in the name of the Father and of the Son and of the Holy Spirit, and teaching them to obey everything I have commanded you" (Matt. 28:19-20, NIV).

Also antithetical to the Great Commission was Peter's cutting off the ear of Malchus, one of the men who came to arrest Jesus of Nazareth in John 18. Instead of mounting an insurrection, Jesus rebuked Peter, reminded him of His mission, and put the ear back on Malchus' head. Additionally, in Acts 1:8, after Jesus rose from the dead and appeared to His disciples, the overwhelming question for the oppressed Jewish people that those gathered brought up immediately was, "is now the time that you have come to restore Israel?" (Acts 1:6, paraphrase).

If Jesus wanted to overthrow Rome and establish the seat of Christian Empire, He could have done so; but instead He acted upon his stated purpose and reality that His kingdom is not of this world. Lastly, before Jesus ascends to heaven, He doubles down on His call from Matthew 28 explaining that the Holy Spirit is coming, not a new empire to subvert the Romans (Acts 1, NIV).

Jesus' words were the opposite of Pope Nicholas V's in 1452 who authored what we know now as the Doctrine of Discovery.[16] Jesus said, *"go out and preach,"* and the Pope said, *"go out and plunder."* The theological foundation for White Supremacy and consequent imperialism birthed at that time dehumanized African and Indigenous people, stripped them of their land and humanity, and laid the foundation for genocide, land theft, environmental destruction, chattel slavery, and horrific sexual violence.

Catholics were not alone in their white-washing of Jesus; Protestants like John Winthrop[17] also needed theological covering and a faith-based framework for the land theft, slavery, and genocide that ensued in his colonies in Massachusetts in 1630. He likened his band of believers to the Israelites and quoted Deuteronomy 30:18, but conveniently replaced "Jordan" with "vast sea,"[18]firmly placing himself and his co-travelers in the Israelite narrative. Thus, those gathered in front of Winthrop, instead of looking out upon the lands and people with the Great Commission in mind; their eyes were set on expanding so-called Christendom.

The Doctrine of Discovery as expressed through Winthrop no doubt influenced Thomas Jefferson when he coined the term Manifest Destiny and claimed the land west of the Mississippi.

His hypocrisy was mind-bending as he enslaved more than 600 human beings over his life, yet called to be liberated from slavery to the British[19]. Jefferson did in practice what Pope Nicholas V and John Winthrop did in their preaching: he literally cut Jesus out of his personal Bible[20] lest he come face to face with the original abolitionist who liberates the captives from physical and spiritual chains.

Sadly, WAFR is not just a problem that impacts those of faith. The town of Lynchburg would surely benefit from an institution that blessed its town instead of threatening it. The entire legal system of the United States would reap the benefits if there were another judge in its highest court who was cognizant of patriarchy and who abhorred sexual violence and alcoholism. And how amazing would it have been for the collective American consciousness if a president with compassion and empathy for communities of color had gone to Charlottesville in August 2017, Puerto Rico after Hurricane Maria, or El Paso after the mass shooting.

With WAFR as the lens and history in the rear view, what is happening in the present day is clear. Trump, Kavanaugh and Falwell Jr. look a lot like the greedy, exploitative, heretical men who came before them and not much like the Jesus they claim to know. They are no doubt religious; but their dedication is to greed, self-preservation, self-gratification and pride. Instead of practicing disciplines to grow in love and kindness, they are committed to behavior that demeans and abuses and arises out of their entitlement as White American men. Jesus' two commandments are to love God and love your neighbor. These three men in accordance with WAFR are only committed to loving themselves and those they deem worthy. Followers of Jesus who desire to be faithful and obedient with our political power must vote against what is self-centered, narcissistic, and self-preserving at the expense of the planet, the poor and the marginalized. Because to vote for what is best for the immigrant, prisoner, hungry and sick is to vote with Christ on the throne of our hearts; not ourselves, or the latest version of Caesar.

Jonathan Walton is the author of <u>Twelve Lies that Hold America Captive: and the Truth that Sets Us Free</u>. He is also an Area Director for InterVarsity NY/NJ focusing on Spiritual Formation and Experiential Discipleship. Recognized as one of "Christianity Today's" 33 Under 33 and one of New York's New Abolitionists, Jonathan was also the recipient of a Young Christian Leaders World Changer award. He has been featured in media outlets such as "New York Daily News," "The Christian Post," and "King Kulture" for his work combatting human trafficking. Jonathan earned his bachelor's degree in Creative Writing from Columbia University and holds a master's degree in the Study of the Americas from City College. He is from Southern Virginia and lives in New York City where he attends New Life Fellowship Church.

On Political Discourse

Comfort, Fear, and Hospitality: Reflections on My Time with Trump Voters
By Jessamin Birdsall

Election Day with Deb

Perched on a well-worn diner stool with my hamburger and Diet Coke, I asked my waitress Deb across the counter how she was feeling about Election Day. Having cast her vote for Trump that morning in the church fellowship hall on the south side of town, Deb reflected:

> *I guess I am scared. But then I saw someone posted on Facebook – it made me think, "okay, no matter who's president, God still is king. The world is out there. We're in our little town. We'll just keep trudging along."*

Back in 2016, I spent several months living and working in Deb's small, white, historically conservative Christian community in the Midwest. I interviewed fifty people and immersed myself in the life of the town to better understand the phenomenon of white evangelical support for Donald Trump. I worked part-time as a diner waitress; participated in church services, Sunday School classes, and Bible studies; volunteered at a Vacation Bible School, crisis pregnancy center, and retirement home; rode alongside farmers as they planted corn and harvested winter wheat; drank Bud Light at the town bar; joined the morning coffee drinkers at McDonald's and a Main Street cafe several times a week; and attended as many community gatherings and events as I could.

Deb's candid statement to me on Election Day 2016 encapsulates several common features of white evangelical subculture in America. These subcultural features helped pave the way for Trump's victory in 2016, and must be challenged in 2020, for the sake of the church and for the sake of the country.

I guess I am scared.

The first sentiment Deb expressed was fear. The people I got to know in Deb's town value continuity, having a clear moral code to follow, and having the freedom and security to govern their lives as they see fit. As many others have written, white evangelicals like Deb (particularly those in more isolated rural communities) fear that these values are under attack. The most common fears shared with me by folks in Deb's town were Islam and the growth of the "LGBT agenda." Both of these threats are framed as threats to the continuity of American culture, to the status of Christian morality, and to the security to practice their faith and raise their children free from intrusion.

It is worth noting that in Deb's town of fewer than 5000 people, there is only one Muslim family and a handful of openly gay or lesbian individuals. The fears of Sharia law being imposed or local churches being forced to marry couples against their conscience are unfounded. However, the widespread consumption of Fox News (consistently in the background at the gym, the barber shop, and people's living rooms) mobilizes more generalized anxieties about cultural change into exaggerated, politicized fears.

But then I saw someone posted on Facebook – it made me think, "okay, no matter who's president, God still is king."

The second feature of white evangelical subculture is to espouse that "God is king" and therefore in full control of all human affairs. In the week leading up to the election, the sentiment I heard most often from people I interviewed was: "Well, God is in control. He knows what's best for America and for the church. Ultimately He's the one who appoints our leaders."

As a fellow evangelical, I agree that God is sovereign. But I have two reservations about the way that I heard evangelical Trump voters rely on God's sovereignty. The first is the use of God's sovereignty as a means of minimizing individual responsibility ("He's the one who appoints our leaders"). On November 8, 2016, God did not miraculously intervene in our voting booths to make Trump win. Rather, 81% of white evangelical voters freely and deliberately ticked the box next to Donald J. Trump. While God is ultimately in control of all things, we are accountable for the choice that we made in 2016 and the choice that we will make in 2020.

The second reservation I have is around the assertion that God's will regarding the election should align with "what's best for America and for the church." Speaking about the things they were most excited about in a Trump presidency, people in Deb's town cited the Mexico border wall, additional screening for refugees, more respect for the police, lower taxes, protection from the encroachment of Sharia law, and protection from the threats of LGBT people to Christian businesses. This list of priorities suggests that when people in Deb's town say that God knows what is best for America, what they mean is that God's will is what is best for *us* – white, native-born, American evangelicals. In this way, the idea of God's sovereignty is inextricable from the idea that God's desire is to bless and prosper his people (white American Christians.)

Paradoxically, white evangelicals like Deb simultaneously claim to take comfort in the sovereignty and protection of God, while voting for the person who most aggressively plays on their insecurities.

The world is out there. We're in our little town.

Not all white evangelicals live in rural white towns like Deb, geographically isolated from people who are ethnically, religiously, or politically different. It is the case, however, that white evangelicals live significantly more socially segregated lives than other Americans.[21] If we look around at the members of our churches, our friendship circles, and our voluntary organizations, we will notice that most people look and think very much like us. Deb's language draws a stark boundary between "the world" and "us," suggesting that the lives of people like her are somehow set apart from wider society. This idea of separation is linked to the values and fears mentioned above. Given the deeply rooted value of continuity, combined with the idea that Deb's rural white evangelical subculture is entirely separate from the "world out there," there is a strong impulse to preserve and protect the subculture from the intrusions and hostilities of the outside world.

We'll just keep trudging along.

The implication of Deb's conclusion is that, regardless of the outcome of the election, we will probably be just fine and keep on living our lives. There is truth in this statement. As people with secure citizenship status, white skin, and membership in our country's majority religion, we can be quite confident of our survival. What this statement fails to acknowledge, however, and what white evangelicals more broadly have repeatedly failed to recognize, is that a victory for Trump has much more serious material and symbolic consequences for people who are not like us. Trump's rhetoric and policies have had deeply damaging impacts on immigrants, refugees, Muslims, Mexicans, and African Americans amongst others.

A failure in hospitality

The morning after the election, I stopped into the diner once again for a cup of black coffee, catching up with a group of older men who have their breakfast together there every morning. After talking about their reactions to the election and the fact that they weren't surprised by the outcome, Jimmy asked me: "When you go back to New Jersey, how do you report your visit with all of us deplorables?"

Over the last four years, I've been reflecting on my time in Deb's town and on my many conversations with her fellow "deplorables." There is much to affirm about Deb's community – the cultivation of farmland over many generations, the centrality of family, trusting relationships between neighbors, and the desire to preserve a traditional moral code. However, there is one very serious weakness of the town, and that is hospitality. On the surface, Deb's town is friendly. Visitors receive warm handshakes in the church lobbies, people smile in the streets, and the Chamber of Commerce works hard to promote tourism. However, as Larry commented at McDonald's one morning, in Deb's town you are "5 minutes a stranger, 50 years an outsider."

One thing that struck me during my time in Deb's town was how often I was asked who my grandparents were. About half of the town's residents trace their ancestry to the original settlers of area. Locating people within locally rooted family trees is an important practice of social categorization. If you are not part of those local family trees, "it is almost impossible to break into that unless you marry in," Pastor Todd told me. While he has been leading a church in the town for nearly five years, during that time only two families have made a significant effort to welcome him and to host him and his family in their homes.

It seems to me that the subculture to which Deb belongs, which is marked by fear of change; equates God's sovereignty with God's desire to bless hard-working white Americans, and positions itself as separate from the rest of society, making it very hard for people like Deb to live out the biblical call of hospitality. This is manifested at the local level, by how people in Deb's town treat outsiders. And it is manifested in how they vote at the national level – supporting a candidate who promises to keep outsiders out and to protect the traditional white Christian subculture.

Hospitality is not easy. It requires displacing fear with love. It requires trusting that God is king not only over your nation but over your neighborhood and home and finances and people who look different from yourself. It requires the courage to engage "the world" with openness and vulnerability rather than withdraw from it.

I am convinced that recapturing the biblical spirit and practice of hospitality is essential to the witness of the church in America and to the wellbeing of our nation in this time. Rather than fearfully seeking to protect our privileges and our way of life, let us open our homes and communities, learn from those who are different from us, and bear each other's burdens. In so doing, we remember and reflect the way that Jesus so generously extends hospitality to each of us.

My hope and prayer for American evangelicals this election year and beyond is that we would internalize and practice these words from Romans 12:10-18 (NIV):

> *Be devoted to one another in love. Honor one another above yourselves. Never be lacking in zeal, but keep your spiritual fervor, serving the Lord. Be joyful in hope, patient in affliction, faithful in prayer. Share with the Lord's people who are in need. Practice hospitality. Bless those who persecute you; bless and do not curse. Rejoice with those who rejoice; mourn with those who mourn. Live in harmony with one another. Do not be proud, but be willing to associate with people of low position. Do not be conceited. Do not repay anyone evil for evil. Be careful to do what is right in the eyes of everyone. If it is possible, as far as it depends on you, live at peace with everyone.*

Jessamin is a PhD Candidate in Sociology and Social Policy at Princeton University. The daughter of missionaries to Japan, she has had a long-standing interest in how culture and ethnicity shape religious identities and practices. While at Princeton, Jessamin has conducted research on white evangelical support for Trump and British evangelical attitudes toward racial diversity and racial justice. Jessamin is also Head of Research and Evaluation at Church Urban Fund, a non-profit tackling poverty and inequality in England.

Left Behind: What American Evangelicalism Has Lost and Needs to Find
By Brandi Miller

> A religion is a system of symbols which acts to establish powerful, pervasive, and long-lasting moods in men by formulating conceptions of a general order of existence and clothing those conceptions with such an aura of factuality that the moods and motivations seem uniquely realistic.
> —Clifford Geertz.[22]

Before the 2008 election, a conservative group in my small rural hometown ran a front page newspaper article questioning whether Barack Hussein Obama was the Antichrist. Obama was identified as such on the basis of a short list of political and personal shortcomings. He was pro-choice, pro-LBTQ, a Democrat, and had a name that triggered anti-Muslim fears associated with 9/11.

My church community took the bait of this propaganda and fear-mongering. Sermons included allusions to losing the country to "the wrong people." Steeped in the scare theology of the *Left Behind* books, my church community described any political practices outside of our understanding of the Bible to be the Antichrist, the mark of the beast, or at the very least, a slippery slope to liberalism. One of their greatest fears for young people leaving for college was that they would become indoctrinated into liberal ideologies at the expense of the gospel. So in November of 2008, at a small private liberal arts college in Oregon, I found myself hiding in my dorm as I cast my vote for John McCain and Sarah Palin.

I voted, unaware of the vast political platform that they represented. I leaned on Fox News talking points and anemic anti-abortion and traditional family arguments. I believed that this, coupled with what I sensed was an imminent, though abstract, threat to this Christian nation; could be thwarted by voting.

My arguments as a young voter were entrenched in this complicated reality. The politics that I was fed and moralized in were predominantly borne of an American Christianity that bore little resemblance to Jesus. Many years passed before I realized that my politics themselves erected a religion full of fallacies and straw man arguments that dictated my political actions. Being American Christian did not mean that I embodied the politics of a follower of Jesus.

The 2020 election is sloganized on the left as a fight for the "soul of the nation."[23] On the right it is a charge to "Make/Keep America Great."[24] Both parties seek that which they see as a more noble vision of reality. These are, at their core, religious visions regardless of purist notions of secularism on the left. These religious ideas are perceptions of the ultimate common good. As such, they seek to establish politics, the public outer working of religion, to see these visions come to pass.

Since the 2016 election of the 45th president, it is clear that the religious vision for a "great America" (aptly) trumps the principles of Jesus himself. Instead of politics existing downstream of religion, the religious right embraces a syncretism of far right conservatism and American Christianity. This blending eliminates the already thin distinction between religion and politics in favor of a divine construction that legitimizes and sanctions the politics of Donald Trump.

There has been a slew of art designed to reinforce a divine mandate in the White House with Trump portrayed with Jesus holding him in office,[25] being prayed for by historic icons,[26] or a variety of memes depicting him as the angel Gabriel, as next to Christ, or depicted as a saint. Oscar Wilde was correct in his assertion that "life imitates art far more than art imitates life[27]" in the onslaught of images of Christian leaders gathering around the president for photo ops and staged photos of the president in front of churches[28] or religious icons.

The result of the syncretism of American religion, propaganda-based iconography and political power is cultish religiosity centered on Donald Trump as God's Messiah sent to buttress patriotism, political power, and global dominance. Regardless of his lack of demonstrable Christ-likeness in his politics, it is clear that pandering to his constituents' desire for Christianized power in the United States has framed him as the president who will "bring America back to God."[29] This is a trade-off: Christian practice and the way of Jesus for American Christian power and utopianism.

Notably, this American "utopia" proves itself to be made more in the image of the religious right and the GOP than the kingdom image of heaven on earth. It is a reality where violence and vitriol are called "law and order" and protecting the property and practices of the powerful triumphs over caring for the basic needs of the most marginalized in our society. "Mak[ing] America Great Again" calls on a mythical past where all could prosper and live freely. This myth centers white men as the litmus test for whether all are free or the nation is great; and centers the rich and corporations to test the strength of the economy. It uses the size of the military to determine safety and the degree to which we, as a nation, have peace.

Reminiscent of the rhetoric of *pax romana,* its assertion is that "peace" comes through the sword. Trump is a master of this rhetoric. In this election cycle alone, the fear-mongering and ad-campaigning center around the notion that "[we] won't be safe in Biden's America"[30] all while showing footage of violence incited over the course of his presidency. This rhetoric obscures the ways in which the GOP, led by Donald Trump, has solidified the context for such civil unrest. This dishonesty, oozing pervasive "us vs. them" ideology, develops fertile soil for the pseudotheocratic cultism in which a word against the policies, practices, and personal life of Donald Trump is equated to being against the will of God.

Crying anti-Christ has proven an effective political tool and was alive and well in the Obama era. Far right evangelical Christians normalized the notion that because Obama appointed pro-choice supreme court judges, worked to legalize same-sex marriage, and was not vehemently pro-Israel, that he himself was anti-American and by extension, anti-God. The ideology of Democrats as anti-Christ produced an epistemology wherein identifying with democratic policies or candidates equates to being against God. Ironically, Obama demonstrated in his personal life and presidency a stereotypical version of a morally astute Christian family man. What this tells us is that it was never about Christian faith, but about cultural Christianity entrenched with politics. In this context, defense of so-called "godly values" functioned more as a Trojan horse for gaining access to political power.

This election cycle, with all of the rhetoric, misinformation, and rampant conspiracy theories, has unearthed the masks that many evangelicals hide behind to cover their support of Donald Trump's racism: the "sanctity of life," Christian freedom (specifically to discriminate against LGBTQ+ people in businesses), the protection of the 2nd amendment (in the name of defending oneself), and pro-Israel politics. This rhetoric equates anyone who does not align with these policies to baby-killing, freedom-hating, restrictive, God haters. This strategy has nefarious consequences- it frames anyone who is not aligned with the leader of this movement or its practices as an enemy or a threat to be negated.

The religious right hijacked what is "godly" and ran the way of Jesus through the American utopian values and tactics of nationalism, order, and global dominance. Jesus comes out on the other side as a sword-wielding, legalistic, capitalist who does whatever it takes to bless the United States. In this context, the basis of American politics on the right has become about generating fear through an abstract threat (Socialism, Marxism, Liberalism) and solidifying it through creating enemies of citizens who oppose the power structures "God" ordained. It measures a nation's godliness by its power, might, and wealth.

Scripture gives us a picture where peace and human co-flourishing is the goal, where enemies receive love, where Christ is the greatest servant of all, where God is known because God's people pursue healing and inclusion instead of power and dominance. It is where people are discipled in the way of Jesus instead of grafted into nationalism disguised as Christianity. God's people get this wrong continually and capitulate to the ways of empire that result in the exploitation of the poor, ethnocentrism, and the coupling of religion and power-gaining politics. God regularly judges nations in Scripture for this trading of shalom and the whole community of creation for individual comfort and prosperity. In these judgments, God gives a litmus test for how we will know that God's shalom way has come: it is that the orphan, the widow, and foreigner are taken care of. In other words, it is not those with political power who are the test of God's peace, but the most marginalized in a society.

One need only look at the cross of Jesus to see how the Trump administration subverts this way of God. Jesus dies at the hands of the government and religious people for claiming to be the God of the marginalized, destitute, and left behind. His murder on the cross is a warning of what happens when religious leaders or the so-called pious and powerful align with political power. Jesus demonstrates on the cross that people are not won over through violence and domination, but through radical forgiveness, indiscriminate inclusivity, and enemy love.

As such, we are given a test of how to find God in politics and what the way of Jesus might look like, even in a political system that is corrupt throughout. We use this test to lean as close as we can to Jesus' way, knowing that no nation will fully politicize the way of God – that was never the point. Our test is two-fold. One, how are the most vulnerable voting and engaging? How are BIPOC and LGBTQ+ seeing themselves in this political moment? How are the poor treated? What is happening to the elderly, to children, and to immigrants? And two, as we look to the cross, do we see hints or calls to the radical forgiveness, enemy love, and inclusivity of the cross and the shalom way that invites all people, regardless of identity to life abundantly in our political options?

With this as a test and principle used in the scriptures, I hold it up to viable options at hand in our two-party system. I hold it up to Donald Trump and see his hatred of enemy, his abuse and demonizing of immigrants, his disregard for the vulnerable, and his radicalizing of violence against the marginalized among us. I see the Christians who support and quote him more than the God that they say upholds him. I see in him echoes of the leaders of Rome, Egypt, Babylon, and Judea in the Scriptures, echoes of violence as a means to peace, rhetoric and fear as a means to social control, and politics as a means to personal deification.

In November I'll cast my vote for Biden/Harris because when presented with the options, I would rather choose a ticket that reflects a semblance of the Jesus way rather than one that names Jesus but doesn't share the religion of politics of Jesus in the Scriptures. I will vote for them because possibility models matter and the image of a woman of color in a position of power offers space for marginalized people to be dignified and lifted up instead of cast to the lowest seats of political tables. I will vote for them, because my own soul requires that I divorce from the cult of the American religious right and look directly at Jesus and his ways instead of at the 45th president who claims him while looking nothing like him. I will vote because at the end of days I don't want to hear from Jesus about my political engagement "Truly I tell you, just as you did not do it to one of the least of these, you did not do it to me."

Brandi Miller is the host of "Reclaiming My Theology," a space to take our theology back from ideas and systems that oppress. She is a staff member and justice program director with a college campus ministry and works at the intersection of faith, justice, and politics.

Our Dreams are Too Small
By Seth Price

The day is June 1, 2020 and the President of these United States has just given a grand speech at the Rose Garden. It is well-received by many. Simultaneously, there are protests around the country surrounding the murders of George Floyd, Breonna Taylor, and numerous others. In his five-minute speech our president offered some haunting words that stand out for me. He said:

> The destruction of innocent life and the spilling of innocent blood is an offense to humanity and a crime against God. America needs creation, not destruction; cooperation, not contempt; security, not anarchy; healing, not hatred, justice, not chaos. This is our mission, and we will succeed. One hundred percent, we will succeed. Our country always wins.[31]

This is the president who has blown dog whistle after dog whistle to stoke fear and divide the country. Under his watch, instead of achieving unity, what has happened is the tattering of our nation through persistent and percussive racial and social injustice.

Evangelicals voted overwhelmingly for Trump in the 2016 election.[32] Since then, I believe that there has been a tectonic shift in the plates of our nation and its churches. I didn't vote for Trump, I couldn't stomach it; but I was not very loud in expressing my reasons why, except among close friends. However, since then I have become increasingly vocal about my concerns and it has cost me dearly. This is a cost I am usually happy to bear; but I must acknowledge that it is ever-increasing. Most recently, a family member cautioned me to be careful what I say and why I say it because he believes the price is too high. He warned, "It might cost you your career" and "it is just not worth it."

Friends, that is a lie.

Back to the Rose Garden: directly after this speech our president walks over to Saint John's Church in Lafayette Park to pose for his infamous photo-op with a Bible in hand. Those peacefully protesting police brutality experience it as tear gas and brute force removing them from Trump's desired backdrop. I am left wondering, what about our Christ?

These past four years, I have tried to picture my Jesus speaking the words of some American evangelical leaders. But I always come up short. I particularly resonate with a parody written by a friend in the form of the Sermon on the Mount:[33]

> 3 Blessed are the powerful,
>   for theirs is the kingdom of America.
> 4 Blessed are those who exalt their exceptionalism,
>   for they are lifted up above all nations.
> 5 Blessed are the proud and boastful,
>   for the world's riches are theirs.
> 6 Blessed are those who consume more than their
> fair share,
>   for their banquet tables are always full.
> 7 Blessed are the retributive,
>   for they punish those they deem the enemy.
> 8 Blessed are the corrupt at heart,
>   for they have made God in their own image.
> 9 Blessed are the culture warriors,

for they have zealously protected their interpretation of Scripture.

10 Blessed are those who persecute the "other,"
for theirs is a very tiny, homogeneous, monolithic kingdom.

This outlook is revolting for several reasons, but most disturbing is the fact that my friend's rewritten Sermon on the Mount so accurately depicts the way we have treated others. I turn on the news and watch pastor after pastor parrot the whataboutisms needed to justify this posture to other image-bearers. This is an addiction.

All too often, the fact that our faith can be separated from or subordinated to our politics is what I have heard. "Turn the other cheek" is just pie in the sky and we must protect ourselves.

I cannot begin to count the times I've been told to turn down my rhetoric with the excuse of "Jesus wasn't political." Jesus was political and I think our framing is off.

All of us are political, even those who don't vote. Churches are a collective of humans expressing collective opinions. They are inherently political, and our pastors, as well as ourselves, have power and influence at our disposal. It is impossible to be apolitical. The problem is the partisanship and the mentality of "othering" that the current climate brings out in church. We are being reduced to Republican versus Democrat, liberal versus conservative, and ultimately–right versus wrong.

For the record, I do think both major parties are guilty here. Both sides are motivated by fear, greed and pride. They lie for their own ends and they discard truth in favor of winning at all costs. They mock and silence their opponents. They abuse and kill innocent human beings[34]. This is clearly not of Christ.

This version of partisan politics that we as the Church practice is going to kill us and all we hold dear because the wages of sin is always death. Jesus called us to be peacemakers who are consumed with seeking wholeness, shalom, justice, and love. It is the definition of following the Way of Christ; to be over- whelmingly and offensively loving, even when it flies in oppo- sition to the partisanship of our politics. You and I must devel- op a new partisanship—one modeled after the words of Jesus. In Luke 19:41-42, as Jesus is entering on a colt into Jerusalem, he says something vitally important: "As he came near and saw the city, he wept over it, saying, 'If you, even you, had only recognized on this day the things that make for peace! But now they are hidden from your eyes'" (NRSV). The text goes on to describe the famous story of Jesus clearing the temple because its leaders have put gold above God.

We are like those leaders. We vote for politicians and sup- port policies that drive the empire, make profits for profits' sake, oppress those living here and abroad, and act in self-in- terest, not a 1 Corinthians 13 type of love.

This is not of God, this is not Christian, and I'm ashamed that at times I still do it. We need a new politic. One that will require us to lay down our power, and possibly be reject- ed by friends and family; one that will call us to surrender to the things that make peace. I know it will be difficult to make peace. This past election we made a collective mistake as a peo- ple searching for the will of God. We wanted a King and in turn forgot the true King.

As you vote, as I vote, we must remember to yield every- thing to the pursuit of love. The call of the church is not to "king-make;" it is to be a prophetic voice to culture. The call of the church is to lead the way and to be the beacon that guides others in a radical, and sometimes painful, way of love. I have no doubt it will be difficult, but I also believe wholeheartedly that it can be attained if only we would live with the humility needed to listen to the call of "The Way" and the conviction to walk in that direction.

Friend, I can hear you now saying, "he's wrong and the church must stand for [insert your political issue here]." I get it,

I really do. My imagination may feel off base here, but I don't believe it is. America's politics and the politics of Jesus stand in opposition to one another and this has always been the reason for us to follow the Way. We, the Church, have dreamed too small and that insufficient vision landed us here. It's time to dream prophetically for something bigger. Together you and I must begin to reform our collective politic.

I fear that if we do not find a new way forward that our public faith may be fractured beyond repair. I simply cannot cast a ballot for Donald Trump as he and those like him hold beliefs that make orphans, oppress the widow, inspire hatred of the other, and demonize those who bear the same divine image you and I do. I am uncertain of what the future could look like under a Biden Presidency; however, I am 100% certain of a downward spiral if the status quo remains in place. Let us all remember that our God is a God of love. He is a tremendous God whose love outruns the speed of light and the expanding universe. He can handle our dream of a nation running un-apologetically after love. Dream with me.

Seth Price is the host of the "Can I Say This at Church" podcast. He lives with his family in Central Virginia and during the day earns a living by working at a bank. Find Seth and the podcast at canisaythisatchurch.com.

What Job is a Conspiracy Theory Doing?
Why American Christians are
Particularly Vulnerable to the Narratives
of the Trump Era
By Matt Lumpkin

1. What job is a conspiracy theory doing?
I recently saw a Facebook post from a friend who lives in Manhattan, the early epicenter of the pandemic in the U.S. It showed a piece of scrawled subway wall note that said:

> Covid 19 was fake. Oprah, Ellen and others been arrested for being perverts so they make us stay home while they are on trial.

I wasn't aware of this particular conspiracy theory so I googled around until I learned that it's a variant on another I had heard. In this one, Bill Gates caused coronavirus as a cover to spread vaccination-based tracking microchips. In this new version, Ellen and Oprah are secretly pedophiles who are under house arrest and they created the pandemic scare to make the rest of us have to stay home so no one will notice that they are on house arrest.

I know. It sounds crazy. How could anyone believe this?

I think that's the wrong question if we want to understand what conspiracy theories like this mean.

A better question is: **what work does this story do for the person who believes it and shares it?**

If Bill Gates or Oprah Winfrey are in control of the pandemic, then that means people – powerful, rich and famous though they may be – are in control of what is happening and there's still hope that people could reverse it.

There are darker, stranger conspiracy theories that have taken hold during the Trump era. What work might they be doing for the people who adhere to them? The QAnon conspiracy postulates that a group of global elites in control of the Democratic party are not only in control of the pandemic, but are pulling the strings on other global events driven by their worship of Satan, hell-bent upon pedophilia and cannibalism. Some even assert that Hillary Clinton and others are in fact a "reptilian" predator race. Recent articles by journalists following both American culture and technology have begun to document the particular resonance of these narratives among American Evangelical Christians.[35] How do we make sense of this? Are American Christians somehow more susceptible to being drawn into this kind of dark fantasy?

2. Where did this come from? When and why conspiracies arise.

So where do these conspiracy theories come from? Stories like this are always around as people respond to new and disorienting circumstances and try to make sense of them. But at times of great social or cultural change when we are struggling to make sense of new threats, fears or anxieties, these stories find a broader audience.

The 2020 pandemic and the growing national response to police violence against Black people created such a context.

Journalist and author, Anna Merlin, in a recent interview about her book on conspiracy theories in America, shares that conspiracy theories:

> ... explain a really consequential world event and how it aligns with *how people already view the world*

... [a conspiracy theory] confirms some political or social element of what they already believe. A timely conspiracy theory is not necessarily a simpler explanation but it is an explanation that allows people to place blame on a specific person. The blame element is really important.[36]

Allowing us to make sense of new and confusing experiences without having to change our mental model of how we already understand the world to work is one of the most powerful and seductive elements of conspiracy theories. They offer us the promise of going back to when the world made sense.

In his book, *The Prophetic Imagination*, Old Testament theologian Walter Brueggemann looks even further back.[37] He writes of how this same dynamic played out in the Jewish communities who produced books of the prophets in the Old Testament; Jeremiah, Ezekiel, Isaiah, and others were at pains to explain their own cultural upheaval.

They had been promised a son of David would always sit on the throne of Israel (1 Kings 9:5), and not a generation later, their throne and temple were destroyed and their leaders led into captivity in exile in Babylon.

They faced the complete erasure of their faith and culture. A new international empire with its own gods was swallowing up nations and tribes, dismantling them, and integrating them into its own new culture. They felt profound disorientation. How could this be? Were the gods of Babylon more powerful than the God of Israel? Had Israel done something wrong?

The prophets answer that last question in the affirmative. They tell a story of a God above all regional and tribal deities who had chosen Israel. But Israel had been unfaithful and was being punished as a result. But still there was a way back for those who would repent and return to faithfulness even in this new reality of exile.

What's important to note here is how these narratives answer the question of **who is to blame**, and **who is called to action** to make things better.

3. Why American Christians are vulnerable.

What the prophets were doing is not unique to their own time. By reaching back and mining their own history for symbols, they lent their prophetic acts and writings resonance and power to stir the hearts of the people who heard them. Reading them from the 20th century, their symbolic acts and extended metaphors can seem cryptic because we don't share their cultural memory.

But that doesn't stop churches from studying them and pastors from interpreting them. In fact, there's a lot of room for creative interpretation in a text that's full of symbols from a culture not your own. Some of that creative interpretation is on display in the popular narratives that emerged during our last great cultural upheaval: the threat of nuclear annihilation during the Cold War.

In the face of the terrifying prospect of mutually assured destruction, many American Christians gravitated to a new story from writer Hal Lindsey called *The Late Great Planet Earth*.[38] In it, Lindsey used the theological framework of Dispensationalism to reassure Christians that God was still in control and to provide a roadmap for what would happen next. Dispensationalism is a distinctly American theological tradition that reads the prophetic books and the Book of Revelation not as meaning-making narratives from their own time and place, but as a kind of book of Nostradamus for foretelling 21st century events. Lindsey's work and the many who followed in his footsteps, popularized "end-times prophecy" and a way of reading Scripture that made it entirely about those of us alive now, living at the end of the world, awaiting Jesus' return.

And like many conspiracy theorists, whenever his predictions failed to come to pass, Lindsey always had a new angle on those same texts to explain how he hadn't been totally wrong, alongside a new batch of tantalizing and terrifying "tribulations" predicted to come.

Many American churches were wholly taken in. Studies of Revelation became popular as generations of Christians squinted at current events through the lens of the "End Times." But unlike the books of the prophets, these narratives didn't demand repentance. Instead they flattered their adherents by centering them in the narrative, casting them as the heroes who were in the know and on the winning side in the coming dark days of war and pestilence. And what call there was to self-examination was for "the world" outside the Church. While Lindsey was among the first to imagine a dark fantasy of coming judgment upon the contemporary church's cultural and political enemies, his work gave rise to a generation of speculative fiction fleshing out his vision avidly shared among American evangelicals.

4. A through line to QAnon.
From my perspective, I see a direct line of continuity between these self-centered patterns of teaching and Bible reading and the current propagation of conspiracy theories like QAnon. Generations of pastors not only taught this kind of thing to their congregations but built these habits of interpreting current events through biblical prophecy or worse, trusting a more well-versed interpreter to do that work for them.

The failure of the American church to perceive Trumpism's betrayal of the way of Jesus is the fruit of a long history: from fundamentalism's century of teaching distrust of government, education, and any authority but its own, all the way up to Dispensationalism. Some journalists have noted that pastors are also feeling a loss of authority they once had.[39] Many have tried and failed to walk their congregants back from the notion that their political enemies are secretly cannibals and lizard-people. But how much of this pattern of questioning all but the authoritative interpreter with special knowledge was created by this kind of leadership and teaching?

5. QAnon, Trump and the current moment: what job is this story doing?

So, in the Trump era, what work does the QAnon story do for the person who believes it and shares it?

QAnon tells a story of a highly placed government intelligence operative who knows what is *really* going on behind the scenes and is sharing that secret knowledge through coded messages online. Those messages say that Trump is working to restore order by defeating a global group of elites who are trafficking children for sex and worse, for Satanic rituals that involve consuming their flesh to achieve immortality.

First, this story does what the Bill Gates and Oprah stories do: it puts a person in control. In the face of a global pandemic, it gives agency to a person and assures us that there is a secret plan to save us all. All we have to do is support our champion: Donald J. Trump.

Second, this story re-centers white, evangelical Christians as the protagonists in the story at a time when they feel they are losing status and power. It has become increasingly difficult to ignore the voices and experiences of Black people, people of color, and gay, trans, and queer people. It explains that those who would advance these narratives are motivated by a hidden, evil agenda. And it reinforces the notion that they will be defeated in the end. Further, the very way the QAnon posts are written activates the habit of interpreting inscrutable texts for symbols and apocalyptic expectations of a world in decline.

Third, this story recasts Trump as the champion, the hero and the self-authenticating authority affirming their identity and the righteousness of their way of life. After decades of being formed by pastors who lead with the same authoritarian style, many American Christians are more ready to follow the loud, blustering orator improvising behind the podium.

Further, Trump's reliance on the authoritarian move of dismissing any critique or inconvenient fact as part of a conspiracy of opponents out to get him feels familiar to congregants accustomed to following pastors who appeal to the same kind of us-versus-them framing. Any critique or opposition is easily waved away as worldly, secular or satanic. Either get in line with the leader or risk being counted among the opposition. This enables Trump to make unsupported claims accusing the press of lying about him or widespread voter fraud while dismissing calls for evidence as just part of the witch hunt. This is the most useful and slippery feature of a conspiracy theory: it can't be disproven because it has deception and obfuscation by a hidden other built into its narrative.

Fourth, and perhaps most powerfully, this story activates strong emotions of disgust and anger at injustice. It's no accident these stories center around our oldest cultural taboos: harm of children, pedophilia, cannibalism. Transgressing these taboos places you outside of human society; monstrous, unredeemable, unworthy of grace, damned. To those who believe it, these people are literal monsters who want to eat their babies. This story serves as a rationale for the disgust and fear they already feel toward their political and ideological enemies and frees them from the difficult obligation to love them as neighbors.

6. What should we do?

The prophets and the author of Revelation weren't the only ones writing stories like these. There were many texts like them from those same tumultuous times; each seeking to make sense of these bewildering new realities. But the communities that survived only kept and passed on the texts that actually worked to help them survive and left the others to be forgotten.

People believe these stories because they help them make sense of a changing world. We can only replace a bad story with one that does a better job.

We can learn a few things from those texts that our predecessors in the faith have passed on to us.

1. They are less interested in finding someone outside the community to blame than they are in searching for their own failures to repent of. Beware any story that flatters you and demands nothing from you. That is more likely a false prophet than a true one.

2. They are more interested in explaining how we got here than in what's going to happen next. Because of the influence of Dispensationalism and its obsession with near term prediction, the popular understanding of the word prophecy is future foretelling. But prophecy in Scripture and the most powerful narratives today help us understand how we got into this mess so we can begin to see our way out.

3. Voices from the margins have a perspective that isn't available from the center. The prophets were written by a people who had lost a significant amount of status. They had gone from being kingly masters of their own destiny to slaves unable to pray in public. The Book of Revelation was written to an early church made up of slaves, women, and outcasts at a time of increasing violent persecution by the Roman empire (which included, by the way, accusations of cannibalism!). These are books not from the center of power but from the margins. The lesson of these books is that if you want to see things from God's perspective, you should be listening to the people on the bottom – those suffering injustice, exclusion, and under threat of complete erasure. In America that means Black people, indigenous people, people of color, as well as queer people.

7. Faithful bearers of the prophetic tradition.

There are still prophets at work in America today. In the summer of 2015, Bree Newsome climbed the flagpole at the South Carolina state house grounds to take down the Confederate flag flying there. The armed security guards who immediately told her to come down didn't know how to respond when she shouted back, paraphrasing David facing down Goliath on the field of battle (1 Samuel 17:45):

> In the name of Jesus this flag has to come down. You come against me with hatred and oppression and violence! I come against you in the name of God! This flag comes down today!

She had reached back into Scripture and dug up a prism through which to view this present reality that shone clear. She was little David, the State was Goliath and the God of the Universe was guiding her hand. And by God, this flag would come down. Two weeks later the South Carolina legislature voted to take it down and keep it down. Just ten days prior, Dylan Roof had committed his own symbolic act of white supremacy, murdering nine Black worshippers who had welcomed him into their prayer service at Mother Emmanuel Church in Charleston, South Carolina. Now, five years later, after waves of protest across the country at the murder of more Black men by the police, the Mississippi Legislature just voted to change its state flag which had prominently featured the Confederate flag.

If the American church is going to survive the Trump era's widespread deception of our people and betrayal of the way of Jesus and the prophets, we will need to turn away from the conspiracy theories that comfort and flatter us, and instead look and listen for prophets, like Bree, who can help us see where we have sinned and illuminate a path of repentance and future hope.

Matt Lumpkin is an ordained Baptist minister and spent his early career as a hospital chaplain. While completing his MDiv at Fuller Seminary he became fascinated with the ways technologies like the printing press and the internet shape religious communities. He's spent the last decade designing and creating digital spaces for education and personal formation for seminaries and startups.

Whatsoever is Good
or
Talking to People Like They Are Not the Devil
By Bart Tocci

I'm 32 years-old, and it has taken me almost all of those years to realize that I like agreement. I like agreement more than you and all your friends do. God gave me an extra dose of empathy, and it makes me good at welcoming people and public speaking and writing. Side effects include decision paralysis and laziness and caring *way* too much about what other people think. But back to the good part: walking in other people's shoes helps me see all sides of an argument. In other words, I change my mind.

This isn't cool in 2020. You can't change your mind. There are a lot of people who would maybe want to change their minds, but unfortunately, they can't. Not now. That would open up a new world of possibilities; the dominoes would fall too fast. If I believe this, then I'll have to believe that as well. One by one they fall ...

I have friends on the right, friends on the left – you do, too, otherwise you wouldn't be here, reading. I don't want to lose those friends and family. I have a cousin who posts alt-right meme news on Facebook – you probably have the same cousin. It's a screenshot of a screenshot of a post and it's usually a Black person who says that racism doesn't exist. It's usually the same Black person. It's Candace Owens. I don't agree with her, but

I respect how much sheer hate she can handle. I can't handle that kind of hate.

I have liberal friends who post the same-but-opposite sarcastic content: biting memes, inflammatory headlines, ready to cancel the next person who uses the wrong vocab word. Their posts condescend, "Just so you know, today is not your day, and you're an idiot if you didn't *know* that." Everything is about *knowledge*. You *must know things*.

My far liberal and far conservative friends are the same: they plug their ears and shout, they consume content that they already agree with, and they unfriend people who disagree with them. "It's not worth putting up with the ignorance and hate," they both say.

You already *know* all this, though, so what do you do with that all-important knowledge? You stay quiet. It's not worth it. You'll never change anyone's mind through a Facebook argument.

No, dammit! Not this time. You're going to act. You furiously type comments in reply to your cousin's memes or your liberal friends' "Just so you know" post. Your finger hovers over the "enter" button.

You delete those comments. Not the right time.

No! It must *be the right time! If you stay silent, you have chosen the side of the oppressor!*

You retype the comments and try to be as calming and pleasant as possible.

You hit enter.

You get destroyed. Your cousin's alt-right gang, or your libfriend's gang, *The People-Who-Think-Just-Like-Me Gang* pile on. Yeah, lousy gang names but, dag *nabbit* they are effective! They are skilled at being loud! And being perpetually online!

When I was in middle school, the *only* way to communicate was through AOL Instant Messenger (AIM). You could personalize your away message; your profile could have clues about your friends or maybe a song that hinted at a girl you liked. For example, one of my away messages was, "There's a log on the fire," from that Eagle-Eye Cherry song, "Save Tonight," and it *really* was about a girl I liked but she had to be freaking Sherlock Holmes to figure that out. My screen name was *Barticusillonius*. It was code: it was my first name, and then *icusillonius*. All my secrets laid bare.

AIM allowed people like me, who were charming and handsome middle-schoolers with undeveloped brains, entirely petrified of any interaction with a human girl our own age, a way to communicate. MAN I was courageous with girls over AIM. No consequences! I would ask girls out; I would ask them if they liked me … actually that's pretty much it. I was fearless! And then in person, we all pretended that AIM didn't exist and that we'd never met before.

That was twenty years ago. We learned how to communicate on AIM by taking in-person communication and translating that to typed messages. Now, we're doing the opposite. We're learning how to argue in person like we do online, and it's dangerous. We're encouraged to "destroy" people who disagree with us. We're encouraged to unfriend people in real life who disagree with us. This is not healthy.

We used to rarely talk about politics. If we did, we spoke face to face with the benefit of nuance, in both tone and body language. I remember asking my friend's mom about who she was voting for. We were big time conservatives; she was a liberal. She said Al Gore. I asked her if George Bush wouldn't be a better choice because, after all, he was the Governor of Texas, and Texas is pretty big, and so he could take that experience and be the President of the U.S.A. I was twelve. She disagreed. She did not "annihilate" me because she was a good person.

Here's my foolish, earnest, and urgent question for people on both the left and right: Can you, for the love of God, love people who disagree with you? I don't know when disagreement marked someone as an enemy, but "Love your enemies" (Matt. 5:44). If you cannot, we have no hope. Can you see the error in the side you support? If you cannot, the work of splitting this country in half will continue, no matter who is elected.

So, the Battle of the Septuagenarians. Trump or Biden. This isn't about policies or appointees, it's not about personal beliefs or tweets or PR or campaign strategy. This election is about unity. It has to be, because if we're not together, if we're fighting between ourselves, we can't move forward. There's a reason Jesus taught, "Blessed are the peacemakers" (Matt. 5:9). Who will work the hardest to keep us together? Who will unite instead of divide? Who cares about everyone, not just some? Who has compassion? Who has empathy?

I like that Biden calls out his own team (left) and the opposing team (right) for violence. He is capable of acknowledging the two sides to the story. I used to think Trump was *unwilling* to do this. Now I don't believe he actually *can* do it. He doesn't have the capacity to acknowledge the problems on his own side. We know this because when anyone on the right has criticized the right, or criticized him, they're done. As evidence of this, there's a 91% turnover rate in Trump's "A Team" (members of the executive office of the president). There are a handful of promotions, but most have either resigned, or resigned under pressure. 91%. You must go back five presidents to get the next highest turnover rate of 78%, with Reagan.[40]

Trump had four years to make things better, and he could not. He is a pot-stirrer. The next four years in Trump's America would mean more stirring, more gasoline on more fire. Yes, Biden has a long list of flaws, and each one of those flaws is matched and far exceeded by Trump.

I'm not going to tell you who to vote for, but I will tell you that I'm not going to vote for Trump.

Don't unfriend me,

Bart

Bart Tocci is a graduate of Calvin College and a former contributor to The Post Calvin blog. He is currently a student at Boston University, studying for his master's in journalism. Bart plays guitar for his church band, he plays hockey every week with old friends, and he would rather talk about anything other than politics.

Brown

By Charles Samuel

I was at home on Election Night in 2016, and I remember the night well for two reasons in particular. The first is obvious: it was the night Donald J. Trump defeated Hillary Clinton to become the 45th President of the United States. And in electing a tabloid-manufactured, reality television-manicured caricature of a person, it felt less like we were making America great again and more like we were giving America an ego boost it didn't need. To borrow from television jargon: 2016 is when America *jumped the shark.*

But I remember that Tuesday night for another reason—an unrelated one involving an election watch party, dinner guests, and a fantastically ruined strip steak. Armed with a much-ballyhooed online recipe, clean cookware & utensils, and all the right ingredients, I neglected the most critical thing of all: the heat.

It's why we didn't end up having steak for dinner.

The difference between browning food and burning it is subtle. Heat forces certain amino acids and sugars in food to interact with each other in hundreds of chain reactions involving hundreds of different new molecules, unlocking hosts of complex flavors and smells and textures. This series of interactions is called the Maillard reaction—what gives cooked meats their golden sears, caramelized onions their piercing umami, and baked breads their crisp crusts.

We credit the science behind the Maillard reaction to French chemist Louis-Camille Maillard, who, in 1912, was the first to describe the complicated interplay between amino acids and sugars in the presence of heat.

But it's important to remember that not all heat is created equal. The same effects you'd expect to see in mere minutes at 300° F would take hours if you were working at a relatively cooler 250° F. The higher the temperature, the faster these micro-interactions occur.

But there's a point of no return. At around 356° F, pyrolysis takes over (instead of the Maillard reaction). That's when strip steaks burn.

It's no coincidence why oven-baked recipes often call for the 350° F standard: it's right at the sweet spot where food browns quick enough but won't incinerate. On a stovetop, 350° F is a shade under *medium temperature*, somewhere between 4 and 5 on a 10-point dial. I had no idea of any of this in 2016. I confidently cranked the cooktop dial up to 10 and realized pretty quickly we'd be ordering out instead.

We undermine the complexity and beauty of the Maillard reaction when we disregard the import of heat. And in my ignorance, I had crossed the point of no return.

Similarly, we undermine the complexity and beauty of *justice* when we disregard the import of *compassion*. While Trump's platform today props up its "law and order" messaging with soaring Evangelical support[41], it largely looks askew at how the Bible colors the interplay between justice and compassion. Justice and equity. Justice and charity.

I believe voting for Donald Trump in 2020 pushes American Christendom past the point of no return—mainly because of the incongruity of his "law and order" plank with a Biblical sense of justice. I am a Christian, and I will not be voting for him.

Lesser Justice

Trump's law and order plank eschews biblically sound social justice for a politically expedient legal justice.

This view of justice is fundamentally flawed in that it distorts the justice of the Bible for a lesser justice of the world. Throughout the Bible, God doesn't encourage legal justice for legal justice's sake. Rather, he warns we miss out on the complexity and beauty of justice when we disregard the dignity of people. It's like trying to enjoy the Maillard effect but ignoring how far you've turned up the stovetop temperature dial.

But the phrase is also troubling because of its racial undertones. "Law and order" was popularized by the Nixon administration in 1968, when they weaponized the slogan as a dog whistle to stoke racial fears among white voters.[42] It was coded and righteous-y rhetoric fixated on *legal justice*. It Othered an entire group of people, and transformed from an en-vogue to long-lasting symbol of the perversion of justice to further political ends.

To emphasize the Bible's version of justice is to think about people first; not politics.

A Counterweight

In the Old Testament, writers use two words in particular to express God's intentions for *legal justice*: *mishpat* and *tzedakah*—neither of which has a true modern English equivalent. While both are important for their literal definitions, they're especially important when viewed through a wider exegetical lens.

Mishpat typically subsumes a positive exertion of legal justice. In Scripture, this is how God's justice is explained; it is of an appropriate and reasonable caliber, and it is ultimately fair. Also, it often protects "the same crowd of people: the widow, the orphan, and the poor."[43] (More on that in a second.)

While *tzedakah* also implies an exertion of justice, Scripture tells us it's a little more nuanced than that. There's a great illustration in Deuteronomy 24:10–13 (ESV):

When you make your neighbor a loan of any sort, you shall not go into his house to collect his pledge. You shall stand outside, and the man to whom you make the loan shall bring the pledge out to you. And if he is a poor man, you shall not sleep in his pledge. You shall restore to him the pledge as the sun sets, that he may sleep in his cloak and bless you. And it shall be *tzedakah* for you before the Lord your God.

Here, *tzedakah* goes deeper than just a performative doling out of justice. In this passage, a poor person offers his only cloak as collateral against a loan. While verses 10 and 11 make it clear the lender is totally within his rights to keep the cloak until the debt has been paid, the temperature seems to change a little bit in verse 12. God raises the dignity of that poor person, conveying in no uncertain terms that administering justice here is not necessarily *the right thing to do*. In fact, in the parallel passage in Exodus 22:27, God rhetorically asks, "In what else shall he sleep?"

God explains his rationale to this apparent flip-flop in the very next line of the same verse: "If he cries to me, I will hear, for I am compassionate." *Tzedekah* goes further than mere justice; Rabbi Lord Jonathan Sacks calls it a "justice tempered by compassion."

So we've got a real complication here. In *mishpat*, there's a focus on the widow, the orphan, and the poor; in *tzedakah*, compassion is a counterweight to indelicate appropriations— or misappropriations—of the law. The anchor of God's justice is a dignifying of people, not a demonstration of power.

Wordplay
Reading into biblical justice is especially jarring when we accept what we should already know: secular and political ladders of power are inherently corruptible.

Isaiah adds a few creative ripples to these terms—*mishpat* and *tzedakah*—bending them past a simple literal reading. As John Goldingay notes in *The Theology of the Book of Isaiah*[44], it's his translation of Isaiah 5:7b in particular that expands how we should interpret these terms

> And he looked for justice [*mishpat*], but saw bloodshed [*mispach*];
> for righteousness [tzedakah], but heard cries of distress [tza'akah].
> (Isa. 5:7b, NIV)

Isaiah's close-but-no-cigar wordplay here is telling. *Mispach* and *tza'kah* are phonetically similar to *mishpat* and *tzedakah*, but they're distortions of what God is seeking here. Instead of justice, he finds bloodshed. Instead of righteousness, there's distress.

According to Goldingay, while "we expect judgment to be exercised in a way that is just … it can be exercised in an unjust way." *Mishpat* — especially when espoused by political opportunists — "can be perverted."

Or it can be blunted. In *Letter from a Birmingham Jail*, Martin Luther King Jr. famously lambasted Christian moderates for following just laws and unjust laws alike. King agreed with Saint Augustine that "an unjust law is no law at all." He writes that churches declaring the need to follow desegregation law for law's sake is inherently—even morally—different from following it "because integration is morally right and the Negro is your brother."[45]

In the book of Isaiah, the prophet also widens the parameters of *tzedakah*. As Goldingay explains, a commonly understood meaning of the word is *righteousness* or "individual holiness… [However, *tzedakah*] is an essentially relational word. It suggests doing the right thing in relation to other people." Isaiah essentially doubles down on what the parallel passages in Deuteronomy and Exodus told us: you cannot have justice without compassion.

In the social upheaval of 1960s America, prominent Christian moderates lost sight of *tzedakah* in favor of law and order. Jemar Tisby writes in *The Color of Compromise* how Billy Graham's response to scenes of civil unrest was to preach more emphatically on the need for "tough laws to crack down on such flagrant disregard for authority."[46] Graham's politics-adjacent Christian messaging was so impactful that it muddied the waters between church and state. In *One Nation Under God*, Kevin M. Kruse writes: "His words and deeds helped make piety and patriotism seem the sole property of the right."[47]

In reorienting around truly biblical justice—around the deeper, wider intentions of *mishpat* and *tzedakah*—it helps to consider Paul's urging in 1 Corinthians 12:12–26 and recognize the tapestries of diversity within the Church body. In exercising justice faithfully, we do so because we believe in the God-given dignity of every person.

Reconciling

It's hard to fight the disappointment of broken promises that Trump made during his Election Night speech in 2016, including a pledge to "be president for all Americans" and to "unify our great country."[48] A quick scan of the unrelenting, coast-to-coast, powder keg protests over the last four years demonstrates how Trump has let down a meaningful subset of society. A scroll through the President's Twitter feed shows a determination to broaden the ruptures of a nation that brands itself as United.

The challenge for Christian voters lies in reconciling the Trump administration's behavior, vocabulary, and policy around the Other—from Mexicans, to Muslims, to refugees, to those from "shithole" countries, to the suffering, to the poor, to the marginalized—with the compassion required from God's demand of a compassion-driven justice.

In Donald Trump's America, we've lost sight of *mishpat* and *tzedakah*. And his platform and message have been antithetical to the nuance of community and diversity Paul highlighted in his letter to the Corinthians. That sort of division just isn't a mistake we can afford again. If we love our neighbors and value each of them as inherently great parts of the sum of all of us, we must embrace diversity, not espouse division.

A lot is at stake at the polls, and Christians have the chance to show up to emphatically change the zeitgeist. Making America truly great requires recognizing all people for their God-given dignity. It's on us to pursue a "justice tempered by compassion."

To brown, not burn.

Charles Samuel is a writer and essayist who writes about the intersection of faith, culture, and politics. He is also the founder of 90odd, a marketing company dedicated to helping social enterprises create, deliver, and scale solutions for some of society's major problems.

What's Love Got to Do With It?
By Erick Schenkel

"The land of the free and the home of the brave;" our American national anthem moves to its stirring conclusion with that statement about who we are as a people. Freedom and courage— those are pretty good values. But what strikes me, as a disciple of Jesus Christ, is what is absent in our national sense of who we are. Love, care and compassion are not core American ideals.

A recent study comparing the beliefs of people from 44 nations offered this set of distinctive American traits: individualism, belief in hard work to get ahead, optimism and religiosity.[49] The first three confirm the absence of love and related virtues as American priorities. One might expect that religiosity would bring some focus on love, but our values shape our religion more than our religion shapes our values. How else can we explain the support that Donald Trump enjoys in the Christian community, despite his personal style and his political policies?

When asked, "What is the greatest commandment," Jesus did not answer, "All the commandments are equally important!" He gave clear priority to love when he answered:

> "Love the Lord your God with all your heart and with all your soul and with all your mind." This is the first and greatest commandment. And the second is like it: "'Love your neighbor as yourself."

All the Law and the Prophets hang on these two commandments." (Matt. 22:37-40, NIV)

Love was the highest value for Jesus and should be the highest value for anyone who would be his disciple. In fact, the apostle John tells us that "God IS love." His very essence, His substance, is love. God is not a loving being. He is love itself.

Much that Jesus and His apostles said about love runs counter to some of our most cherished American beliefs. For example, loving one's neighbor as oneself is clearly a challenge to our individualism and competition. The apostle Paul counsels, "Be kind to one another, tenderhearted, forgiving one another, as God in Christ forgave you" (Eph. 4:32, NKJV). Kindness and tenderheartedness are not usually thought of as American values. They are too soft. In a recent book on the absence of mercy in our public life, an American businessman laments:

> Showing mercy is often seen as weakness. Feed the poor? They should work for a living, we think ... The business world—the world I'm familiar with— can be particularly unmerciful. It's predicated on a far more Darwinian "survival of the fittest" mode of operation than of anything predicated on God's curious calculus.[50]

In another famous passage, Paul exhorts Christians:

> Love is patient, love is kind. It does not envy, it does not boast, it is not proud. It does not dishonor others, it is not self-seeking, it is not easily angered, it keeps no record of wrongs. Love does not delight in evil but rejoices with the truth. It always protects, always trusts, always hopes, always perseveres. Love never fails. (1 Cor. 13:4-8, NIV)

The tone of our national political discourse utterly fails when measured against this standard! Imagine trying to say with a straight face, "President Trump is patient, he is kind. He does not envy, he does not boast, he is not proud. He does not dishonor others, is not self-seeking, is not easily angered, he keeps no record of wrongs. He does not delight in evil but rejoices in the truth."

Perhaps Jesus' most difficult teaching on love is His command to love our enemies—to turn the other cheek. This seems to run counter to our national tendency toward self-assertion, and once again, our president, Donald Trump, goes further than most, proudly staking his political life on the philosophy, "Hit me and I'll hit you back twice as hard."[51] Was Jesus wrong in what he taught?

Here is how Catholic Bishop Robert Barron; Fr. explains Jesus' words about how to respond to unfair attack:

> "If someone strikes you on the right cheek, turn and give him the other." No one in Jesus' time would have used the unclean left hand for any kind of social interaction. Therefore, to strike someone on the right cheek was to hit him with the back of the hand, and this was a gesture of contempt, reserved for slaves and social inferiors. Faced with this kind of aggression, Jesus says, one should neither fight back nor flee; rather one should stand one's ground and turn the other cheek. He thereby signals to the aggressor that he refuses to live in that person's spiritual and psychological space. And he mirrors back the aggressor's aggression, shaming him into self-awareness and prompting conversion.

Bishop Barron tells a story about a time when Mother Theresa approached a baker, begging some bread for a starving child. The baker spat in her face. She stood firm, looked at the baker and said "That was for me, now can you give something for the child?" Bishop Barron concludes, "Naïve? Impractical? Tell that to Gandhi, Martin Luther King Jr., and John Paul II, all of whom effected massive social changes through creative employment of Jesus' teaching. The Christian churches need to recover their confidence in this method and to teach it, at the very least to their own congregants."[52]

Another practitioner of this kind of love was Congressman John Lewis, whose funeral is being celebrated as I write these words. His skull was fractured as he crossed the Edmund Pettus Bridge in the historic 1965 Selma march for voting rights. He was arrested at least 45 times in non-violent protests for civil rights. He served in the U.S. House of Representatives for 33 years, and was called "the conscience of Congress."[53] In a radio interview late in his life, Lewis looked back on his life and his politics:

> The movement created what I like to call a nonviolent revolution. It was love at its best. It's one of the highest forms of love. That you beat me, you arrest me, you take me to jail, you almost kill me, but in spite of that, I'm going to still love you. I know Dr. King used to joke sometime and say things like, "Just love the hell outta everybody. Just love 'em."[54]

Love is always costly. It is all too easy for me, as a middle-class white American, to blithely ignore what it costs heroic African Americans like John Lewis to respond in love to our continuing national history of hatred and abuse toward people of color. I am painfully aware that my privileged socio-economic status often blinds me to the suffering of marginalized people around me and how unwilling I am to pay the cost of love. I live like the rich man in Jesus' parable (Luke 16:19-31) who failed every day to see the plight of poor Lazarus and was condemned for his callousness. As a follower of Jesus Christ called to make love my core value, I am learning to look beyond my own interests and to empathize with others. As I learn, I am compelled to lament our national history of racism, including enslaving and oppressing African Americans and carrying out genocide against native peoples. I am concerned by the plight of those in dire need in America today—the ill who cannot afford health care, the unemployed parent who cannot feed their family, the immigrant in need of safety, the LGBTQ+ student who is bullied. I am appalled when America proudly boasts its ability to bring "shock and awe" while indifferently killing tens of thousands of civilians in an unjustified war. I am sorry for the state of the environment that we are leaving to our children. Yes, addressing these issues will be costly; love is always costly.

I am also moved by the cry of the unborn child who is unwanted and unprotected, and by the hopelessness of the young woman who bears that child. I am frustrated that our two major political parties force Christians to choose between love for the unborn and love for the born. I am most deeply offended by the cynical Faustian bargain offered to Christians by Donald Trump, who has promised Christians that he will oppose abortion in exchange for their loyalty to him regardless of who else he hurts. How can we say we love the one whom we have not seen, when we do not love those whom we have seen?

It is tempting to match Trump's divisive rhetoric insult for insult, but the recent direction of the Republican People's Party (CHP) in the Republic of Turkey offers another alternative. This party recently won an astounding victory over the ruling Justice and Development Party (AKP) in the Istanbul mayoral election by employing what they call a strategy of "radical love." They fought against the polarizing authoritarian populism of Recep Tayyip Erdoğan by refusing to address him with angry rhetoric, by showing genuine concern for the pain of his conservative supporters, and by focusing on listening to and responding to the real needs of the people on whose frustration Erdoğan has built his political base. Their blueprint, the *Book of Radical Love*, authored by party member Ateş İlyas Başsoy, quotes the Sufi poets of Turkey's Muslim tradition as its foundation.[55] The words of Jesus can provide the foundation for an American movement of radical love that remakes our national politics.

Love belongs in the public square; it deserves a place at the center of our civic discourse. Russian Christian author Leo Tolstoy described over 100 years ago, in a letter published by Mohandas Gandhi, how people who sincerely believe in the power of love can embrace horrifyingly unloving behavior in their public life:

> Thus it went on everywhere. The recognition that love represents the highest morality was nowhere denied or contradicted, but this truth was so interwoven everywhere with all kinds of falsehoods which distorted it, that finally nothing of it remained but words. It was taught that this highest morality was only applicable to private life — for home use, as it were — but that in public life all forms of violence — such as imprisonment, executions, and wars — might be used for the protection of the majority against a minority of evildoers, though such means were diametrically opposed to any vestige of love ... And such a teaching, despite its inner contradiction, was so firmly established that the very people who recognize love as a virtue accept as lawful at the same time an order of life based on violence and allowing men not merely to torture but even to kill one another.[56]

One of our contemporary prophetic intellectuals, Cornel West, often reminds us, "Justice is what love looks like in public."[57] We need to see more of her out there. No political principles, claiming to be derived from the Bible, may supplant her. None can compare with her. Those of us who claim to be Christians, ignore her to our everlasting peril. When all the public policy principles are weighed and evaluated, the words of the apostle Paul will forever stand, "The greatest of these is love."

Erick Schenkel has served as a pastor, a cross-cultural missionary, and an organizational leader, including six years as Executive Director of the "Jesus Film Project," a sub-ministry of Cru. He holds a PhD in American religious history from Harvard University and is the author of <u>The Joys and the Hopes: An American Evangelical Discovers Catholic Social Teaching</u>.

On Discernment in Voting

Vote Like the Beatitudes Matter
by Mark Scandrette

Just before the midterm elections in 2018 I did something spontaneous. I jumped on a bus to join the Vote Common Good tour. Along with a dozen other Christian leaders, I spent three weeks visiting towns and cities across the heartland that supported Donald Trump's 2016 bid for the U.S. presidency. In town squares, truck stops and parking lots we hosted public conversations about faith and politics. Reporters from *The New York Times*, *The Guardian*, and NPR traveled with us, curious about whether evangelical Christians might be open to changing the way they vote. On the tour we asked people to consider how the teachings of Jesus, and particularly the Sermon on the Mount, might inform our civic engagement and voting practices.

For most evangelical Christians, considering a change in voting means choosing any alternative to the Republican party, which has relied on the evangelical vote since the 1980s. The widespread assumption is that the GOP represents what we Christians care most about. By participating in the tour, I risked offending friends, family, and supporters of my ministry who believe that voting Republican is the only viable option for a Christian. After announcing my participation in the tour, I received angry letters that led to difficult conversations. Despite the personal costs, I chose to go on the tour because of the ways I'd seen the cause of Christ affected by the decisions and behavior of Trump— who claims to be a Christian.

A watching world assumes that since 81% of white Christians voted for Trump; his speech and behavior reflect the attitudes and beliefs of those who claim to be followers of Jesus. I regularly travel internationally to train pastors and leaders. They often quiz me about Christian support of Trump. The clarity of their outside perspective gives me pause: "Mark, what are our brothers and sisters in the U.S. thinking? How do they not see how misguided this is?" One leader in particular said, "I'm concerned that by not speaking out about Trump we are inoculating an entire generation to the gospel."

I came of age during the culture wars of the 1980s, listening to James Dobson on Christian radio and reading periodicals like James Dobson's *Citizen Magazine* and Phyllis Schlafly's *Eagle Forum* Newsletter. Although my parents weren't particularly political, as part of a churchgoing military family, my views were largely shaped by what I was exposed to inside the conservative evangelical bubble. I grew up paranoid about Communism, fearful of feminists, and suspicious of anyone who wasn't clearly aligned with a conservative agenda. Conspiracy theories abounded and even trusted faith leaders like Billy Graham and Chuck Colson were considered suspect because they associated with people on the other side of party and religious lines.

The Christian apologetic writings of Francis Schaeffer were formative for me, so I paid careful attention when his later work took a decisively right-wing turn. Books like Peter Marshall and David Manuel's *The Light and the Glory* led me to believe that from Christopher Columbus to George Washington, divine guidance established the United States, a country founded on explicitly Christian principles that were under attack by liberals. It was our job to fight for the return to a Christian America. As a teenager, I protested abortion clinics. In my University Honors program, I presented a political science paper on how the religious right's participation in politics was essential to returning America to its former greatness. At age 21, after I gave a rousing speech about personal responsibility, I was nominated to be the local precinct chairman of the Republican party. When Bill Clinton defeated George H. W. Bush in the 1992 presidential election, I sat in stunned silence and wept. It felt like the end of the world!

That ended up being the last time I cast all my votes for Republican candidates. So what happened?

As a teenager I became a follower of Jesus. While reading the four gospels I fell in love with a revolutionary rabbi/messiah who spoke about the Kingdom of God and invited his disciples to follow his radical ethic of love: forgive relentlessly, don't worry, love your enemies, sell your possessions, and give to the poor. I started asking myself, *if Jesus walked the earth today, would he be in a brick-columned church or bank, or hanging out with the poor and forgotten on the wrong side of town?* Prompted by my faith, in college I started crossing boundaries of class and race. I taught children's Bible clubs in the Black neighborhoods of Tuscaloosa. I volunteered in the adolescent unit of the Alabama state mental hospital. Eventually I left school to work at an inner-city ministry serving low income and unhoused families in Minneapolis. I began having first-hand experiences that contradicted what I had always been told about liberals, minorities, immigrants and "welfare moms." I learned that the "good old days" when America was supposedly governed by Christian values were also the days of slavery, segregation and terror lynchings. Women and non-white people didn't have the right to vote. Gay people were often beaten to death by angry mobs with impunity.

I've spent a lifetime trying to reconcile my involvement in politically conservative Christian circles with the revolutionary life and teachings of Jesus. The message of Jesus was inherently political. At the beginning of his public life, he stood up in the synagogue and used Scripture to declare his purpose as a liberator: "The Spirit of the Lord is on me ... to proclaim good news to the poor, freedom for the prisoners ... to set the oppressed free ..." (Luke 4:18-20, NIV). Jesus brought healing and hope to people in physical and mental suffering. He spoke truth to power, turning over tables and chasing out the currency venders taking advantage of the poor. He invited his disciples to make the healing of the world their highest priority: "Seek first the kingdom of God and God's justice" (Matthew 6:33 DRB).

How does the world become better? When we decide to use our power for good. The whole universe is God's creative realm. You and I have been given a small piece of that as our personal "kingdom" to manage. Your body. Your mind. Your time. Your money and possessions and the influence you have in relationships. We are being invited to imagine the world as it could be and take action to make it that way. What we do matters.

As a privileged white male, the dominant systems work to my benefit. It's easy to feel less urgency about changing unjust systems when they benefit us and insulate us from the pain they cause. The book of James says, "If anyone, then, knows the good they ought to do and does not do it, it is sin for them" (James 4:17, NIV). If we aren't actively working for change on both personal and systemic levels, then we are complicit in keeping things the way they are. It's true that the systems are broken, but we are that system. If we want to see change, it will have to begin with us – with our hearts and minds, our actions, our voices and our votes.

My sense is that most of us evangelical Christians think of politics as a dirty and divisive business. I often hear people say, "All politicians are crooks, so I choose not to be involved." I've said myself, "Our country won't change until hearts are changed, so rather than working for change through laws or policies I'm praying that God will change hearts." The one day we are supposed to be political is on election day in November, when it's our duty to vote to protect the lives of the unborn – even though data shows that there is no statistical correlation between abortion rates and which party is in power.[58]

Gradually I realized that I'm invited to care about everything our Creator cares about: the dignity of human life at every stage, care of Creation and future generations, just and sustainable economic policies, and care of immigrants and the poor, to name a few. To do this I must be civically engaged and spiritually attuned. Rather than being a single-issue voter, I must look carefully at the policies and platforms that best support the greater good of the Kingdom of God. I don't believe that one party's platform reflects the full range of God's desires for humanity and creation. I agree with what Francis Schaeffer once wrote, that as Christians we are invited to be cobelligerents – meaning that rather than being strictly aligned with one political party, we support policies and candidates from multiple parties that best reflect all the values of the Kingdom of God.

On the Vote Common Good tour, we invited congressional candidates from both parties to participate in our events. Knowing that our gatherings were faith-voter-oriented, they talked candidly about their own spiritual lives and motivations for seeking public office. A surprising number of Democratic candidates were self-professed Christians, though it was obvious that many of them weren't used to talking about their faith in public. Over a meal I said to one candidate, "So you're a Christian; why don't you talk about your faith on the campaign trail?" Her response was instructive. She said, "The Republican party uses faith to pander to religious voters and I believe that lacks integrity – especially when it is clear the candidate is insincere."

I believe we need Christians involved in both parties helping candidates develop platforms and legislation that reflect the shalom of God's Kingdom. And we can encourage and keep them accountable to those priorities. But what this calls for is much more civic engagement than most of us are accustomed to. Many of us scarcely know the names of the elected officials whose leadership shapes life in our neighborhoods and cities.

I'll be the first to admit that, at best, I've been inconsistent in my civic engagement. I know that real system change requires sustained involvement, beginning at the local and grassroots level.

At our Vote Common Good events, I greeted people as they arrived and asked, "what brings you here tonight?" One person's reply particularly struck me. She said, "I'm here tonight because I'm a Fox news orphan." I asked her to say more, and she explained: "I grew up in what I would describe as a devout and loving Christian home. My parents were key leaders in our church and taught me to be loving, kind and ethical. They spent many years doing foster care and going on mission trips. They gave me a wonderful example. But since my dad's retirement, he spends his days watching Fox news and he's become increasingly fearful, angry and judgmental. Even though I'm not interested in talking about politics, he insists on spending family gatherings ranting about immigrants, the poor and minorities. What happened to my loving and Christlike father? He didn't teach me to act or speak that way!" As she spoke, tears welled up in her eyes.

So many of us are disturbed by the polarization and incivility that characterizes current political discourse. The media industry knows that the best way to attract clicks, eyeballs, and revenue is to stoke conflict, alarm, and controversy. If you want to see how pervasive this mentality is, try going a day or a week without using language that labels, stereotypes and divides – words like liberal, conservative, fascists, or socialists. See how it shapes your heart and interactions in new ways.

I believe the Beatitudes provide wise guidance for the posture and values that might shape how we engage in public discourse and how we vote:

Blessed are the poor. Am I affirming God's care and provision or acting from anxiety and a mentality of scarcity and greed? Does my vote support the well-being of everyone, including the poor and most vulnerable in our country and around the world?

Blessed are those who mourn. Am I willing to acknowledge and lament the ways I have participated in or benefitted from systems and structures of oppression? Does my vote help repair the damage caused by native genocide, slavery, structural racism, and past international aggressions?

Blessed are the meek. Do I recognize people from all walks of life as being made in God's image with inherent dignity and worth? Does my vote support human equality and basic human rights?

Blessed are those who hunger and thirst for justice. Do I agree with God's holistic agenda of seeing heaven's dream established on earth? Does my vote support justice for the alien, the poor, the widow, and the oppressed? Does my vote support providing care to "the least of these:" the hungry, thirsty, sick, naked and imprisoned?

Blessed are the merciful. Do I look with compassion at my fellow humans or scapegoat and speak and act with judgement and contempt? Does my vote support restorative justice instead of retribution?

Blessed are the pure in heart. Do I value honesty and integrity within myself? Do I expect the same from public officials? Does my vote support candidates that exhibit honesty, integrity and responsibility for inevitable mistakes?

Blessed are the peacemakers. Do I recognize that we are each part of God's larger family, or do I tend to emphasize what divides us? Does my vote support candidates who seek unity, civility, and policies that promote domestic and international cooperation and peace?

Blessed are those who are persecuted for justice. Am I prepared to choose the good, no matter what it costs me personally? Does my vote support the common good over what might benefit me?

Jesus said, "You are the light of the world... let your light shine ... that they may see your good deeds and glorify your father in heaven" (Matthew 5:14-16, NIV). We are powerful creatures who shape the world by our choices. At a time when corporations and billionaires effectively buy politicians and shift legislation toward their own interests and away from the common good, we urgently need to let our voices be heard. May we use our bodies and our votes to do justice, love mercy, and walk humbly.

Mark Scandrette is an internationally recognized expert in practical Christian spirituality. He cofounded Reimagine, a center for integral Christian practice. His most recent books include Belonging and Becoming, Practicing the Way of Jesus, *and more. Mark teaches in the Doctoral program at Fuller Seminary and is on the creative team for the 9 Beats Collective, a project exploring the beatitudes as a 21st century vocabulary for Jesus' way. He is passionate about efforts to create safe neighborhoods for all people.*

Voting as a Citizen of the Kingdom of God
By Michael F. Kuhn

Recently I listened to a well-known evangelical leader as he commented on the 2020 presidential election. In his words, every "true believer in Christ" is obliged to vote for the Republican candidate. For him, the deciding factors are abortion and a traditional understanding of marriage (i.e., between a man and a woman). The truth is that a growing number of "true believers in Christ" are considering the issues in the 2020 election more broadly and arriving at different conclusions. The issues I outline below represent where I am now in an ongoing process of discernment. I share these thoughts as an invitation to positive dialogue and a witness that not all "true believers" can endorse the current administration.

I will elaborate under three headings: 1) Jesus' teaching and implications for Christian engagement in politics, 2) Leadership character and implications for policy, and 3) Acknowledging complexity.

Jesus' Teaching and Implications for Political Engagement
Jesus' first and primary message was that the "kingdom of God" had come in his person and work.[59] He called all people to ultimate loyalty and obedience to that kingdom. He did this in a society awash in political zealotry and strident anti-colonialism, Rome being the colonizing power. A nationalistic pro-Hebrew stance would have been immensely popular with his compatriots. Satan's attempt to entice Jesus, offering him worldly power in Luke 4:5-7 reveals that the issue of political

leadership was alive and well. Jesus' response to the temptation reveals that he refused to lower his kingdom's standards to embrace political power. In fact, he called his people to repent and embrace loyalty to God as their true king. To enter this kingdom of God, one had to follow Jesus resulting in a total life transformation.

The current administration has appealed to popular sentiment among Christians that their faith is under siege. The president promised to return power to his evangelical constituency: "Christianity will have power … If I'm there, you're going to have plenty of power, you don't need anybody else."[60] Given that Jesus rejected political power, thoughtful Christians are asking why the promise of power should be so alluring to his followers.

For the Christian, it is simply wrong-headed to expect any human society or government to adequately represent and uphold the values of Christ's kingdom. America can only be a vessel of good in our world as it realizes its own alienation from God and acts to bring about restorative justice and righteousness among its people. In short, we cannot hope for the kingdom of God in Washington. We hope that Washington will be influenced and corrected by the kingdom of God as the kingdom infiltrates its structures and institutions with the gospel of peace. This is America's hope for a role of distinction in service to its people and the world.

This understanding of the kingdom of God in the person and work of Jesus Christ resists uncritical endorsement of either political party. Policies on either side of the American political spectrum (left and right, Democrat and Republican) alternately support or undermine values that are consistent with the kingdom of God as understood through the Bible and the history of the church. Therefore, the American church must reflect on a wide array of issues that impact public life and lead to a more just and peaceful society.[61] Endorsing one party as the "Christian" option contributes to a dangerous polarization of society and gags the prophetic voice of Jesus' kingdom.

Accordingly, a refusal to vote for the current administration is not an endorsement of every value upheld by the Democratic party. I especially grieve that party's embrace of abortion, which I discuss further below. Furthermore, I acknowledge positive contributions of the current administration to our country's well-being, including the maintenance of a vibrant industrial and business sector accompanied by a robust market for investors. However, critical areas of Christian concern have deteriorated under the current administration. These include justice for the poor and vulnerable, care of creation, preserving human rights and dignity, racial and ethnic reconciliation, and restraint of violence.

Leadership Character and Implications for Policy

The rhetoric and actions of the current administration have undermined the confidence of many that it can lead with integrity. Leadership is not merely utilitarian or functional. It is the product of the leader's character. Nor can it be isolated to a leader's personal choices. The leader's character inevitably infiltrates the decisions and policies of that leader. The policies of the current administration reflect in great measure the character and vision of the president.

In the lead-up to the 2016 election, I was concerned by candidate Trump's history of business dealings (six filings for corporate bankruptcy by Trump-associated businesses),[62] his liaisons with porn stars, and his recorded comments revealing a demeaning attitude towards women. After the election, I hoped the weight of public office would influence the president for good. But personal entitlement remains the pattern of the president's decision-making. The following are a few examples.

The just rule of law is basic to any society, but the current administration believes itself to be above prosecution by law. This is disturbing and ironic for a president who claims to be the "law and order" president. Perennial lawsuits[63] and partisan backscratching have conspired to protect a president who surrounded himself with aides who violated the law for his benefit. Moreover, the president uses the power of his office to pardon his friends who have been convicted of criminal behavior. The president was impeached by a democratic House of Congress. I listened attentively to the proceedings and became convinced that the president did indeed make military aid to a vulnerable ally conditional on a favor that would influence the American election. The Republican-led Senate rejected impeachment. If the Senate did not wish to impeach the president, it could have, at minimum, reprimanded him, reining in his excesses with accountability. On the contrary, its vote gave the president his vindication. One lone Republican senator had the courage to vote against his party. That senator has since been the continual object of the president's public scorn.

This abdication of oversight by the Republican party to the president's agenda is a deep concern. Rather than update and amend its party platform, the Republican National Committee simply reaffirmed the 2016 platform noting its continued support for the president's "America first" agenda. Amid questions of legality and precedent, the president used the White House as the venue for the 2020 Republican Convention. I cannot escape the conclusion that whatever serves the president is deemed right.

Leaders should inspire unity of vision for the common good of a society. Our present leadership has contributed to a loss of dignity in civil discourse, partisanship, denigration of opposing views and blame-casting. The free press has become his personal nemesis, resulting in a downward spiral of polarization and hate speech.

Numerous leaders of integrity with proven track records have found it impossible to serve the current administration. Resignations include four chiefs of staff, four national security advisers and four press secretaries in less than four years. Two of these are seasoned military leaders, John F. Kelly[64] and James Mattis,[65] both of whom have issued public statements against the current leadership. Other top military leaders have uncharacteristically spoken out against their Commander in Chief.[66] This reality is puzzling for an administration that is known to be "pro-military." It begs the question why these seasoned veterans of America's most respected institutions cannot function under the president's command.

Emma Lazarus' poem, engraved on the pedestal of the Statue of Liberty expresses a value enshrined in the history of our nation:

> Give me your tired, your poor,
> Your huddled masses yearning to breathe free,
> The wretched refuse of your teeming shore.
> Send these, the homeless, tempest-tost to me,
> I lift my lamp beside the golden door!

In contrast, "America first" is our president's motto. While appealing to the masses, its application in public policy yields injustice and oppression. The rejection of refugees from numerous war-torn countries has divided families and deprived many of the world's most oppressed people of security and hope.[67] The president points to the threat of Islamic terrorism to support these policies. In fact, UN resettlement policies provide a more thorough vetting of refugees than student or business immigrants, not to mention touristic arrivals. Resettled victims of war and natural disasters have posed no credible threat to American security.[68] In a similar vein, the president has promised to secure the southern border by building a wall. Additionally, he rejects a path to citizenship for undocumented immigrants born in America. These are the symbols of the president's immigration reform. The problem of border security and immigration is complex and cries out for holistic solutions. The president's unilateral proposals portray a society that prefers to hoard its blessings rather than welcome those in need.

Our nation continues to reap the bitter fruits of its social sins of dislocation of Native Americans, slavery, Jim Crow laws,[69] segregation, housing inequality and a penal justice system that disproportionately punishes people of color.[70] The president has made clear that acknowledgement of these realities is unpatriotic and a rejection of American values. On the contrary, it is an indicator of an authentic love of country. For the Christ-follower, awareness of social and personal sins should be reflexive. Our country will not mend itself by refusing to acknowledge systemic injustice and thereby refusing to uproot the remnants of racial discrimination.[71] The current administration, while touting its record in employment of minorities, has shown itself inept to bring about a thorough justice that will return peace to our streets and cities.

Sadly, the same unwillingness to acknowledge oppression translates into foreign policy. The president acclaims his "deal of the century"[72] for peace in the Middle East along with the relocation of the U.S. embassy to Jerusalem and naturalization of Israeli relations with the United Arab Emirates. In his recent acceptance speech, the president claimed he had established peace in the Middle East which no president before him has been able to accomplish. Let us be clear. This is arrogance and political naivete. I lived in the Middle East for nearly 30 years. Peace cannot be made without including oppressed minorities (e.g., Palestinians) in the decision-making process. It is a disturbing pattern of exclusion of the oppressed, imposition of a solution built on military and economic might with denial of any recourse for the oppressed to a higher authority. In a word, it is bullying applied to foreign policy.

Additionally, the inability to balance the science of medicine with the interest of economic vitality is proving disastrous. Rather than proceed cautiously to reopen the country after the COVID-19 lockdown, the president rejected common sense precautions and spread disinformation related to the virus. Of course, we the American people must accept responsibility as we failed to act on what we knew, preferring our enjoyment and social activities over health, security and love of neighbor. As a result, the United States has the worst record of any developed country in dealing with COVID-19.

Concerning the environment, biblical faith entrusts humanity with the role of "dominion" in the created order. Far from being a license to exploit creation, humankind is to lovingly care for it as an act of worship of its Creator. I do not find this care of creation in our current leadership whose sole motivation appears to be economic prosperity. While the provision of jobs and trade is important to a society, wisdom seeks to balance short-term gain with long-term care of creation.

Gun violence in our nation's schools and neighborhoods is at an all-time high. The current administration frames the issue in terms of Second Amendment rights, rather than the right to life and security. The politicization of the issue is due to the funding of progun lobbies provided to their candidates of choice. A kingdom of God response must analyze the issue as more than merely upholding the Second Amendment to the Constitution. Refusing to do so is a moral failure and a victory for those who pad their bank accounts on the perpetration of violence. If life is a gift of God, Christ-followers must advocate for its preservation, which means taking a fresh look at the issue of guns and violence in America, including common sense gun laws that do not violate the spirit and intention of the Second Amendment. Sanctity of life applies from conception to natural death.

Acknowledging the Complexity

Rarely are moral choices "all or nothing." The issues that concern Christ followers in the 2020 election do not all align on either side of the political spectrum. Voting calls for discernment, not blanket endorsement. The appointment of supreme court justices is a vital area of Christian concern which will have a long-term impact on our nation's application of law. For many Christians, the appointment of conservative justices to the Supreme Court is reason enough to vote for the current administration. The focus of concern is abortion. To be clear, I grieve the Democratic platform's embrace of abortion and strongly agree that life is the gift of God and may not be taken by human beings. Abortion must not be cast as a "reproductive right" as is the case in the Democratic party platform. While legislation is part of the solution, I am skeptical that such a deeply rooted problem can be resolved by legislation alone and I applaud the efforts of Christians in the areas of pregnancy counselling, fostering, adoption and economic support for un-wed mothers. Overturning *Roe v. Wade* is not the only front in the struggle for the sanctity of life.[73] If *Roe* is overturned, abortion will still be available but only in certain states. I wonder if this partial victory should be the church's objective or if a more holistic and long-term approach must be kept in view.

Many Christians worry about the looming specter of en-larged government control in fiscal and social systems—a le-gitimate concern. For instance, the Democratic party is more inclined than their Republican counterparts to institute govern-ment control of medical care. Though Christians will differ, the number of uninsured coupled with soaring medical costs plead for consideration. At any rate, by most assessments, govern-ment has not become "smaller" over the past three Republican administrations. National debt has snowballed and taxation, especially for the middle class, has not changed significantly. Personally, I do not find this argument a compelling reason to vote for the current administration.

Loving America and Hoping for True Greatness
Given the beauty and promise of America, Christ-followers should continue to hope for and work toward:

Leadership that is transparent, conciliatory and committed to the common good through healing our nation's deep divisions.

The just and equitable application of law across all sectors of society.

Societal structures that uphold the dignity of all human beings and uplift the downtrodden to become productive and secure members of society.

A society that, aware of its blessings, expresses the generosity and grace of God to the peoples of the world.

A nation that is aware of its history and committed to righting our societal wrongs, eliminating systemic injustice.

Leadership that carefully weighs the science of climate change and acts for the long-term good of God's creation.

Leadership that values human life by embracing the science of pandemic mitigation.

A society that courageously ensures life and safety for its most vulnerable, from the womb to natural death.

The American heritage of democracy and human rights has brought hope to the peoples of the world. Indeed, the civil rights demanded by our minorities today and in the past are enshrined in the very founding documents of this union. We have the ideological and material resources to make America greater, but American greatness must not be reduced to economic prosperity. Might does not make right. American greatness must include justice for all and extend mercy to the downtrodden. Followers of Jesus will contribute to this end by belonging with abandon to the kingdom of God and bringing the light of wisdom to our public discourse. May God preserve our union and grant us leadership of integrity and truth.

Michael Kuhn teaches Biblical Theology and Muslim-Christian relations. He has taught at the Arab Baptist Theological Seminary (Beirut, Lebanon); Fuller Theological Seminary and Covenant College (adjunct). He is an ordained minister of the Evangelical

Presbyterian Church and serves with the International Theological Education Network, teaching itinerantly and assisting developing world theological institutions. He has authored several books in the areas of Muslim-Christian relations and spiritual formation. Mike is married to Stephanie and they have three daughters, two sons-in-law, and seven grandchildren.

Look to Your Lord

Anonymous

The tension was palpable as Jesus knelt, tracing in the dirt with his finger. The religious leaders exchanged smug glances with one another. Now they had him. Jesus had often eluded their traps with clever answers, but now he had only two choices. Both choices were bad. Again they prompted him, "So what do you say?" Would he say "yes" and condemn the woman to be stoned to death, provoking the Roman rulers who had not sanctioned the execution? Would he dare say "no" and go against the Law of Moses itself? It would be unthinkable that a man considered a prophet might forsake the Law. Yes, now this troublemaker Jesus would be forced to provoke Rome, and his end was near. Again, they prompted him, "So what do you say?"

Jesus saw deeper than either Rome or the religious leaders when considering his answer. Jesus saw the injustice of the question itself. The religious leaders were liars, using their religion to cloak their power schemes. They cared nothing for justice. They had no respect for the Law of Moses nor the God who gave it. The Law commanded that both the man and woman be stoned to death. But they had brought only the woman. She had been "caught in the very act" so where was the man? Why didn't they bring him also? He might have been a religious leader or powerful man, shielded from punishment by a community that valued him and reviled her. To condemn her would be unjust, and to deny the law would be unjust. There would be no justice done here today with either bad choice offered to Jesus.

Look to your Lord. Instead of settling for the "lesser" of two evils, Jesus attacked the injustice of the system. His answer stunned the religious leaders. He rejected both of their unjust choices, and instead exposed the unjust system that produced them. Each man among the religious leaders, confronted with his own sin, walked away. Nowhere in the Scriptures do we ever find Jesus choosing one evil path because it is less evil than another. He never endorsed an injustice as necessary. When he saw systems of injustice, he turned over tables and drove out the unjust system.

My family and I serve as missionaries in the Middle East. We work preaching the Gospel of Jesus Christ, planting churches, and fostering church planting movements. We give glory to God for the churches he has raised up, and all those he has brought to the truth of Jesus Christ. We are truly seeing a transformative movement in a region that has long been closed to the gospel.

I hesitated to write this article because of the damage it might do to our ministry. Missionaries coming from especially partisan regions of the United States simply don't enjoy the liberty to speak their opinions on the social and political issues facing our nation today. Their gospel work may be attacked in retribution by those who put the wrong kingdom first. Because of this I asked to write this article anonymously.

Some years ago, I commented that Franklin Graham should return to his successful gospel ministry instead of becoming a political pundit. Why should an ordained minister abandon working for the Kingdom of God to devote his passions and resources to a kingdom of man? We have too many political pundits already, and not enough bold preachers of the gospel. This question angered a deacon, a thoroughly partisan man, at one of our supporting churches. Though the pastor objected, they cut our missionary support. A church pulled away from

Kingdom building because a deacon's partisan politics were offended. I have to guard my words more closely among my own people, the Church, than I do among Muslims. Let that sink in.

Look to your Lord. Are we not told in Hebrews 12 "Let us fix our eyes on Jesus, the author and perfecter of our faith?" Are we not told "Seek first the Kingdom of God?" Kingdom confusion is rampant. Being a good Republican voter has nothing to do with the Kingdom of God. Equating a political loyalty with faith in Jesus is rank idolatry—no different than equating a golden calf with the Almighty God. Someone may disagree with your politics, or your vote, and still be a faithful follower of Jesus. Do not believe those who make political affiliation a requirement for salvation.

If you've spent more time trying to send illegal immigrants "back to where they belong" than you've spent sharing the gospel with them, you are putting the wrong kingdom first. If you've spent more time campaigning to shut down mosques than you have spent talking about Jesus with Muslims, you are putting the wrong kingdom first. If you've spent more time pushing for political solutions to social issues than you've spent feeding the poor, you are putting the wrong kingdom first. If you've spent more time complaining about Black Lives Matter on Facebook than you've spent helping impoverished minority communities, you are putting the wrong kingdom first. America will not honor God by shutting our borders, abandoning the poor, and locking up children in cages. We will honor God by honoring the values of his Kingdom: mercy, justice, and peace.

So, I cannot be silent when presented with the political abomination that has grown in our nation. People are actually equating loyalty to the Republican (or sometimes the Democratic party) with allegiance to the Cross of Christ. Partisan loyalty has, in many areas of the country, become a litmus test for fidelity to Jesus. How did we reach the point where political zealots are successfully interposing their banner before the Cross of Christ?

Look to your Lord. Don't let anyone tell you that you must vote for a candidate because his party is God's chosen party. Don't fall for the insistence that you must vote for an ungodly man because of a political strategy. Voting for a Presidential candidate who may appoint anti-abortion Supreme Court Justices is a strategy which has failed from the outset. The current Supreme Court, which just reaffirmed Roe v. Wade in June 2020, has 5 Republican and 4 Democratic (Presidential) appointments.[74] In the 2016 Whole Woman's Health v. Hellerstedt case, a 4-4 appointed Supreme Court (Republican-appointed Justice Scalia had recently died) produced a 5-3 ruling upholding Roe v. Wade. In the 1992 Planned Parenthood v. Casey ruling, a 6-3 Republican-appointed majority upheld Roe v. Wade. The original Supreme Court ruling establishing abortion in Roe v. Wade in 1973 was made by a Supreme Court with 7 Republican appointees and 2 Democrat appointees. Six Republican-appointed Justices voted in favor of Roe, along with one Democrat-appointed Justice. The two dissenters against Roe were appointed one by a Democrat, the other by a Republican.

In every major challenge to Roe v. Wade, Republican appointments have had a majority (or equality) and in every case the Supreme Court has ruled in favor of abortion. Republican appointees have never been outnumbered in any vote. Republican-appointee votes created Roe v. Wade, and Republican-appointee votes have upheld it in every major case.

I am strongly pro-life. I have marched in pro-life rallies. One of our ministries is pregnancy crisis help for expectant mothers. I don't support abortion in any form. But I also realize that voting for Republicans gave us Roe v. Wade and voting for Republicans has done nothing to overturn it. The strategy of voting for Supreme Court appointments is a failed lie. It has distracted us from looking at so many other issues where our society is failing to value and encourage life.

Look to your Lord. We cannot say that we are pro-life if we only value life in the womb. Christians should be the first to support public schools and school lunch programs. We should be the first to protest locking immigrant children in cages. We should support healthcare for all Americans. We should value increased social services for pregnant women and new mothers. Our proposals on these issues reflect whether or not we actually value life, as we claim.

Can we truly justify voting for a party that fails to value life on any front except abortion, and fails on that front? Should we not rather be looking at other means to value life, and to reduce abortion? Isn't it incumbent on followers of Jesus to look for better answers than the ones we are offered?

We should vote for candidates and parties who offer life-affirming policies. Support for medical care, birth control, programs that curb domestic violence and sexual abuse, strengthening and expanding adoption, paid maternal leave, and nutritional programs are the sort of life-saving programs that reduce the number of women seeking abortion. Community development and job training programs have a better track record than judicial appointments. Opposing the legalization of abortion does not make us pro-life. It is not enough.

Look to your Lord. Look to his example. Jesus did not condemn the woman who was trapped in an unjust system. Neither did he excuse her sin. Abortion is a sin. We can and should hold on to that idea. But the way to combat the sin issue is to look to our Lord, and his standard of justice.

Look to your Lord when you vote. Look for someone who walks as Jesus walked. Look for someone who reflects the character of Jesus. Look for someone whose values align with the Kingdom of God.

Would Jesus?

By Anne Blackwill

It seems to me that Christians should live and work and, yes, vote in ways that are akin to our Lord. Can you imagine Jesus separating children from their parents and then forgetting where he put them? Would the Son, who together with the Father brought forth Creation, urge America to systematically strip protection away from land and sea in favor of big business? Would he applaud us for backing out of the Paris Climate Accord? Would Jesus, who gave his life for the whole world, smile as America narrows its national identity, alienates its friendly neighbors, and insists that America can be great only if it denies access to the rest of the world?

Ask Matthew, a tax collector, who upon meeting Jesus gave back everything he had taken unjustly. Would Jesus approve of a tax plan that piles more wealth on the wealthiest and further entraps America in the life-damaging gap between the haves and the have-nots?

Ask Luke, himself a doctor. Would Jesus praise national leadership that denies science and further drives our nation into a prolonged pandemic with all its terrible costs, both to life and to economic stability?

Ask Paul, who preached that the gifts of the Spirit of God are the opposite of egoism and self-aggrandizement. Would Jesus embrace a leader who instinctively chooses division over love, animosity over peace, and who, very discernably, lacks either patience or self-control?

Only recently I realized that I have never honestly prayed the first part of our Lord's prayer: "Thy kingdom come, thy will be done, on earth as it is in heaven." Somehow this seemed something I couldn't really hope for – or even earnestly ask for – in this present day. But Jesus taught this prayer to his disciples for their very present guidance, their protection, and their understanding of what is real. If we abandon this part of our Lord's prayer and vote, not in keeping with who Jesus is and who he asks us to become; but for some perceived benefit, economic or moral, that we might possibly gain with our vote, we could do damage to our nation and find ourselves working counter to God's kingdom.

As believers we cannot live – or vote – divided from our deepest selves. We cannot simply say that we live in a fallen world and that all politics and politicians are flawed. Jesus taught his disciples to judge a tree by its fruit. We have watched this particular tree for almost four years now, and we need to carefully evaluate the fruit it has given us. Are we as a nation more unified and more just? Are we more hospitable to the stranger, more loving to those in need? More truthful? Is the fruit of this present tree consonant with our Lord's character and kingdom work? Would Jesus, looking at us as a nation over the last four years say, "Well done"?

Anne Blackwill is a former literature professor with an under-graduate degree from Wheaton College and a PhD. from Stanford University in English and Humanities. She served as Adjunct Professor of English at Gordon College for over twenty years prior to retiring, and has over forty years of teaching experience from academic institutions as diverse as Beirut College for Women, the U.S. Naval Academy, Tel Aviv University, and Working Men's College in London. Throughout her career she has maintained a commitment to education for incarcerated men and women, of-fering college-credit courses in four different prisons, including ten years at MCI-Norfolk through the Boston University Prison Education Program. In 2019, she spent three months in Lesvos, Greece teaching ESL to asylum seekers.

On Immigration

The Yeast of Herod

By Robert Chao Romero

In this time of pandemic, all of us have adapted. I learned to teach my classes at UCLA by Zoom. I made homemade disinfectant wipes with alcohol, essential oils, and paper towels. I scavenged for toilet paper (and even gave it away as a birthday present), and most recently, I made homemade bread. With store-bought packets of yeast in short supply, I also learned how to make "wild yeast." By combining flour, water, naturally occurring fungus from the air, and time, you can make your own wild yeast just like they did in Jesus' day. The yeast is "alive" and bubbles when it's happy. It's like a pet. You feed it regularly, and you can even name it. When you mix it into dough and heat in an oven, a chemical reaction occurs, releasing carbon dioxide, and the bread rises.

Jesus uses this timeless metaphor of yeast to describe the Kingdom of God:

Again he asked, "What shall I compare the kingdom of God to? It is like yeast that a woman took and mixed into about sixty pounds of flour until it worked all through the dough." (Luke 13: 20-21, NIV)

Like yeast working its way through a batch of dough, the Kingdom of God brings unity to all things in heaven and on earth under the love and reconciliation of Christ. "For God was pleased to have all his fullness dwell in him, and through him to reconcile to himself all things, whether things on earth or things in heaven, by making peace through his blood, shed on the cross" (Col. 1:19-20). Furthermore, like yeast, the Kingdom of God should work its way through the dough of our individual lives so that it transforms every aspect of who we are, shaping us more and more into the character of Jesus and bearing the fruit of the Spirit (Gal. 5:22-23). Through the Body of Christ, this same Kingdom yeast should leaven the dough of society and transform it according to the biblical values of mercy, justice, and compassion for our neighbors, immigrants, the poor, and those on the margins of society. God wants to transform all of us, and all things. Nothing and no one is left out. This holistic focus of the good news is referred to by Latino theologians as "misión integral." In the words of René Padilla, misión integral is "the mission of the whole church to the whole of humanity in all its forms, personal, communal, social, economic, ecological and political."[75]

More than 2,000 verses of Holy Scripture speak about God's heart of compassion for immigrants and the poor. In fact, Jesus warns us soberly in Matthew 25 that our response to them is a barometer of the sincerity of our relationship with him. If we truly know Jesus, then we will express hospitality to immigrants, feed the hungry, clothe the naked, care for those who are sick, and visit those who are in prison (Matt. 25:31-46). In short, compassion for those on the fringes of society is a sign that the yeast of the Kingdom of God has transformed us through relationship with Jesus. Conversely, a callous heart toward immigrants and the poor is evidence that we have not submitted ourselves to the leavening influence of our Lord.

As a follower of Jesus in a pluralistic democracy, I will cast my vote in November for the candidate who most aligns with these clear biblical values and whose stated policies will allow for social compassion to flourish toward the common good of our diverse nation.

As a pastor, professor, and immigration attorney, I have observed painfully the suffering of millions of Latino immigrants and their families under the Trump administration. Though claiming to embody the biblical values of the evangelical church, the current administration has blatantly disregarded the Scriptures, which unequivocally command followers of Jesus to demonstrate compassion and mercy for immigrants and the poor of our nation. I personally witnessed fellow immigrant pastors arrested and separated from their families, UCLA students torn from their parents, and friends who are "Dreamers" suffer physically, emotionally, and educationally from the abolishment of Deferred Action for Childhood Arrivals (DACA). On a national and international level, the immigration policies of the Trump administration have led to many other unconscionable arrests and deportations that violate not only biblical principles, but also the U.S. Constitution and international law. Under the direct guidance of Trump, lawful asylum seekers were separated from their children and placed in cages. A 10-year-old girl with cerebral palsy and a mother with a brain tumor were detained after receiving hospital treatment. Parents have been arrested while dropping their children off at school and driving to the hospital to give birth. A victim of domestic violence was detained and threatened with deportation after testifying against their abuser in court.[76] The list is long and egregious. These xenophobic policies and actions violate both the spirit and the letter of Scripture, such as Leviticus 19:33-34: "When a foreigner resides among you in your land, do not mistreat them. The foreigner residing among you must be treated as your native-born. Love them as yourself, for you were foreigners in Egypt. I am the Lord your God." According to my biblical conscience, I cannot vote for Donald Trump; for to support his reelection would lead to the further persecution of Jesus who, according to Matthew 25, appears to us in the faces of the millions of immigrants who have suffered under this racist administration.

The Bible not only uses yeast as a metaphor for the Kingdom of God, but also as a warning about political leaders who would feign religious identity for the sake of wealth and political power. "And he cautioned them, saying, 'Watch out – beware of ... the yeast of Herod'" (Mark 8:15, NRSV). The family of Herod appropriated a nominal Jewish faith for the sake of wealth and political power under the Roman Empire.[77] The Herodians portrayed themselves as faithful Jewish believers, but in practice obeyed God's Law only when it was convenient. Herod the Great was installed as "King of Judea" by the Roman Senate in exchange for serving as puppet ruler of the Roman empire. He was known for colossal building projects, including the renovation of the Temple in Jerusalem and the construction of fortresses and pagan cities, aimed at garnering the favor of both Rome and the Jewish community. Herod the Great was also known for his narcissism, and violent and despotic rule. He had a bodyguard of 2,000 soldiers, used secret police to monitor his subjects, prohibited protests, and removed opponents by force. In addition to the Massacre of the Innocents (Matt. 2:16-18), Herod the Great also murdered one of his wives and three of his children. In fact, he was so worried that no one would mourn his death that he ordered a large group of respected leaders to attend his funeral and be murdered on the spot, so that genuine mourning would be present at his burial. Thankfully, his deranged requests were never carried out. In sum, the yeast of Herod may be summarized as religious and political compromise in exchange for wealth and power. As a disturbing representation of this unholy fusion of religion and politics, Herod the Great earned the ire, and near revolt, of the Jewish people, by placing a Roman Eagle outside the Temple of Jerusalem.

The yeast of Herod dangerously leavens the political administration and campaign of Donald Trump. As I pen these words, I reflect with great concern upon Vice President Mike Pence's speech from the Republican National Convention in

2020. His words unabashedly conflate evangelical Christian identity and Republican politics in the millennia-old pattern of Herod. Rather than fusing the Temple and the Roman Eagle, however; Pence confuses the Cross of Christ with the American Bald Eagle and the flag of the United States:

> Let's fix our eyes on Old Glory and all she represents ... let's fix our eyes on the   author and perfecter of our faith and freedom, and never forget that "where the spirit [SIC] of the Lord is, there is freedom," That means freedom always wins.[78]

The United States is not the Kingdom of God. And Donald Trump is not its king. To claim an equivalence between the reelection of Donald Trump and the triumph of Christianity is an old trick. It follows Herod's playbook. Like Herod 2,000 years ago, Trump appropriates a nominal religious faith for the sake of wealth and power. He claims to be a Christian, but has also proudly stated publicly that he has never asked God for forgiveness. He says that he follows Jesus, but ignores biblical teachings on both a personal and social level. Trump is known for lying, bullying, predatory sexual behavior, and eviscerating his perceived enemies—all in contradiction to the teachings of Jesus (Matt. 5:37, 5:44; John 4:1-42, Mark 14:1-11, Matt. 28:5-8). Moreover, as has been discussed at length, the vast majority of his social policies ignore the thousands of verses of Scripture which command us to demonstrate mercy and compassion toward the marginalized.

Like Herod, Trump is also a builder. His towers are a monument to himself, and he has even touted the construction of "the wall" as a building project aimed at currying favor with millions of white evangelical Christians whom he claims to represent. Similar to Herod, moreover, Trump is known for violence of word and action, as well as for clamping down on constitutional protest of those he disagrees with. His political rhetoric, or "yeast," has labeled me, and millions of other Latinos as "drug dealers," "criminals," and "rapists," and cast suspicion on our legitimacy as equal citizens of the United States.[79]

Such anti-immigrant rhetoric is sadly nothing new in the United States and is the product of the centuries old heretical theology of "Manifest Destiny."[80] According to 19th century Manifest Destiny, Mexicans and Native Americans were culturally inferior, and therefore could be stripped of life, land, and liberty by Anglo Americans who were God's true people, divinely destined to rule North America. These same racist attitudes also led to the exclusion of and discrimination against Italian, Greek, Russian, Polish, Jewish, African, Asian, and Middle Eastern immigrants to the United States in various forms from the late nineteenth century until 1965. Today, Manifest Destiny has morphed into "Make America Great Again." MAGA supporters directly infer that "true Americans" are white evangelicals like Mike Pence, Franklin Graham, Jerry Falwell Jr., and their constituencies. As in decades past, Latino, African American, Jewish, Asian American, and Middle Eastern Americans, are viewed as inherently suspect, even if we are U.S.-born citizens. A few of us are granted honorary membership within the MAGA club, but only if we support Trump and assimilate into the cultural values and norms of white evangelicalism. By casting us collectively as unassimilable criminals, rapists, and disease-ridden; Trumpism casts doubt upon our dignity as children of God, equally made in His image. Tragically, the yeast of MAGA and Trumpism has thoroughly worked its way deep into the dough of American politics and society over the past four years, and our nation is beginning to mold and rot. The lungs of American democracy have become poisoned by the toxic mold of white nationalism, racial division, and provocation, which are markers of the flesh, not of the Spirit of God (Gal. 5:16-26). In November, as brothers and sisters of the Body of Christ, may we begin the process of detoxification together.

Robert Chao Romero is an associate professor in the departments of Chicana/o Studies and Central America Studies, and Asian American Studies at UCLA. He received his PhD from UCLA in Latin American History and his JD from UC Berkeley. He is the author of Brown Church: Five Centuries of Latina/o Social Justice, Theology, and Identity; The Chinese in Mexico, 1882-1940, and more. He is also an ordained minister and faith rooted community organizer.

Christ in the Stranger
By Alexia Salvatierra

On August 6, 2020, the *Los Angeles Times* published an article entitled "Children Fleeing Danger Come to the U.S. for Refuge and are Expelled."[81] It tells the story of two children, 12 and 9 years old, whose uncle was killed by MS-13 in Honduras and who ran away to make the long trek to the United States to join their mother.

The boy had saved a video on his cell phone of a hooded man with a rifle, saying the boy's name and threatening to kill him and his sister. Upon arriving in the U.S., the children were held for three days in Border Patrol custody before being returned to Honduras without having received any hearing where they could have presented the evidence of the video. They are now with another uncle who himself is planning to flee. Their rapid expulsion occurred under the emergency declaration issued in March.

While this is clearly a tragedy for these children and their loved ones, we do need to recognize the broader context. Most countries have sealed their borders under COVID. However, in the case of this federal administration, this action is unfortunately characteristic of their modus operandi, with roots and implications far beyond this historic moment.

I have been working with immigrant ministry and the struggle for immigrant justice for roughly forty years, through multiple Republican and Democratic administrations. I have never seen an administration so profoundly committed to restricting immigration. According to the Migration Policy

Institute's recent report, this administration has implemented over 400 restrictive regulations and policy changes, almost all unilaterally (without any participation by Congress.) Our immigration system has never been as effective, just, logical and humane as many of us would wish – but since January of 2017, we have experienced a whole other level of cold-heartedness. Many people know about the separation of children from their parents at the border. I could give many examples of similar stories. Three actions that particularly reveal this fundamental stance:

Refugees Caps: The reduction of the cap on refugees from the average of 80,000 per year (through Republican and Democratic administrations) to 18,000.[82] The United States is not responsible to care for every refugee or asylum-seeker in the world, but if the Statue of Liberty is true of us at all, we are responsible for our fair share. A famous stanza of the poem written on the base of the Statue of Liberty by Emma Lazarus reads "Give me your tired, your poor, your huddled masses yearning to breathe free, / The wretched refuse of your teeming shore." This line is an eloquent manifestation of the commitment that the U.S. showed in our leadership in the drafting and ratification of the Universal Declaration of Human Rights in 1948. Article 13 of the Declaration states "Everyone has the right to seek and to enjoy in other countries asylum from persecution."[83] A friend who works for an international refugee ministry shared with me that they are panicked. Given that refugees are at the highest number internationally in history; there is no practical way that international refugee agencies can make up for the gap that this administration has created.

Returning Asylum Seekers to Danger: Asylum can be legally requested either from outside the U.S., typically from a refugee center in a safe third country, or at the U.S. border. We call those whose applications are accepted from outside the U.S., "refugees" and we call those who apply at the border and whose claims are deemed legitimate "asylum-seekers." However, the criteria are exactly the same. This administration recently instituted a requirement that asylum seekers must apply for asylum to countries they pass through before being allowed to apply to the U.S. – even if those are countries that are known for human rights abuses. For example, this administration has formed Asylum Cooperative Agreements with Northern Triangle countries such as Guatemala. These are the kinds of agreements that the U.S. makes with safe third countries. In 2017, according to federal records, over 25,000 asylum cases were approved; the majority were from China, El Salvador and Guatemala.[84] The asylum seekers from El Salvador and Guatemala whose cases were approved had fled their countries on the grounds that their government could not protect them from organized crime syndicates that are controlling increasingly large territories throughout Central America. This human rights crisis continues, with the homicide rates in these countries among the highest in the world.[85] The Lutheran Church in El Salvador is a sister synod with our Southwest California Synod; we hear the stories from our brothers and sisters about ongoing assaults, rapes, torture and murder – often by corrupt police working in tandem with MS-13 and other gangs. The United States ratified the 1951 Refugee Convention which requires "non-refoulement;"[86] we have agreed not to send people back to a country in which they are in danger.

Work Permit Delays: The Acting Director of the Department of Homeland Security recently proposed that asylum seekers whose cases are in progress in the U.S. would have to wait a year to receive a work permit – to discourage "trivial" applications.[87] The assumption that someone who has a genuine fear of persecution would not need to work for a year is truly bizarre and lacks even the pretense of empathy.

When I think about these kinds of decisions and actions on the part of the current administration, I compare them to Psalm 72[88], which is a prayer for the king that describes the nature of a godly government. The Psalm mentions the needy four times. The godly governor will save the children of the needy, deliver the needy who cry out, take pity on the weak and the needy, and save the needy from death. He will also judge the afflicted ones with justice and deliver the afflicted ones who have no one to help. He will do all of this because "precious is their blood in his sight." In other words, a godly government treats people in need as if their lives were precious. I have friends and family who support the current administration because of their commitment to protect the unborn. While I agree that abortion is a tragedy, when I read Psalm 139's beautiful proclamation of the sacred worth of every life, I am clear that this worth does not end at birth. If we are to judge our leaders with the scriptures as a yardstick, I think we have to look at their overall commitment to save the lives of the needy and not only those who are in a particular phase of life. What about children who are fleeing violent persecution in the countries of origin and have no one to protect them?

If none of our options for national leadership protects and defends the needy in every way, what do we do? Do we stay away from the political arena entirely? Many of my friends who are Hispanic evangelical leaders are talking about that very option.

I cannot do that for a simple reason. When I was young, I served as a missionary in the Philippines during the pro-democracy movement against the dictator Ferdinand Marcos. Before going to the Philippines, I was not sure that we had a truly democratic system in the United States. I define a democracy as a system in which everyone has an essential role in the process of public decision-making. I thought that our votes, voice and influence made no difference in the decisions of the powerful. Then, I had first-hand experience of a country without a functioning democracy. I realized how precious democracy is and how deeply thankful I am for the U.S. system with all its faults and flaws. The principle of stewardship calls us to use every gift for God's service and to fulfill His purposes. How do we become good stewards of the gifts of democracy? If we do not use them to the best of our ability, we are committing the sin of the man in the parable of the talents who hides his talent in a napkin instead of investing it.

As I look at imperfect choices for government leaders, I look at their overall values, commitment and character. One aspect of character that I look for is humility. A humble person can listen and learn. I have seen Christian humility in political representatives (of both parties). I have personally experienced that they can successfully be called to meet a higher standard.

When I think about a godly government's response to those in need, I remember the words of Matthew 25. Whatever we do to the poor, the sick, the prisoner and the stranger, we do to Jesus directly and personally. In the end, the bellwether question for me is how a leader treats Jesus as He comes to us in his distressed disguise. All ancient peoples believed that a country was affected by the leaders' relationship with God. I believe that there is truth in that ancient perspective. Psalm 72 goes a step farther; it says that "all nations will be blessed through him." All nations will be blessed by a godly leader of any nation. The reverse is also true. May we choose leaders whose overall perspective and decisions will bring blessing to us all.

Rev. Dr. Alexia Salvatierra is a Lutheran Pastor with over 40 years of experience in congregational (English and Spanish) and community ministry, including church-based service and community development programs, congregational/community organizing and legislative advocacy. She serves as Assistant Professor of Integral Mission and Global Transformation as well as Coordinator of a Professional Certificate program for Hispanic pastors and church leaders at Fuller Theological Seminary. She coordinates the Ecumenical Collaboration for Asylum Seekers and serves on the leadership team of Matthew 25/Mateo 25, a bipartisan Christian network to protect and defend families facing deportation in the name and spirit of Jesus. She serves as a consultant (training, facilitating, organizing and leading strategic planning) for a variety of national/international organizations, including World Vision, InterVarsity Christian Fellowship, and the Christian Community Development Association. She co-authored Faith-Rooted Organizing: Mobilizing the Church in Service to the World with Dr. Peter Heltzel.[89]

Restaurando Esperanza

By Miluska E. Aquije

It was November 9, 2016 and I stood on the subway platform, waiting for the 6 train. New York City scurried around me, always hustling and bustling. The train roared in and screeched to a stop. Like the train, my soul roared and screeched with the pain of hopelessness. I wondered, am I living a nightmare or a repeat of antebellum times? I am a first generation Latina immigrant and the first to graduate from college in my family. My Peruvian mother made the brave choice to cross the border, bringing me when I was only four. Being undocumented, I already dealt with discrimination, but now I was hearing Trump claim that Mexican immigrants were "bringing drugs, bringing crime. They're rapists."[90] Though I am not Mexican, I have many dear friends who are and they are by far the most hardworking people I know. How can he say that about my *hermanos/as*? Our community hasn't brought what he said in his speech. Actually, America has contributed to the rise of gangs in Latin America, like MS-13 that originated on American soil.[91] I thought the American people would actually correct Trump's racism but I was shocked when they did not.

As I watched my Facebook feed throughout 2016, many people who I called friends all of a sudden started posting material from the Trump campaign, agreeing with him. I froze as I saw long-time friends and others who worshiped with me on many occasions expressing anti-immigrant beliefs. At the time, I was taking a seminary class entitled "Slavery and the Church in the Antebellum Era." It opened my eyes to how American

Christianity manipulated scripture to support slavery instead of stoking compassionate concern for human freedom and salvation. I read many works of preachers in the 1800s who used Scripture and the science of their day to explain how slavery was of God, and how enslaved Africans were subhuman. The same undertone I read in these writings of the 1800s was now in my Facebook timeline as friends posted in favor of Trump. Fear washed over me. Was history repeating itself for our immigrant communities? Or had white Americans always thought people of color threatened them? Had racism always existed in their "Making America White Again" hearts and I just never saw it? So many questions left me overwhelmed.

When Trump was elected, I saw so many on the TV screen jumping up and down in excitement while I was in disbelief. Even the Ku Klux Klan came out of hiding, emboldened by Trump. The celebration of his racist, sexist and xenophobic campaign was unbelievable. What would this mean for us, the immigrant community? Would our undocumented family and friends be safe? Would I be safe as a Dreamer/Deferred Action for Child Arrivals (DACA) recipient? As I recall my post-2016 election memories, it was a miracle that I continued pressing forward trusting in God beyond the xenophobia that was so prevalent. Personally, the Trump administration made me distrustful of the white American community. I felt unsafe calling this country that raised me, home.

People misunderstand the immigration system. Not everyone has the same path to citizenship. I've heard judgmental comments about "illegal entry" implying all of us from our respective countries had equal access or opportunity to be accepted by the strenuous visa process. Or, the age old "just get married" in order to become a citizen. Being undocumented, I feel targeted by both narratives. The first implies my parents had all the means necessary in our home country Peru to file for a visa. They did not. The second implies the complete stripping away of my human choice of my life partner. Shouldn't we who are suffering in the margins have the same opportunity to pursue happiness in marriage and choose someone to say "I do" to without the limiting factor of him/her being a U.S. citizen?

These narratives kept me skeptical and guarded. Unfortunately I didn't properly process my feelings and my anger grew into hate. I couldn't for the life of me see a white American the same. I wished I could ask those who said, "You don't belong here," then where do I belong? I've been in the United States for the past 29 years. Its culture and customs are my own. I don't remember anything from Peru except what I've been taught about our language, traditions and music. Still, I am questioned. Are you purely American? What's your ancestry? The pride of white Americans due to their privilege can feel insurmountable.

What really crushed my heart was seeing my Christian white American brothers and sisters saying "yes" to sending us, the undocumented community back to "where we came from." People practiced patriotism and xenophobia and uttered lifeless words as they sang worship songs such as "Jesus at the Center." How could I ever trust my Christian white American community again?

And a woman was there

Theologically, this time wasn't such a whirlwind for me, thanks to my amazing Alliance Theological Seminary (ATS) graduate experience, which helped me see God loved all parts of me, and grieved with me. The study of God, ourselves, and our viewpoint of our world is part of our theology. My professors helped me understand God to be present with all His children's stories regardless of gender, marital status, ethnicity, race, socioeconomic status, and documentation. God loves us all. They encouraged me to always go back to the text to accurately interpret Scripture and to learn the history of misinterpretation.

I held onto the story of Jesus becoming a refugee child as God revealed to Joseph in a vision to flee to Egypt to escape the killing of children. Jesus, the promised Messiah, had to flee for safety in disobedience to the law of the land. I embraced the story of Ruth who as a foreigner clung unto the God of Naomi and trusted him without understanding what would come next after she lost her husband. Her story of being found in the field by the kinsman redeemer Boaz helped me understand God's heart for me and all who are undocumented.

In 2019, I read the book *Hermanas: Deepening Our Identity and Growing Our Influence*. Co-author Noemi Vega Quiñones wrote an essay called "*Mija* Leadership" about the *atrevida*, the courageous woman with the issue of blood. I was captivated, tearful, and forced to see this woman in a completely different way. The bleeding woman understands my hurt and pain of being undocumented. She faced this terrible condition of bleeding for twelve years. Though it was a physical condition, as a Jewish woman, it meant much more for her. She would be avoided and had to avoid others because people with unclean conditions in Jewish law were perceived to contaminate the spaces they occupied. As Ms. Quiñones' put so eloquently:

> Thus, they were most likely void of community, relationship, and touch until they were healed. Even then, they had to provide sacrificial offerings to the priest in order to be declared clean. Days of uncleanliness and separation from community might have been difficult to bear, but can you imagine *years* of such void?[92]

I cry just thinking of what it means for a woman in our society today to be without support, especially those who share my undocumented status. We are taught to cook, clean and work, yet keep our secrets to ourselves. It took me years to trust anyone outside of my immediate family with my status.

I, too, am the bleeding woman, stuck in a system which doesn't see my humanity. Trump's administration doesn't see the tears I shed as I watch both my parents suffer from their status. They were not able to say goodbye to their mothers, my grandmothers, who only live through their stories in my heart. I never had the opportunity to meet my grandmothers before their passing due to the ten-year ban I would receive as punishment for my "illegal entry" as a child. Most of us who are undocumented enter without a visa. This is considered "illegal entry" under immigration law. The punishment for "illegal entry" is a ban on reentry into the United States for 10 years unless one receives a pardon. Undocumented people, including those like me who came as children, are subject to deportation and have no means to adjust that status because there hasn't been immigration reform since 1986.[93] Trump's administration doesn't see my struggle with anxiety which resurfaced strongly with their attempts to dissolve DACA, a program which is erroneously thought to grant amnesty but only protects us from deportation, never giving us a status except permission to work. Trump's administration doesn't see the societal pressures I have to overcome to find my voice in the midst of the fear, hate, and distrust they use to dehumanize us and justify their discriminatory policies.

She came up behind him

The bleeding woman was an *atrevida*, courageous in knowing her truth of being marginalized, but choosing not to isolate herself and seek Jesus in spite of how society would see her and her condition. How she approached him speaks volumes: as it is said in two gospels "she came up behind him" (Mark 5:27; Luke 8:44, NIV). She didn't dare approach him face to face but overcoming fear and shame she boldly reached for her miracle. I understand her posture vividly as I have felt shame with my own undocumented story. Shame for the number of years suffering without a pathway to citizenship, internalizing unworthiness and inadequacy as truth. Ashamed to tell others for fear of losing their respect and avoiding the pain of people's sympathy or "suggested" solutions, as if I haven't exhausted every possibility to adjust my status. Yet, I've abided in Jesus because behind him I am covered, protected and seen—not uncovered, in danger, and rejected. I am the bleeding woman who has come behind Jesus reaching out in hope of a better future for us, the undocumented immigrant community.

Daughter, your faith has healed you

Jesus, the Son of God called the bleeding woman "daughter" after he felt her touch. He asked his disciples who did it and she in fear and trembling told him her truth. I understand the bleeding woman's fear and trembling because I still wrestle with it. It is not easy to live in between knowing whether or not you'll be deported just because of people's political perspective.

I'll never forget the day after Trump's election. On auto-pilot, I traveled to work in NYC's subway system but saw a swarm of sullen faces on the trains. People on phone calls with voices breaking, some crying, others sitting on the train with blank stares. New York City was grieving. I tried to hide behind my work. My supervisor came to me with watery eyes and a shaky voice. She shared her uncertainty for her family who had a blended status. This means members of her family were both documented and undocumented. She didn't know what would happen to them.

Later, I witnessed the fear of a group of female Muslim undergrads pleading with their professor to pardon them from class as they had to leave early for their safety. Unfortunately, unsympathetic, the teacher responded abrasively, informing them of their need to make up the work. All of these factors were cumulative bricks on my glass heart; and I shattered. My eyes filled with tears, a lump formed in my throat, and in a desperate need for privacy, I raced to the restroom. I found a stall and unraveled.

Quiet tears escaped and the knot in my throat softened only to tighten again as I heard two young Muslim friends trying find the safest way to study late in the library. That evening I hit my breaking point on the phone with my mentor who was angry as well with the results of Trump becoming president. She reminded me that I wasn't alone and if I ever needed shelter, her home was open and prayed over me with reassuring words which imprinted in my soul reminders of whose I was. I was a daughter of the King of Kings, who is over rulers and principalities, despite the circumstances and hardships of a Trump presidency.

As the Trump administration dehumanized me, I was confronted by my own dehumanization of white Americans in New Life Fellowship Church's Racial Reconciliation Conference in 2017. I heard Sandra Van Opstal[94] speak wonderfully of God's heart for unity and standing in mutuality for our hurting immigrant communities. She spoke with tears on not just singing worship songs in Spanish, but caring for our Latino community in the midst of profound hardship. I cried inconsolably. After her talk, we debriefed in groups and spoke about what impacted us the most. For the first time I shared my anger against the white American Christians who dehumanized my immigrant community with their xenophobia. A white American brother spoke through tears and told me, "On behalf of them, I apologize. I am so sorry for the hurt and pain it caused you." Tears just flowed; and I could feel myself being healed. God came to me in this brother's wonderful words of reconciliation which immediately brought to mind the many white Christians who mentored and counseled me on my journey. How did I dare forget? Due to the pain of others' xenophobia, I forgot the Christ-loving community that loves and supports me.

My hope will continue in Christ and I thank you for reading my story. The 2020 election is in your hands. As an undocumented Latina pastor who is a Dreamer and DACA recipient, I pray with all my heart you may choose wisely who you place in power in our nation. I don't have the right to vote, nor do my parents and the millions undocumented in all our nation striving to survive in this global pandemic. Remember your vote for a candidate is also a judgment on us, your undocumented immigrant neighbors. If you do not know someone who is undocumented, now you do. We are more than just a number. We are a people who just like you are in the pursuit of love, happiness, dreams and goals for our families and future generations.

My hope for all who are undocumented is for you to know you are not alone. I, too, as an undocumented single pastor with Afro-Peruvian and Peruvian-Italian roots, lament with you. I lament all the times you've never heard that God loves you and is for you regardless of your documentation, because you are a child of the King of Kings and Lord of Lords. I apologize for all the racist, discriminatory, xenophobic comments you've received from the faith community. I'm deeply sorry for all of the rhetoric which has affected your heart and soul.

I apologize for all the ways you, too, our dear beloved Afro-Latino community, have heard Scripture manipulated to tell you to "honor the law by going back to where you came from,," making you feel less than, just as the enslaved did. You are not what people say you are. You are who He says you are. I apologize for not speaking my story sooner and advocating for you as it took me time to get out of the shadows of telling my undocumented story but also recognizing my own Black heritage. Through my grandmother's roots on my father's side I am Afro-Peruvian. I grieve with all who are Afro-Latino, my dear brown church community who suffer the injustice of police brutality. I recognize my privilege because I have lighter skin and lament with you those who don't recognize our African origins. I ask for forgiveness on their behalf and will continue to fight for you. *No estan solos!*

I recently had a conversation with a German friend of mine. I shared with my friend that I watched a documentary on the life of Dietrich Bonhoeffer, and was alarmed by the Nazis' usage of Scripture to justify the Holocaust. My friend with much sadness and confidence told me this was true. He recited the history of his people with a humble repentance from the atrocities it caused and the Nazis' misusage of Scripture. He was absolutely aware of the pain, suffering, and grief this history left for decades. He also said that Trump's politics reminded him of the same fear tactics and manipulation he saw in Hitler's campaign. I was shocked hearing my friend's response and also comforted. I was shocked as I saw history repeating itself, yet I was comforted in seeing the humble repentance of a German native reciting his history many generations after the Holocaust. Perhaps one day, generations after the Trump administration, Americans will recite history and recognize and own all the pain and suffering caused to people of color. I hope to be living to see this unfold. But even if I don't this side of heaven, after America is gone, there will come a day when our stories of suffering will be told, and all will repent of what America did to us.

Miluska E. Aquije (Milly) is many things. As an educator, a spiritual advisor, a mentor, and a Dreamer - among so much else - Milly supports her community with a unique passion and vibrancy. Her current professional experience includes serving as the Discipleship Pastor with Reconcile Brooklyn, and as the founder of Hoping Greatly, where she uplifts others through her story of resilience as an undocumented immigrant. She holds degrees from Nyack College and Hunter College, as well as a certificate from the City Seminary of New York.

On Abortion

The Real Origins of the Religious Right
By Randall Balmer

One of the most durable myths in recent history is that the religious right, the coalition of conservative evangelicals and fundamentalists, emerged as a political movement in response to the U.S. Supreme Court's 1973 *Roe v. Wade* ruling legalizing abortion. The tale goes something like this: evangelicals, who had been politically quiescent for decades, were so morally outraged by *Roe* that they resolved to organize in order to overturn it.

This myth of origins is oft repeated by the movement's leaders. In his 2005 book, Jerry Falwell, the firebrand fundamentalist preacher, recounts his distress upon reading about the ruling in the Jan. 23, 1973, edition of the *Lynchburg News*: "I sat there staring at the *Roe v. Wade* story," Falwell writes, "growing more and more fearful of the consequences of the Supreme Court's act and wondering why so few voices had been raised against it." Evangelicals, he decided, needed to organize.

Some of these anti-*Roe* crusaders even went so far as to call themselves "new abolitionists," invoking their antebellum predecessors who had fought to eradicate slavery.

But the abortion myth quickly collapses under historical scrutiny. In fact, it wasn't until 1979—a full six years after *Roe*—that evangelical leaders, at the behest of conservative activist Paul Weyrich, seized on abortion not for moral reasons, but as a rallying-cry to deny President Jimmy Carter a second term. Why? Because the anti-abortion crusade was more palatable than the religious right's real motive: protecting segregated schools. So much for the new abolitionism.

Today, evangelicals make up the backbone of the pro-life movement, but it hasn't always been so. Both before and for several years after *Roe*, evangelicals were overwhelmingly indifferent to the subject, which they considered a "Catholic issue." In 1968, for instance, a symposium sponsored by the Christian Medical Society and *Christianity Today*, the flagship magazine of evangelicalism, refused to characterize abortion as sinful, citing "individual health, family welfare, and social responsibility" as justifications for ending a pregnancy. In 1971, delegates to the Southern Baptist Convention in St. Louis, Missouri, passed a resolution encouraging "Southern Baptists to work for legislation that will allow the possibility of abortion under such conditions as rape, incest, clear evidence of severe fetal deformity, and carefully ascertained evidence of the likelihood of damage to the emotional, mental, and physical health of the mother." The convention, hardly a redoubt of liberal values, reaffirmed that position in 1974, one year after *Roe*, and again in 1976.

When the *Roe* decision was handed down, W. A. Criswell, the Southern Baptist Convention's former president and pastor of First Baptist Church in Dallas, Texas—also one of the most famous fundamentalists of the 20th century—was pleased: "I have always felt that it was only after a child was born and had a life separate from its mother that it became an individual person," he said, "and it has always, therefore, seemed to me that what is best for the mother and for the future should be allowed."

Although a few evangelical voices, including *Christianity Today* magazine, mildly criticized the ruling, the overwhelming response was silence, even approval. Baptists, in particular, applauded the decision as an appropriate articulation of the division between church and state, between personal morality and state regulation of individual behavior. "Religious liberty, human equality and justice are advanced by the Supreme Court abortion decision," wrote W. Barry Garrett of *Baptist Press*.

So what then were the real origins of the religious right? It turns out that the movement can trace its political roots back to a court ruling, but not *Roe v. Wade.*

In May 1969, a group of African-American parents in Holmes County, Mississippi, sued the Treasury Department to prevent three new whites-only K-12 private academies from securing full tax-exempt status, arguing that their discriminatory policies prevented them from being considered "charitable" institutions. The schools had been founded in the mid-1960s in response to the desegregation of public schools set in motion by the *Brown v. Board of Education* decision of 1954. In 1969, the first year of desegregation, the number of white students enrolled in public schools in Holmes County dropped from 771 to 28; the following year, that number fell to zero.

In *Green v. Kennedy* (David Kennedy was secretary of the treasury at the time), decided in January 1970, the plaintiffs won a preliminary injunction, which denied the "segregation academies" tax-exempt status until further review. In the meantime, the government was solidifying its position on such schools. Later that year, President Richard Nixon ordered the Internal Revenue Service to enact a new policy denying tax exemptions to all segregated schools in the United States. Under the provisions of Title VI of the Civil Rights Act, which forbade racial segregation and discrimination, discriminatory schools were not—by definition—"charitable" educational organizations, and therefore they had no claims to tax-exempt status; similarly, donations to such organizations would no longer qualify as tax-deductible contributions.

On June 30, 1971, the United States District Court for the District of Columbia issued its ruling in the case, now *Green v. Connally* (John Connally had replaced David Kennedy as secretary of the Treasury). The decision upheld the new IRS policy: "Under the Internal Revenue Code, properly construed, racially discriminatory private schools are not entitled to the Federal tax exemption provided for charitable, educational institutions, and persons making gifts to such schools are not entitled to the deductions provided in case of gifts to charitable, educational institutions."

Paul Weyrich, the late religious conservative political activist and co-founder of the Heritage Foundation, saw his opening.

In the decades following World War II, evangelicals, especially white evangelicals in the North, had drifted toward the Republican Party—inclined in that direction by general Cold War anxieties, vestigial suspicions of Catholicism and well-known evangelist Billy Graham's very public friendship with Dwight Eisenhower and Richard Nixon. Despite these predilections, though, evangelicals had largely stayed out of the political arena, at least in any organized way. If he could change that, Weyrich reasoned, their large numbers would constitute a formidable voting bloc—one that he could easily marshal behind conservative causes.

"The new political philosophy must be defined by us [conservatives] in moral terms, packaged in non-religious language, and propagated throughout the country by our new coalition," Weyrich wrote in the mid-1970s. "When political power is achieved, the moral majority will have the opportunity to re-create this great nation." Weyrich believed that the political possibilities of such a coalition were unlimited. "The leadership, moral philosophy, and workable vehicle are at hand just waiting to be blended and activated," he wrote. "If the moral majority acts, results could well exceed our wildest dreams."

But this hypothetical "moral majority" needed a catalyst—a standard around which to rally. For nearly two decades, Weyrich, by his own account, had been trying out different issues, hoping one might pique evangelical interest: pornography, prayer in schools, the proposed Equal Rights Amendment to the Constitution, even abortion. "I was trying to get these people interested in those issues and I utterly failed," Weyrich recalled at a conference in 1990.

The *Green v. Connally* ruling provided a necessary first step: It captured the attention of evangelical leaders, especially as the IRS began sending questionnaires to church-related "segregation academies," including Falwell's own Lynchburg Christian School, inquiring about their racial policies. Falwell was furious. "In some states," he famously complained, "It's easier to open a massage parlor than a Christian school."

One such school, Bob Jones University—a fundamentalist college in Greenville, South Carolina—was especially obdurate. The IRS had sent its first letter to Bob Jones University in November 1970 to ascertain whether or not it discriminated on the basis of race. The school responded defiantly: It did not admit African Americans.

Although Bob Jones Jr., the school's founder, argued that racial segregation was mandated by the Bible, Falwell and Weyrich quickly sought to shift the grounds of the debate, framing their opposition in terms of religious freedom rather than in defense of racial segregation. For decades, evangelical leaders had boasted that because their educational institutions accepted no federal money (except for, of course, not having to pay taxes) the government could not tell them how to run their shops—whom to hire or not, whom to admit or reject. The Civil Rights Act, however, changed that calculus.

Bob Jones University did, in fact, try to placate the IRS—in its own way. Following initial inquiries into the school's racial policies, Bob Jones admitted one African-American, a worker in its radio station, as a part-time student; he dropped out a month later. In 1975, again in an attempt to forestall IRS action, the school admitted Blacks to the student body, but, out of fears of miscegenation, refused to admit *unmarried* African-Americans. The school also stipulated that any students who engaged in interracial dating, or who were even associated with organizations that advocated interracial dating, would be expelled.

The IRS was not placated. On January 19, 1976, after years of warnings—integrate or pay taxes—the agency rescinded the school's tax exemption.

For many evangelical leaders, who had been following the issue since *Green v. Connally*, Bob Jones University was the final straw. As Elmer L. Rumminger, longtime administrator at Bob Jones University, told me in an interview, the IRS actions against his school "alerted the Christian school community about what could happen with government interference" in the affairs of evangelical institutions. "That was really the major issue that got us all involved."

Weyrich saw that he had the beginnings of a conservative political movement, which is why, several years into President Jimmy Carter's term, he and other leaders of the nascent religious right blamed the Democratic president for the IRS actions against segregated schools—even though the policy was mandated by Nixon, and Bob Jones University had lost its tax exemption a year and a day before Carter was inaugurated as president. Falwell, Weyrich and others were undeterred by the niceties of facts. In their determination to elect a conservative, they would do anything to deny a Democrat, even a fellow evangelical like Carter, another term in the White House.

But Falwell and Weyrich, having tapped into the ire of evangelical leaders, were also savvy enough to recognize that organizing grassroots evangelicals to defend racial discrimination would be a challenge. It had worked to rally the leaders, but they needed a different issue if they wanted to mobilize evangelical voters on a large scale.

By the late 1970s, many Americans—not just Roman Catholics—were beginning to feel uneasy about the spike in legal abortions following the 1973 *Roe* decision. The 1978 Senate races demonstrated to Weyrich and others that abortion might motivate conservatives where it hadn't in the past. That year in Minnesota, pro-life Republicans captured both Senate seats (one for the unexpired term of Hubert Humphrey) as well as the governor's mansion. In Iowa, Sen. Dick Clark, the Democratic incumbent, was thought to be a shoo-in: Every poll heading into the election showed him ahead by at least 10 percentage points. On the final weekend of the campaign, however, pro-life activists, primarily Roman Catholics, leafleted church parking lots (as they did in Minnesota), and on Election Day Clark lost to his Republican pro-life challenger.

In the course of my research into Falwell's archives at Liberty University and Weyrich's papers at the University of Wyoming, it became very clear that the 1978 election represented a formative step toward galvanizing everyday evangelical voters. Correspondence between Weyrich and evangelical leaders fairly crackles with excitement. In a letter to fellow conservative Daniel B. Hales, Weyrich characterized the triumph of pro-life candidates as "true cause for celebration," and Robert Billings, a cobelligerent, predicted that opposition to abortion would "pull together many of our 'fringe' Christian friends." *Roe v. Wade* had been law for more than five years.

Weyrich, Falwell and leaders of the emerging religious right enlisted an unlikely ally in their quest to advance abortion as a political issue: Francis A. Schaeffer—a goateed, knickers-wearing theologian who was warning about the eclipse of Christian values and the advance of something he called "secular humanism." Schaeffer, considered by many the intellectual godfather of the religious right, was not known for his political activism, but by the late 1970s he decided that legalized abortion would lead inevitably to infanticide and euthanasia, and he was eager to sound the alarm. Schaeffer teamed with a pediatric surgeon, C. Everett Koop, to produce a series of films entitled *Whatever Happened to the Human Race?* In the early months of 1979, Schaeffer and Koop, targeting an evangelical audience, toured the country with these films, which depicted the scourge of abortion in graphic terms—most memorably with a scene of plastic baby dolls strewn along the shores of the Dead Sea.

Schaeffer and Koop argued that any society that countenanced abortion was captive to "secular humanism" and therefore caught in a vortex of moral decay.

Between Weyrich's machinations and Schaeffer's jeremiad, evangelicals were slowly coming around on the abortion issue. At the conclusion of the film tour in March 1979, Schaeffer reported that Protestants, especially evangelicals, "have been so sluggish on this issue of human life, and *Whatever Happened to the Human Race?* is causing real waves, among church people and governmental people too."

By 1980, even though Carter had sought, both as governor of Georgia and as president, to reduce the incidence of abortion, his refusal to seek a constitutional amendment outlawing it was viewed by politically conservative evangelicals as an unpardonable sin. Never mind the fact that his Republican opponent that year, Ronald Reagan, had signed into law, as governor of California in 1967, the most liberal abortion bill in the country. When Reagan addressed a rally of 10,000 evangelicals at Reunion Arena in Dallas in August 1980, he excoriated the "unconstitutional regulatory agenda" directed by the IRS "against independent schools," but he made no mention of abortion. Nevertheless, leaders of the religious right hammered away at the issue, persuading many evangelicals to make support for a constitutional amendment outlawing abortion a litmus test for their votes.

Carter lost the 1980 election for a variety of reasons, not merely the opposition of the religious right. He faced a spirited challenge from within his own party; Edward M. Kennedy's failed quest for the Democratic nomination undermined Carter's support among liberals. And because Election Day fell on the anniversary of the Iran Hostage Crisis, the media played up the story, highlighting Carter's inability to secure the hostages' freedom. The electorate, once enamored of Carter's evangelical probity, had tired of a sour economy, chronic energy shortages and the Soviet Union's renewed imperial ambitions.

After the election results came in, Falwell, never shy to claim credit, was fond of quoting a Harris poll that suggested Carter would have won the popular vote by a margin of 1 percent had it not been for the machinations of the religious right. "I knew that we would have some impact on the national elections," Falwell said, "but I had no idea that it would be this great."

Given Carter's political troubles, the defection of evangelicals may or may not have been decisive. But it is certainly true that evangelicals, having helped propel Carter to the White House four years earlier, turned dramatically against him, their fellow evangelical, during the course of his presidency. And the catalyst for their political activism was not, as often claimed, opposition to abortion. Although abortion had emerged as a rallying cry by 1980, the real roots of the religious right lie not in the defense of a fetus but in the defense of racial segregation.

The Bob Jones University case merits a postscript. When the school's appeal finally reached the Supreme Court in 1982, the Reagan administration announced that it planned to argue in defense of Bob Jones University and its racial policies. A public outcry forced the administration to reconsider; Reagan backpedaled by saying that the legislature should determine such matters, not the courts. The Supreme Court's decision in the case, handed down on May 24, 1983, ruled against Bob Jones University in an 8-to-1 decision. Three years later Reagan elevated the sole dissenter, William Rehnquist, to chief justice of the Supreme Court.

Randall Balmer is the Mandel Family Professor in the Arts & Sciences at Dartmouth College. His most recent book is Evangelicalism in America. A version of this article first appeared in "Politico Magazine" on May 27, 2014. It is reprinted here with permission.

Do Pro-Lifers Who Reject Trump Have 'Blood on their Hands'?

By David French

I don't often post the trolling, angry tweets that I receive on a daily basis, but I thought I'd make an exception to launch a longer, important discussion that we simply don't see enough in American Christianity: How do politics impact abortion rates in the United States? It has been almost 50 years since *Roe v. Wade* was decided. What have we learned?

Or let's put it another way, since I'm not voting for Donald Trump in 2020, is this tweeter correct (@DavidAFrench, August 21, 2020)? Will I have the "blood of dead unborn children" on my hands?

> **The Other Jack** @richard18682884
> @DavidAFrench @Tracinski You are an anti-Christ that bears false witness daily. And should your new 'side' somehow win, you will have the blood of dead unborn children on your hands when you face judgment.
> August 21st 2020
> **2** Likes

I'm going to give a short answer to this question and a long answer. The short answer is no. The long answer, which is going to dive deep into the legal, political, and cultural realities of the abortion debate, isn't likely to please any partisans. So buckle up.

Decades of data and decades of legal, political, and cultural developments have combined to teach us a few, simple realities about abortion in the United States:

1. Presidents have been irrelevant to the abortion rate;
2. Judges have been forces of stability, not change, in abortion law;
3. State legislatures have had more influence on abortion than Congress;
4. Even if *Roe* is overturned, abortion will be mostly unchanged in the U.S.; and
5. The pro-life movement has an enormous cultural advantage.

If the points above don't seem to make sense to you, then you're likely unfamiliar with the way that decisive numbers of Americans think about abortion—not in crystal-clear terms of life versus choice (or "baby" versus "clump of cells"), but through much hazier and subjective reasoning. This means that absolutists are consistently frustrated with the political process. Unless Americans change, that process will not yield the results they seek.

But while many millions of Americans are hazy about the politics and morality of abortion, it's apparent they have a bias about the *practice* of abortion. In their own lives, pregnancies are both increasingly rare and increasingly precious, and thus abortion is in steady decline, no matter who sits in the Oval Office.

Before I walk through the points above, I want to share with you two key pieces of data. The first is a chart showing the American abortion rate since *Roe*.[95] It's compiled by the pro-choice Guttmacher Institute, and while the data isn't perfect, it's perhaps the best dataset we have:

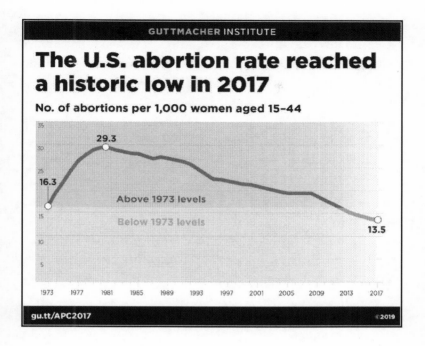

I've posted this before, and a number of commenters have responded with two immediate questions. Does this account for medication abortions? Also, isn't this decrease merely an artifact of declining American birth rates? After all, if there are fewer pregnancies per woman, then it stands to reason there will be fewer abortions.

The first response is easy. Guttmacher data takes into account[96] medication abortions and notes that the overall rate is declining in spite of an increase in medication abortions.

But what about America's declining birth rate?[97] That response is also easy. Yes, America's birth rate has declined, but at nothing like the rate of decline in the abortion rate since 1980. At the same time, we also have data not just about the abortion rate, but also about the abortion *ratio*—the number of abortions per 1,000 pregnancies that end either in abortion or live birth. And that abortion ratio is in steep decline as well.

Guttmacher reports a 13 percent decline[98] in that ratio between 2011 and 2017—a period that represents the last five years of the Obama presidency and the first year of the Trump administration. Broader historical data shows the ratio peaking (and staying relatively high throughout the 1980s—at between 346 and 364 abortions per 1,000 pregnancies) before plunging since 1990 to the current ratio of 184[99]

With these numbers as a backdrop, let's walk through politics, law, and culture.

1. Presidents don't really matter.

Let's begin with a pop quiz. Who is the most pro-life president in the modern history of the United States? A surprising number of contemporary Republicans have a quick answer—Donald Trump. Not only is this answer wrong—other presidents have passed more substantial pro-life policies—the fact that any person could credibly think that's the case is symbolic of historic presidential irrelevance.

For example, Trump is rightly praised for enacting new Title X regulations that required physical and financial separation of Title X projects from abortion-related activities. This decision has caused Planned Parenthood to withdraw from the Title X program.[100] But the Trump rule is less strict than Title X rules promulgated under the Reagan administration.[101]

Moreover, Trump has hardly "defunded" Planned Parenthood. In fact, Planned Parenthood received record-high taxpayer funding in 2019,[102] performed a record-high number of abortions, and its affiliates received $80 million in coronavirus bailouts earlier this year.[103]

Unlike George W. Bush—who signed into law a born-alive infant protection bill and a partial-birth abortion ban—Trump has not signed a single significant piece of pro-life legislation. But even Bush's historic legislation merely nibbled at the edges of the abortion challenge. It's exceedingly rare for babies to be born alive after botched abortions, and partial-birth abortion was barbaric but thankfully infrequent.

Yes, Republican presidents use the bully pulpit to advance the pro-life cause (and Trump is to be commended for speaking to the March for Life). And yes, Democratic presidents use the bully pulpit to hail "reproductive choice." Remember when President Obama said that if his daughters made a mistake, he didn't want them "punished with a baby?"[104]

Regardless of the tweaks to the law, regardless of the bully pulpit, look back again at the numbers above. The abortion rate declines. The abortion ratio declines. They declined during pro-life and pro-choice presidencies. They declined when George W. Bush was president, and they declined when Barack Obama was president. If the decades-long trend holds, they'll decline no matter who wins in November.

But astute readers will note I haven't mentioned perhaps the president's primary theoretical influence on abortion—judicial nominations. Have presidents (or the justices they've appointed) meaningfully moved the needle on abortion law since *Roe*? No, they have not. Let's take a closer look.

2. Supreme Court justices are instruments of stability in abortion law.

I started the last section with a pop quiz. Let's start this section with another. How many of the current Supreme Court justices have recently and unequivocally stated that *Roe v. Wade* and *Planned Parenthood v. Casey* (the two cases securing a constitutional right to an abortion) are bad law? Exactly one out of nine.[105] It's George H.W. Bush appointee Clarence Thomas.

The rest just voted to apply some variant of the *Casey* undue burden standard to a Louisiana statute requiring abortion doctors to have admitting privileges at a local hospital. The court struck down the Louisiana law by a complicated 4-1-4 vote, but one thing was clear—only Justice Thomas cast the abortion right in doubt, and no one else joined in his dissent.[106] In fact, abortion jurisprudence has been relatively stable and intact since 1992.

To be fair, the state of Louisiana did not ask the court to overturn *Roe*, but Thomas stated his opinion. Any justice could have joined him. They chose not to. CNN later reported that Trump's most recent Supreme Court appointee, Brett Kavanaugh, had urged the justices to sidestep the merits of the case entirely.[107]

Now, you might object that previous presidents were "RINOs." They didn't have the *guts* to pick good justices. They wouldn't *fight* like Trump does to put his man or woman on the court. But here again the historical record is not their friend. Even though previous justices were subject to filibusters, Republican presidents did, in reality, succeed in putting on the court justice after justice who had expressed opposition to *Roe*—including some of the most infamous abortion "squishes" in modern Supreme Court history.

As Carrie Severino recently noted,[108] even justices David Souter, Anthony Kennedy, and Sandra Day O'Connor critiqued *Roe* before they joined the court. Souter filed a brief that called abortion "the killing of unborn children." Kennedy once called *Roe* the "*Dred Scott* of our time." O'Connor wrote that the court's abortion decisions "have already worked a major distortion in the Court's constitutional jurisprudence."

Each of those justices joined the majority in *Casey* to preserve the right to an abortion. For almost three decades, the Supreme Court lesson has been clear—put not your trust in judges to rescue America from the moral stain of abortion.

3. State legislatures are more effective than Congress.

One of the most frustrating aspects of modern right-wing political debate has been the claim that the conservative movement didn't "win" before Trump. A conservative movement that was raised from the ground up to celebrate federalism ended up disregarding immense and substantive gains in state governments. For millions of populists, all that really mattered was the presidency.

For many reasons—including the state of abortion law—this is a profound mistake. In reality, the astonishing advance of the conservative movement in American states *during the Obama administration* yielded more concrete pro-life gains than anything the Trump administration has accomplished. Again, here's a Guttmacher chart:

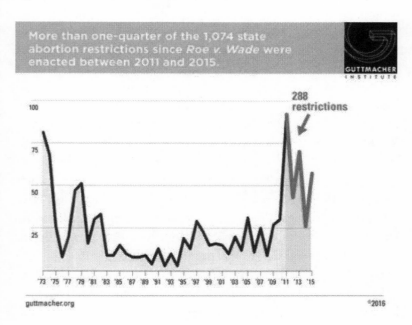

In fact, given this reality, it's not too much to say that losing or winning state elections has proven to be more directly material to the law of abortion than 40 years of federal electoral contests. To understand the extent of state regulation, this piece[109] compiles the sheer totals of state laws that regulate public funding, gestational requirements, waiting periods, parental involvement, physician involvement, and a host of other regulations and restrictions.

But given the extent of state legislation, doesn't this make the Supreme Court even *more* important? After all, the court ultimately rules on the constitutionality of these regulations, and while overruling *Roe* and *Casey* won't ban abortion nationally, it will grant these same states the ability to more heavily regulate abortion or even ban it within their borders.

Not so fast ...

4. Overruling *Roe* won't touch the vast majority of American abortions.

This section might be the most dispiriting for pro-life readers. After all, overruling *Roe* has been the Holy Grail for the national pro-life movement for decades. End *Roe*, and you liberate the states. End *Roe*, and you can finally start working to ban abortion. So long as *Roe* stays, the law will remain unjust. It will permit the killing of innocent, unborn children.

But America is a very big, culturally and religiously diverse country. Support or opposition to *Roe* is hardly spread out evenly across the nation, and while there are many states that regulate abortion as much as they can, other states have passed laws to expand abortion access, and almost 100 million Americans live in states that provide public funding[110] for abortions (the Hyde Amendment[111] prohibits direct federal Medicaid funding for abortion, but it does not bind states).

One of the results of cultural and legal diversity is that states have wildly different abortion rates, and many of the states that have passed the strictest abortion laws already had low abortion rates. This interactive chart[112] is a bit outdated (the data is from 2014), but still useful. It shows abortion rates varying from a low of 5 per 1,000 women (Utah) to a high of 29 in New York state. That's immense variation.

The consequence is that overruling *Roe* would have a disproportionate effect in states with already-low abortion rates. A recent study[113] calculated a potential 32.8 percent decrease in the abortion rate "for the regions at high risk of banning abortions." But for the nation as a whole, the abortion rate would likely shrink by only 12.8 percent.

That's right, even if the pro-life legal movement locates its Holy Grail, almost 90 percent of the American abortion regime would remain intact. The work of the pro-life movement would have to continue, largely as it continues today.

5. But still, the pro-life movement has one immense advantage.

Earlier in this newsletter, I described the thinking of millions of Americans as "hazy" and "subjective."[114] They don't fit neatly into a "pro-life" or "pro-choice" binary, either philosophically or politically. In fact, this muddled reality is one reason for the enduring abortion stalemate in American national politics. There just aren't enough single-issue voters to materially tip the balance of power.

But yet despite the muddle, the abortion rate and ratio continues to fall, and it's fallen dramatically. Why?

Last month researchers at Notre Dame issued a remarkable and interesting study called "How Americans Understand Abortion."[115] Their study wasn't a simple poll that asked its subjects if they were "pro-life" or "pro-choice"—or whether they supported *Roe*. Instead, they conducted 217 in-depth interviews of a representative sample of the American population. Interestingly, abortion was not disclosed as the topic of the interview during recruitment.

The findings are fascinating. I could write an entire newsletter on its contents, but here are the top-line conclusions:

1. Americans don't talk much about abortion.
2. Survey statistics oversimplify Americans' abortion attitudes.
3. Position labels are imprecise substitutes for actual views toward abortion.

4. Abortion talk concerns as much what happens before and after as it does abortion itself.

5. Americans ponder a "good life" as much as they do "life."

6. Abortion is not merely political to everyday Americans, but intimately personal.

7. Americans don't "want" abortion.

Each point is worth discussing. Each point is vital. I found the first point particularly poignant and the last point particularly pertinent. How many truthful, heartfelt conversations have you had *in your entire life* with friends or family about abortion? And no, I'm not talking about political conversations. I'm talking about genuine, transparent, and intimate conversations about personal lives.

In reading the study, it became clear to me that if you want to save unborn life, then improving the conditions of conception, birth, and post-natal life for mother, father, and child are vitally important. This is how real people work through abortion questions:

Americans focus much of their attention on abortion's preconditions, alternatives, and aftereffects. We heard contemplations such as, What was the nature of the relationship between conceiving partners? Was it consensual? How did they approach pregnancy prevention, if at all? Was there sufficient knowledge about potential outcomes? What kinds of support (financial, relational) are available to people facing unplanned pregnancies? What are the stages of prenatal development? What health situations would put a mother or baby at risk? What does it take to raise a child (financially, parentally)? What impact does having a child have on professional aspirations, or on reputation, or on permanent ties between conceiving partners? What roles do (or can) men and women play in parenthood? How accessible is a choice like adoption? What are the conditions of children in foster care? This list of questions continues. The point here is that opinions on myriad social issues and corollary personal decisions frame attitudes well beyond the procedural "yes/no" or "right/wrong" of an abortion decision.

So, if all these questions come into play, and if the combination of Americans who are solidly pro-choice or more moderate in their attitudes vastly outnumber those Americans who are solidly pro-life from conception until natural death, then what is the pro-life movement's immense advantage? It's the last point. It's the fact that abortion is not, ultimately, what people want:

None of the Americans we interviewed talked about abortion as a desirable good. Views range in terms of abortion's preferred availability, justification, or need, but Americans do not uphold abortion as a happy event, or something they want more of. From restrictive to ambivalent to permissive, we instead heard about the desire to prevent, reduce, and eliminate potentially difficult or unexpected circumstances that predicate abortion decisions (whether of relationships, failed contraception, lack of education, financial hardship, or the like). Even those most supportive of abortion's legality nonetheless talk about it as "hard," "serious," not "happy," or benign at best. Stories from those who have had abortions are likewise harrowing, even when the person telling it retains a commitment to abortion's availability. (Emphasis added.)

This is not the "shout your abortion" mindset of a tiny, tiny online fringe. The nation is full of women who want to have their children.

In other words, pro-life Americans may not be approaching a culture biased in favor of their *political* position, but they are approaching a culture that is biased in favor of the pro-life outcome—the birth of a child who is loved. And that bias is manifesting itself in a decades-long shift to a culture that is viewing pregnancy as increasingly purposeful and increasingly precious.

I'm not arguing that national politics don't matter at all. A blue wave could end the Hyde Amendment and result in direct federal funding of abortions. The best available data[116] indicates that would result in more abortions (though it's far from clear that it would stop the overall decline in abortion rates and ratios), and it's a reason why pro-life Americans should resist a Democratic takeover of the Senate.

But if you're pro-life, the encouraging reality is those things that matter most—your relationships and your local political community—are the things over which you have the most influence. The things that matter the least—the presidency and national politics—are those things most removed from your daily life.

But I've been around the pro-life movement enough to know that we often get this exactly backwards We're most passionate about the president. Yet too many of us are less interested in the crisis pregnancy center down the street. Without forsaking national politics, we can reverse that intensity, and if we reverse that intensity through loving, intentional outreach, we will reinforce the very decision the data and our experience tells us a woman *wants* to make.

David French is senior editor of "The Dispatch." A version of this article first appeared in "The Dispatch" on August 23, 2020 and is reprinted with permission. The original article can be found at: https://frenchpress.thedispatch.com/p/do-pro-lifers-who-reject-trump-have.

The Unbearable Lightness of Being "Pro-Life"

Anonymous

I was a freshman in college on September 11, 2001, the day the Twin Towers went down. It was the first time in my life that I had seriously paid any attention to politics at all. For a breath, a heartbeat, we experienced a sense of unity as a nation. By September 13, it had evaporated. The country was soon deeply, evenly, and bitterly divided on the question of whether we should go to war.

As a Christian, I thought the answer for myself and for all Christians was obvious. "You must not murder" is one of the Ten commandments. Our Jesus is the Prince of Peace, who preaches forgiveness "seventy times seven" times—and every pastor or Christian author I've ever heard has interpreted this to mean unlimited forgiveness. Our God is the creator God, arcing the universe toward the renewal of all things, not Shiva, the destroyer. He loves justice, but warns that vengeance belongs to Him alone. He tells us that our fight "is not against flesh and blood," but against spiritual forces of darkness. These are not fringe verses plucked out of context; they are fairly central concepts of the faith.

So I was shocked to realize that the vast majority of Christian America didn't seem to be taking into account the basic tenets of Christianity that were, in my eyes, so eminently applicable to the situation at hand. Instead, people who never seemed to care about theories of any kind before were suddenly throwing around the words "Just War Theory," never being terribly clear what the theory actually was, or on the connection between Saddam Hussein and Osama bin Laden, but nonetheless certain that it justified America going to war in Iraq.

Over nearly two decades since then, the division between the two Americas has only gotten worse. I understand now that when America began to rip in two, it was not a random rupture, but a tear along a perforation. We were already riddled with holes.

Many of those holes were directly connected to America's most intractable and ongoing dispute: the abortion debate.

I was a child the first time someone asked me if I was pro-life or pro-choice. I thought it was a trick question. Life? We're all in favor of life! If not, we wouldn't be living. Choice? America is the land of the free; isn't choice and freedom what we are all about? So I said,

"Both!"—cleverly, I thought.

"You can't be both," my friend said. "They're against each other; you have to pick a side." I decided to find out what these two sides believed and see which one I agreed with.

The answers my research turned up were fairly simplistic. Sometimes a woman gets pregnant without meaning to. She would like to not be pregnant. But then there is a baby inside and the baby, presumably, would like to live. Ending the pregnancy would kill the baby.

One side seemed to be making the point that a woman should be free to do what she wants with her own body, and that seemed reasonable.

The other side seemed to be making the point that a person who is alive should get to keep on living, especially if they haven't done anything wrong, and that seemed very reasonable, too. Overall, it did seem like the right to keep on living trumped other needs, so I decided I must be "pro-life."

At the same time, this clearly wasn't about a good side versus an evil side, but rather a tough situation of competing interests. The pro-choice team wasn't wrong in saying that everyone should get to have control over their own body, insofar as such a thing is possible. This situation was like so many others that people face every single day, in which people with conflicting interests reach compromises and find ways to try to satisfy the needs of both parties.

So it seemed that, even if the baby's need to live trumped the woman's needs, there must still be ways to try to meet her needs as well: to make pregnancy and parenting less hard, to make it easier for her to carry and keep or give up the child, and most of all, to prevent those awful, no-win situations from occurring in the first place.

For years, I didn't give the matter much more thought. I was in my early 20s when I got a call from my friend Amanda. She and her husband had tried for quite a while and finally had successfully gotten pregnant. But it turned out baby Taylor wasn't developing properly at all. She was suffering in the womb, and she would die as soon as she left it. Amanda was an emotional wreck. She didn't know what to do. But eventually she decided that the only kindness available for her to give her baby was to end Taylor's suffering and send her back to the arms of Jesus.

She told people that it was a miscarriage. To her, that's what it was. She didn't need judgment and condemnation on top of her physical and emotional pain.

It was the first and, to this day, the only time (to my knowledge) that someone I personally knew got an abortion. And it wasn't at all like the picture that had been painted for me, of promiscuity and unsafe sex and selfish post hoc choices. As my college roommate went on to become a specialist in maternal-fetal medicine, I learned how very many situations like Amanda's there were, and even worse. In so many cases, and especially with later-term abortions, it was the last thing in the world that the mother wanted—but it was a medical necessity.

This complicated the matter of whether abortion should be legal. I wanted it to be available for situations like Amanda's, and my former roommate's desperate patients. I didn't want it to be used thoughtlessly, but as a last resort. And as I finally began to pay attention to the pro-life, pro-choice debate, I began to see how ugly, exhausted and endlessly hypocritical the whole thing was. Both sides saw and treated each other as monsters, refusing to listen to or make any allowances for the other side's better points. Pro-choicers accused pro-lifers of trying to control women's bodies and behaviors and having no interest in actually preventing unintended pregnancies. Pro-lifers played right into this with pushes for "abstinence-only" sex education and removing access to contraception wherever possible. Pro-lifers saw pro-choicers as indiscriminate and selfish baby-killers, and it sometimes seemed true that pro-choicers were ignoring all of the many other choices women had for avoiding pregnancy, as though they were in fact fighting for the right to have indiscriminate, unsafe sex and never have to face the natural, biological consequences.

Worst of all, both sides seemed to completely ignore the role of men in the whole situation, even though "men cause 100% of unwanted pregnancies" (as Gabrielle Blair so eloquently elucidated in her 2018 article by that title—an absolute must-read).[117]

Neither side seemed terribly interested in changing the behaviors of men that cause so many unintended pregnancies. Men have the easiest birth control option *ever*—condoms are cheap, available last-minute, no side effects—and yet all of the onus is typically on women to avoid pregnancy, as well as virtually all of the consequences when they do not.

Another aspect of the whole situation struck me as particularly odd. A Christian perspective maintains that a human is a combination of the physical body and the spiritual. The fact that we have souls is a primary difference between humans and animals.

A purely secular and scientific perspective doesn't ask about the presence of a soul. A thing is alive, or not alive, based on whether it has cells that are undergoing respiration and replication. A virus, as I understand it, is that ever-confusing middle ground, the thing that replicates but does not respirate, but most things are pretty simple: Granite – not alive. Dog – alive. A once-living thing is dead and begins to decay when the cells are no longer respirating and replicating.

So the thing inside of a pregnant woman—whether we called it a blastocyst, an embryo, a zygote, or a fetus—unless it died, it was alive, and it was able to die *because* it was alive, and furthermore it was a living thing with unique, human DNA.

The one thing we do not and cannot know about it, from a scientific perspective, is whether God has put the soul in yet or not. And we also don't know from a biblical perspective. The Bible doesn't tell us that the soul enters the body at the moment of conception. We as Christians respect the body of a living human because we know that it is made by God and in some mysterious way in the image of God, but we don't actually know at what moment God puts a soul into that body. Given that 10-20% of known pregnancies end in miscarriage, and an unknown number of pregnancies miscarry before the woman ever knows she is pregnant, it seems likely to me that God *doesn't* necessarily put a soul into every fertilized egg. In fact, a few instructional verses from the Old Testament actually seem to treat unborn children as not bearing the full value of a human—like the ones where two fighting men who cause a miscarriage are not put to death, but charged a fine (Exodus 21:22-25), or the ones where a jealous husband can have the priest give his wife a drink that causes her to miscarry if she's been sleeping with someone else (Numbers 5:11-31). Then again, when John leapt in his mother Elizabeth's womb at the arrival of Mary pregnant with Jesus, I'm guessing John's soul and body were acquainted with each other at that point. My point is that God is omnipotent, and would have the ability to control when a baby's body and soul come together, would He not?

So it seems strange to me that the secular, supposedly scientific side of the debate treats unborn children as "not-human" until they are some nebulous stage of "big enough," and the Christian side of the debate treats every abortion situation as murder, no matter the circumstances. Doesn't the "science" side have every reason to believe that a human life begins at conception? Doesn't the Bible give us enough of a sense of God's omnipotence that we Christians can give folks a little grace?

If we did, what might that grace look like—and how might it actually result in fewer abortions? Maybe it looks like providing food and housing assistance to families that are struggling. Maybe it looks like workplace policies that reward, rather than punish, women who bear and raise the next generation. Maybe it looks like valuing and paying fairly for women's work, including "pink-collar" jobs that are essential to our thriving as a nation—and perhaps even the work of caring for children or elders (*Can you imagine? There are countries that actually do this!*). Maybe it looks like providing support to the families of people with disabilities rather than leaving them to fend for themselves, often drowning in poverty as marriages fracture under the stress. Maybe it looks like treating people with disabilities as valuable members of society. Maybe it means free prophylactic birth control for everyone. Maybe it means taking more seriously unmet needs in women's health.

I believe that grace looks like a whole host of policies and cultural mores that make pregnancy and parenting more of an unadulterated joy, as God intended, and less burdened by the hardships and brokenness of our world. And to me, over the years, these have been the policies proposed and enacted primarily by Democrats.

In fact, starting in college and repeating countless times over the years since, I have been shocked at the willingness of Christians to vote for politicians and promote policies grounded in emotions of fear, selfishness and greed, hard-heartedness and unforgiveness toward those who are lesser or undeserving in some way. The God of the Bible instructed his people to welcome the stranger, to forgive debts (yes, even monetary ones!), to stand up for the marginalized. Jesus tells us that we are caring for him when we give a drink to the thirsty, when we visit someone in prison, when we clothe the naked. He commended the woman who gave literally her last pennies to see the work of God done in her world. I don't see Jesus spending a lot of time holding back his blessings from the sinful, and I don't see him telling us to, either. He doesn't call people "illegal;" he calls them his own. He doesn't tell us to hoard our tax dollars so we can use them as we see fit. Jesus said to give to Caesar that which is Ceasar's—and Caesar didn't even have food stamps or Medicaid; he just threw bread to people who came to the Coliseum to be entertained by enslaved people murdering each other.

Ultimately, our ability to show the world what Jesus is like has been crippled by our desire to fight human battles instead of spiritual forces of darkness. My heart breaks for the hearts broken, the souls and decades lost, by Christians pointing accusing fingers instead of reaching out hands of grace and love. We don't see that the more we attack the other side, the more they defend and counter-attack. We can't expect them to listen to any of our points if we never listen to any of theirs.

What if we had approached the whole pro-choice/pro-life battle differently from the beginning? What if we had focused on building a culture in which we worked to end unintended pregnancies? What if we had a culture and policies in which men were truly held responsible for the children they fathered instead of putting all of the onus on women? What if the child support system had real resources and teeth? What if we didn't accuse women of being "welfare queens" but actually saw their children as precious image-bearers of God, worthy of quality food and medical care and education? *We could have prevented hundreds of thousands of abortions every year for decades* if we hadn't been so focused on our side winning the narrow legal battle, feeling right and righteous in our own eyes, and instead focused on the bigger picture.

Because the reality is, nobody wants an abortion. Not even the most staunch pro-choice activist goes out and gets pregnant so she can have an abortion. An abortion is always seen as the solution to a problem—and we could, in so many cases, prevent that problem. It starts with listening, with a heart of grace.

We watched the Twin Towers go down, and then watched our country torn in two, never coming back together. Children were born and raised and went off to college in a world where the Twin Towers never existed. I saw my friends vote over and over for politicians who took away welfare benefits and healthcare, and made it harder and harder for people to come to America; and as long as those politicians were "pro-life," none of the rest of it seemed to matter. In fact, being against gun control was a positive, and no one even talked about the death penalty. Over time, all of those other positions became easier and easier to justify (if they were ever difficult), and they eventually calcified as the positions of the "evangelical voter."

By now, partisan politics have become the de facto religion of America, even among those who call themselves Christian and evangelical. Many Americans are fine with marrying someone of another religion but can't fathom marrying someone who votes for the other party. (I remember telling my girlfriends from my urban church about my new boyfriend, now husband: "I think he might be ..." I bared my teeth nervously

"... a Republican." Eight women literally gasped in unison.) Today, amid a global pandemic, people are treating public health issues as first and foremost political issues. We're also in a months-long reckoning with racism, but peaceful protesters and looters are treated with equal disgrace, and both the extreme right and the extreme left seem to be devolving into violence. On my social media feeds and in real life, everyone seems simultaneously outraged by the issues that divide us, and exhausted by the outrage and division. A few more years on this tragic trajectory, and it wouldn't be surprising to see our country embroiled in a second civil war.

It has to stop. *We* have to stop this.

We have to stop treating those who disagree with us as evil. Our fight is not against flesh and blood, but against the spiritual forces of darkness—and those forces are seeing great success. They are tearing our country and our families apart along partisan lines—and honestly, I don't even think that's their main goal. That's just collateral damage. The Enemy gets what he wants when people's hearts are suffering and souls are dying because the folks who are supposed to represent the way of Jesus have become obsessed with supporting a political party that no longer seems to care about the poor, the marginalized, or the oppressed. The Enemy has used the abortion debate to get us to hate other humans instead of hating him. We, on both sides of the partisan divide, have feared, mocked and vilified children of God.

No more.

No more.

A year ago I became a mother myself, and when I hold my sweet son, even the idea of him dying, in the womb or any other time, chokes my throat and drops a stone into my stomach. I may hate the idea of abortion with every fiber of my being ... but I don't have to hate people who are pro-choice. In fact, God tells me not to. "Forgive them, for they know not what they do."

And from the freedom of forgiveness and grace, I can think creatively about how to eliminate, or nearly eliminate, the need for abortions. We, together, could build a culture in which men are held as responsible as women for their children, and take equal responsibility for preventing unwanted pregnancies. We, together, could ensure that prophylactics and quality reproductive education are available to all. We, together, could end rape culture instead of asking if she was asking for it. We, together, could make sure that struggling families have no problem accessing food and housing and clothing and medical care. We, together, could ensure that both men and women get parental leave, and create workplaces that celebrate and support pregnant and breastfeeding mothers and all parents. We, together, could close the wage gap for men and women (and especially for women of color, who so often are the primary breadwinners for their households).

And maybe, we will discover that this was what being pro-life really meant all along.

Where Love Ends
Anonymous

Disciples of Jesus know that God persistently asks us to consider what we might love more than him. "You won't sacrifice that, huh? What if I wanted you to?" "You say you won't live in that place or take that job. How about for me?" "What if I was the one asking you to help that person instead of them?" God always questions the limits of our love so that we might find more of his love, which knows no limits, on the other side. I love this about him.

Unfortunately, I and those like me often find that love for us is beyond those limits. I have a disability caused by a genetic mutation. Throughout my life, when it came to including me in social activities, games and sports, lessons, or job opportunities, there were always friends, coaches, teachers, and employers who shrugged and said it would be too hard. My parents had to fight for me to be in a mainstream school. Friends and dates were tough to find. I'm still working through the insidious anxiety of the constant exclusion, rejection, and doubts about my abilities.

But as disabled people know, being outside the limits of love can get much darker. Over the summer, a woman recorded a conversation she had with a doctor in Texas telling her that the hospital decided to stop treating her husband for COVID-19 because even if the treatment was successful, he would have a low quality of life. Why? He was quadriplegic and had a traumatic brain injury.[118]

The belief among medical practitioners that disabilities detract from the value of life itself is familiar to disabled people. Last year, I went to a new doctor who asked if I was going to have children any time soon. She wanted to inform me that there were treatments nowadays for ensuring that children did not have my condition. I naively asked what the treatment was. It was early detection of the genetic mutation in fetuses, and abortion. Of course. I should have known. One of this doctor's colleagues once asked me to participate in a survey he was conducting of patients with my condition to assess – what else? - their quality of life.

Experiences like these lead the disability community to almost uniformly oppose physician-assisted suicide. The risk is too high that a doctor will readily believe a disabled person's desire to die is rational. And in most places, it is only disabled people who can request this treatment, which is discrimination. Everyone else gets suicide prevention. We get assistance.

Abortion raises similar risks. Parents afraid of life with a disabled child opt to terminate. Individual choices add up, decimating whole populations of disabled people. American parents, for instance, abort two-thirds of fetuses diagnosed with Down Syndrome.[119]

Here is where I depart from much of the disability community, who believe that the bodily autonomy of pregnant people requires that we should fight discrimination in abortion while keeping it legal. That, too, is a boundary on love. The decision not to allow a life to exist is a determination of that life's value. This fetus cannot be born because – fill in the blank. The people in that blank aren't valuable enough to warrant birth.

But valuable to whom? The individual parent might value the life enough to give birth under different circumstances which society prevents. So society's willingness to invest in those people, the people in the blank, matters.

And here is where I depart from the Republican pro-life movement. They too have borders around their love; a wall, if you will, reinforced with concrete conservative ideology. If, for instance, you think America is both exceptional and a meritocracy, then why invest in anyone? An individual's poverty is nothing more than their failure to avail themselves of the opportunities America offers. Their anxiety about how they will raise a child betrays their lack of faith because in all things, America works for our good. If they choose abortion, they, or their doctor, or someone deserves punishment. Trump knows his Christians think this way. They will not connect his desire to slash benefits, increase policing, segregate public and private housing, heap scorn on vast swaths of people, or any number of other issues to parents calculating whether they want to raise a child in this world.

The only way that anyone seriously argues Trump is pro-life is by pointing to the Supreme Court. But overturning *Roe v. Wade* will likely have a marginal impact on the abortion rate, which in any case has "been plunging since 1990."[120]

So, how do you fight for life? Invest. Invest your prayer, your money, your time, and your love in vulnerable people. Fight for disability rights and disability pride so expecting parents won't be afraid after a diagnosis (and so we won't have so many bigoted doctors). Do everything you can to make sure people have housing, and food, and mental health care, and regular health care, and money; lots of money. Stop demeaning people. Shout "Black lives matter!" from the rooftops. And listen; for God's sake, listen to people whose lives are not like yours. Then fight alongside them. If your politics or your feelings give you pause here, I hope you reconsider the line you've drawn.

Also, vote for Joe Biden. The boundaries of Donald Trump's love are basically the outline of his own silhouette. Fortunately, he is not our model. Our model is the city of our King, which does actually have walls; beautiful, enormous walls that John spends 10 entire verses describing (Rev. 21:12-21). But then do you remember what he says? "On no day will its gates ever be shut" (Rev 21:25, NIV).

May his kingdom come.

On Decolonization

Interceding for the Soul of America
By Danielle Espiritu

It's an interesting position to write about American politics as a Kanaka Maoli who loves Jesus.[121] It's almost like asking the exiles about the Babylonian Empire or the Jews of Jesus' day for their thoughts on Rome. Whether it be the mass death that swept across our islands and devastated a population of nearly one million before 1778, causing it to dwindle to just above 40,000 a century later; the illegal overthrow of Queen Liliʻuokalani, Hawaiʻi's last reigning monarch at the hands of American missionary descendants backed by the might of the U.S. marines in 1893; or the continued occupation of our islands by the United States government and subsequent attempts to strip us of our lands, language, culture, and identity; we have become intimately familiar with the pouli, the darkness.[122] It's a good thing the book of Genesis reminds us that life began in darkness.

> In the beginning God created the heavens and the earth. The earth was formless and void, and **darkness** was over the surface of the deep, and the Spirit of God was moving over the surface of the waters (Gen. 1:1-2, NASB)

> I kinohi hana ke Akua i ka lani a me ka honua. He ʻano ʻole ka honua, ua ʻōlohelohe; a ma luna nō o ka hohonu ka **pouli**. Hoʻopūnana ihola ka

'Uhane o ke Akua ma luna o ka wai. (Kinohi 1:1-
2).[123] [Emphasis added].

When I read the account from Genesis 1, I cannot help
but feel as if we are in the thick of that first night. Before light.
Before breath. In the depths of the void, the weight of the
night can sometimes feel unbearable. Here we find ourselves
in the midst of a global pandemic; mounting economic crises; a growing racial divide evidenced by the continued murder
of Black men and women; and the devaluing of human lives
along racial, economic, gender, political, religious, and cultural
lines. The dark of the night is sometimes so thick it's hard to
breathe ...

I remember all too vividly the night of Trump's election.
I recognize now that the stillness and rush of those memories
are consistent with trauma. It's as if everything was happening
in slow motion as the world around rushed by. Past the initial
shock, the looming cloud of sorrow began to set in. Four years
... Knowing that I needed to find a safe place to fall apart, I
went to visit a friend, and through the glow of street lights
and on the mat of woven hala, we lay on the floor and wept.[124]
There weren't any words, not yet, just tears and the comfort
of knowing we weren't alone. Perhaps then the next four years
wouldn't seem so long ...

Ho'opūnana ihola ka 'Uhane o ke Akua ma luna o
ka wai (Kinohi 1:2)

The Spirit of God was moving over the surface of
the waters (Gen. 1:2, NASB)

As it was during the creation of one honua (the earth),
and our own forming in the darkness of another honua (the
womb), our spirits recognized the vibration of ke Akua's presence, brooding and hovering (ho'opūnana) above.[125] And

though we sensed it, all that flowed out were tears and the sounds of lament.

> In the same way, the Spirit helps us in our weakness. We do not know what we ought to pray for, but the Spirit himself intercedes for us through wordless groans. (Rom. 8:26, NIV)

In times of darkness, when we are completely undone, what else is there to do but to cry out, allowing those tears to become prayers for tomorrow and trusting the Holy Spirit with the rest? As we wept, we planted seeds of prayer for our children, grandchildren, and generations yet to be born (Ps. 126:5-6). We joined with mothers and grandmothers, fathers and grandfathers who, through times of sorrow, sowed prayers of hope for us long before we entered this world.

> "Those who sow with tears will reap with songs of joy." (Ps. 126:5, NIV)

I suppose it's true that seeds must enter a time of darkness and take root before they pierce forth into the light ...

'Ī MAILA - The Power of Voice
From the start of the 2016 presidential campaign, Donald Trump's words had been insensitive, crude, and essentializing. Though many either laughed or shrugged them off, his language and demeanor carried both a pride and contempt that felt dangerous to me.

> I ka 'ōlelo no ke ola, i ka 'ōlelo no ka make.

> In the spoken word there is life/healing, in the spoken word is death. (Mary Kawena Pukui 1983)[126]

This ʻōlelo noʻeau, or proverb, reminds us of the power of our words to bring both life and death. As Kānaka, we are taught that the words we speak have mana (power) that affect the physical and spiritual environments beyond what we might know or experience in our lifetime.[127] Each thought released in speech becomes like a seed planted that will eventually bear fruit. We see this reflected in our language as, "hua," the word for seed is present in both the word "hua ʻai", or "fruit" (literally "seed that is eaten"), as well as in "hua ʻōlelo", or "word" (literally "seed of speech").[128] Thus, there is the constant reminder that the seeds we sow, through our prayers, thoughts, words, and actions, will indeed yield fruit of some sort. It is our responsibility and privilege to be incredibly mindful of the fruit we cultivate for ourselves and for future generations. Proverbs 18:21 reflects these sentiments exactly: *The tongue has the power of life and death, and those who love it will eat its fruit.*[129] (NIV)

Jesus' life on earth was a perfect example of ke Akua's original intention for us as people. Doing nothing apart from His Father, He demonstrated how to operate in grace, speaking a truth that disrupted unjust systems and brought healing and repentance. We see Him consistently rebuke the Pharisees and religious teachers, who had become condemning, exclusionary, and elitist. Instead, He intentionally transcended the social, political, religious, and cultural barriers of His time in order to seek out and elevate those considered outcast in society.

In the gospel of John, a woman caught in the act of adultery was brought before Jesus by a group of scribes and Pharisees (no mention, of course, was made of the man she was found with, who by the law should also have been held accountable). In this instance, Jesus' words had real power to bring death to this woman. However, He invited those without sin to cast the first stone, shining light on the truth that each one of her accusers was a sinner. One by one, they left. After affirming that He would not condemn her, Jesus instructed the woman to go from there and to leave her life of sin (John 8:3-11).

Jesus used His voice to speak truth that challenged the religious authorities of His day. His proposition that the one without sin be the one to cast the first stone called into question their façade of holiness and superiority. Furthermore, when viewed alongside another encounter Jesus has with women in all four gospels, we see His intentionality to elevate female voices in a male dominant society (John 4:5-42; Matt. 26:6-13; Mark 14:3-9; Luke 7:36-50; John 12:1-8).[130] In this instance, Jesus used his voice as a man to challenge other men and to extend grace to a woman threatened with death, not only saving her physical life but also drawing her closer to the Lord.

We are called to do the same. Considering Jesus' example, I think it important to ask: *How might Donald Trump's words and actions reflect the superiority and contempt that Jesus called into question? How might a failure to address these issues create a silence that has critical and potentially devastating effects?*

MOʻOʻKŪʻAUHAU & MOʻOLELO - Genealogy & History

Moʻokūʻauhau, the Hawaiian word for genealogy, evokes the image of a sequence of vertebrae, interlocked and positioned together. Each one, affected by those who've gone before, sets the foundation for those who will come after. In Hawaiian tradition, the moʻokūʻauhau of an aliʻi (chief) would be chanted as the child was being born, beginning with the start of the universe in pō (the time of night/darkness) and continuing to the present day, so as to remind the young one of their kuleana (responsibility, privilege, authority) to their people as well as to the rest of creation.[131] While the significance of this is often lost in American culture, the Bible is full of references to genealogies of people that are woven through the telling of their stories (moʻolelo).[132] In an Indigenous worldview, there is a constant recognition that everything has both a moʻokūʻauhau and moʻolelo, from the people we encounter, who carry with them stories of the communities, lands, and waters that have fed and raised them, to the physical water we drink, which traveled for years through layers of rock and soil before making its way to our homes. We all have a genealogy leading back to the start of creation; it is remembering those stories that helps us to understand our responsibility to see beyond ourselves and to honor the many intersecting lineages that comprise our lived experience.

Moʻokūʻauhau and moʻolelo help to put into perspective the painful and problematic pieces of Trump's call to "Make America Great Again." This rhetoric reflects a convenient forgetting and an intentional dismissal of the moʻolelo (histories and stories) of sin and pain tied to these times of perceived American "greatness." From slavery to genocide to the stealing of nations, the cries of lament made by those who have born the cost of "greatness" are often overshadowed or rationalized by stories of "American" success.

From 1946-1958, the Marshall Islands, a small group of atolls in the Pacific, suffered incredible loss as a result of nuclear weapons testing done by the United States during the U.S. arms race with the Soviet Union.[133] The U.S. not only tested 67 nuclear weapons on the Marshall Islands, the largest being 1,000 times stronger than the bomb dropped on Hiroshima, but a number of miscalculations resulted in the direct contact of entire communities with radioactive nuclear material. Marshallese were told these bombings were, "for the good of mankind."[134] Rather than immediately evacuate or inform the Marshallese of the dangers of nuclear fallout, the U.S. government capitalized on these miscalculations and used them as an opportunity to study the effects of nuclear radiation on live human subjects.[135] The accounts are horrific – vomiting, hair and fingernail loss, miscarriages and "jellyfish babies," birth defects, and cancer, not to mention the ongoing health effects caused by a reliance on imported, canned food now that traditional foods could not be grown on some islands.[136] These are the stories of real families, like those of my former students now living in Hawaiʻi. Atolls enduring heavy bombing, such as Bikini, have now become unlivable – their people never able to return to the islands that raised them.

Here we see the direct impacts of the fear and exceptionalism characteristic of the Post-WWII era. During this period, the pursuit of American "greatness" and the fear of the communist "enemy" led to policy and action that brought death and a rhetoric that rationalized it. And though glossed over as having happened in America's distant past, let's not forget that these atrocities took place in my grandparents' lifetime on a small group of islands not far from their own.

Though President Trump is not engaged in an arm's race, his investment in oil and corporate interests have had devastating effects on Pacific Islander and Indigenous communities, including the Marshall Islands. Since Trump's election, his administration has been working to dismantle over 100 major climate and environmental policies.[137] These actions directly threaten the ability of entire nations to remain in their homelands, as Pacific Islanders living on atolls have already experienced salt-water inundation due to sea level rise. These issues, though classified as "environmental," also speak directly to basic human rights and people's ability to subsist and to engage in cultural practices tied directly to their lands and waters. Should these islands become uninhabitable, entire nations will be forced to leave their homelands as refugees.[138] This blatant disregard for other people, cultures, and lands and the intentional dismantling of legislation that would protect them does not reflect the heart of the gospel.

Perhaps this is a critical moment to ask: *What "greatness" does America desire to establish and at what cost? Is it possible for true "greatness" to be built on the lands and backs of unwilling participants?*

Then they said, "Come, let us build ourselves a city, with a tower that reaches to the heavens, so that we may make a name for ourselves; otherwise we will be scattered over the face of the whole earth." (Gen. 11:4, NIV)

Our early ancestors' rationale for attempting to build a city with a tower that would reach to the heavens was motivated first by a desire for **greatness**. By making a name for themselves, they would be able to elude the command to "fill the earth" (Gen. 1:28). Thus, they began to establish a monolithic city and ultimately chose self-sufficiency and desire for power in place of the relationship and obedience for which they were created. Out of a **fear** of losing control, they attempted to build the world's first empire.

In *Unsettling Truths: The Ongoing, Dehumanizing Legacy of the Doctrine of Discovery,* Mark Charles and Soong-Chan Rah highlight the ways in which Trump's platform taps into a deep-seeded belief that America is different and fundamentally better than the rest of the world.[139] This belief in American exceptionalism works in tandem with a rhetoric of fear. When describing immigrants at a 2015 campaign event, Trump stated, "They're bringing drugs. They're bringing crime. They're rapists."[140] Stemming directly from his comments and the racist ideology that undermines them, Trump's proposed policies on immigration called for the militarization of borders, the deportation of millions of undocumented immigrants and "criminal aliens," increased criminalization of those with expired visas, and a temporary ban on immigration for individuals from nations "tied to Islamic terror."[141]

Over the last four years, the Trump administration has worked to dismantle programs that afforded human rights protections for some of our most vulnerable populations. By breeding a culture of fear and leading the cry to "protect American communities and jobs," Trump has been able to institutionalize policies that criminalize and incite violence toward immigrant families and communities.[142] This has resulted in terror for undocumented immigrants often fleeing poverty and political violence: policing of borders, travel restrictions from countries deemed threatening, and the violent separation of families and caging of children. These acts of "protection" go directly against the biblical command to "love thy neighbor," the "stranger," and the "alien" (Lev. 19:34; Jer. 7:5-7; Matt. 5:43-44).

Furthermore, rather than seeking to honor and listen to Indigenous communities, Donald Trump and his administration have consistently supported policy placing economic and business interests above the health of Indigenous people and the lands and waters that feed us. Likewise, communities voicing outcry against systemic, racial injustice and murder are cast as violent, irrational criminals and threatened with the use of military force "needed" to bring a semblance of "control" and "peace."

This doesn't feel like the gospel of grace that Jesus gave His life to demonstrate. Instead, it seems alarmingly similar to the sin committed at the Tower of Babel.

MOʻOMEHEU - Culture & Healing

In response to our early ancestors' desire for control, ke Akua gave us our cultures (Genesis 11; Acts 17:26-28). Moʻomeheu (culture) brings up the image of a series of tracks or footprints left by those who came before. Understood through the lens of Acts 17:26-28, it can also be interpreted as a set of clues that the Creator has placed in each cultural heritage, with the hope that we would seek Him.[143] By perfect design, the Lord determined our times, seasons, and boundaries that we might travel, footprint by footprint, down the moʻokūʻauhau that points us back to Him. In uncovering the fullness of the moʻolelo (histories, stories) of our ancestors, and in learning to honor the beautiful pieces of Him hidden in others, we are meant to grope for Him that perhaps we might find Him in the connection for which we were created (Ps. 78, Acts 17:26-28).

I've sometimes heard Americans refer to America as a "melting pot," often with a sense of pride at the array of cultures and people represented. I commend the desire for diversity, but I wonder if it is truly reflective of the Creator's intent.

> After these things I looked, and behold, a great multitude which no one could count, from **every nation and all tribes and peoples and tongues**, standing before the throne and before the Lamb, clothed in white robes, and palm branches were in their hands ... (Rev. 7:9, NASB) [Emphasis added]

Revelation depicts a "great multitude" of diverse languages, nations, and people worshipping before the Lamb. Here we see the Lord's beautiful heart for diversity. However, through the stories of pain and suffering woven throughout America's genealogy, it is evident that this country has failed to demonstrate a value for true, biblical diversity and justice. The melting pot of American culture has instead done much to suppress, and in some cases destroy, the rich language and cultural reflections of the Lord seen through His people – an undoing of the beautiful work presented in Acts 17 and a reminder of the folly of Genesis 11. Unfortunately, those added or forced into America's pot who are not seen as "American" either melt away or are burned at the bottom.

As a way to understand this trauma, we might consider the concept of "han" offered by Korean theologians. Young-Hak Yun explains han to be, "a sense of unresolved resentment against injustice suffered ... a feeling of acute pain of sorrow in one's guts and bowels."[144] This depiction of han aligns beautifully and painfully with Hawaiian perspectives of healing, viewed as the peeling back and release of layers of trauma, exposing areas of the na'au (guts, intestines; mind, heart, center) that are knotted. Kala, the act of forgiveness literally means "to loosen, untie, free or release" bringing to mind the unknotting and releasing of the transgressor.

Included below is a verse from a prayer and song entitled, "Ke Aloha o ka Haku," "The Lord's Mercy," written and set to music by Queen Lili'uokalani in 1895 during her time of imprisonment.[145] Held captive by the same missionary descendants who had overthrown her, these words express her heart's cry and that of a nation in mourning.[146]

Ke Aloha o ka Haku
The Lord's Mercy

Mai nana inoino
Na hewa o kanaka
Aka e huikala
A maemae no

Oh! Look not on their failings,
Nor on the sins of men,
Forgive with loving kindness
That we might be made pure

(Translation, Lili'uokalani) [147]

And with the grace and example of Jesus and that of our ali'i (chief), I say: E kala aku au iā 'oe e Amelika. I forgive you, America. I release you to heal, grow, restore, and be restored as the Lord leads you.

I have offered several momi (pearls) from our own culture and history that will hopefully help the Americans reading this to navigate this time of pō particularly leading into and following the upcoming election.[148] While I am very concerned with the outcome of November and what it will mean for those I love who will bear the brunt of its results, and while I will continue to hope for a future that reflects the Creator's heart and design for justice and healing, the Spirit has also asked me if I would be willing to intercede for the soul of the American people. Who am I that I should object?

And so, with the tears shed throughout the course of this writing and through tears now, I offer these as prayers for you:

I bless you. I pray the gentleness, courage, faith, and endurance of my people be released to you, and I pray you receive whatever is needed to pursue the Creator's plan for your people. I bless you to know, feel, and see ke Akua's heart for you and for others, and I bless you with vision and strength to see the dawn before it's come and to remain there until it does.

I bless your voice to carry the love and light of Jesus – to bring good news to the afflicted, to bind up the brokenhearted, and to proclaim liberty to captives and freedom to prisoners. I bless you to be oaks of righteousness that reflect beautifully the Lord's heart for justice, restoration, and redemption; and I bless you to rejoice in the Lord, carrying fully His mantle of salvation and of righteousness.[149]

Amene.

Danielle Espiritu is a Kanaka Maoli educator from Kāne'ohe, O'ahu currently living with her 'ohana in Waimalu in the moku (district) of 'Ewa. She is of Chinese, Samoan, Native Hawaiian, Korean, Puerto Rican, Filipino, and European descent, and honors the people, lands, and genealogies that have shaped her. Dani and her community are passionate about justice and pursuing the Lord's heart and presence. They seek to live lives that bring healing, reconciliation, and abundance to both 'āina (land, that which feeds) and kānaka (people) by restoring balance and right relationship, and they stand on the shoulders of many po'e aloha 'āina (patriots, lovers of the land) who held fiercely to their love for their lands, their people, and for Iesū (Jesus).

The Fullness Thereof

By Randy Woodley

CHANGE YOUR LENSES, please. Okay, maybe you can't simply change lenses right now, but would you at least notice the lenses you are currently wearing? If you are like, say, 99.9 percent of us in the U.S., you have been influenced by a very particular set of perspectives that interpret life from an Enlightenment-bound Western worldview.

All of our lenses have various perspectival tints, but Western worldviews seem to have several in common, including the foundational influence of Platonic dualism, inherited from the Greeks. This particular influence absolutizes the realm of the abstract (spirit, soul, mind) and reduces the importance of the concrete realm (earth, body, material), disengaging them from one another. In dualistic thinking, we are no longer an existing whole.

Western worldviews tend to have other related assumptions—such as hierarchy, extrinsic categorization, individualism, patriarchy, utopianism, racism, triumphalism, religious intolerance, greed, and anthropocentrism. But the influence of dualism empowers these other concerns.

What difference would it make if life were viewed instead as a fundamental whole, if the earth itself were seen as spiritual? And how would such a worldview square with Jesus' approach to such matters?

A few encouraging facts as we approach these questions:

- Most of the rest of the world does not understand life through a Western worldview. We in the West are the anomaly.
- Jesus was not an Enlightenment-bound Western thinker. He thought more like today's premodern Indigenous people.
- Not one writer of the scriptures saw life through a Western lens.
- Indigenous Peoples of the world have an advantage over Western thinkers in that there is still enough premodern worldview intact among North American and other Indigenous people to relate to the premodern Jesus and the premodern scriptures. They can bring new kinds of hope to today's earth climate crisis, if we allow it.

Jesus understood humanity's relationship with the earth differently than we do. He spoke to the wind, to the water, and to trees; closely observed the habits of birds, flowers, and animals; and called his disciples to model their lives after what they saw in nature. In Matthew 5, during his Sermon on the Mount, Jesus said, "Do not say, 'By heaven!' because heaven is God's throne. And do not say, 'By the earth!' because the earth is his footstool" (34b-35a, NLT).

Jesus was making a point about making vows, but one of the many byproducts we see from this short exchange (and from his whole life) is Jesus' view of the whole world, including earth and heaven, as sacred. Jesus understood the balance between the earthly and the heavenly realms, and he certainly understood the relatedness of both ("on earth as it is in heaven"). Jesus was firmly planted in the construct that "the earth is the Lord's and all that is in it."

The predominant themes and subject matter of Jesus' stories were natural, such as fish, flowers, birds, sheep, oxen, foxes, earth, trees, seeds, harvests, and water. There were many mechanical inventions during Jesus' time, but the record reflects he paid little attention to them. His was a world of keen observation, where God was wondrously alive and at work in creation.

In Jesus' worldview, he laid to waste the fallacies of Platonic dualism that exist in our modern era and that presume the earth or the body or anything earthly is less spiritual than the mind, the spirit, or things more abstract. To Jesus, as it should be to us, the earth is wholly spiritual, as are our bodies.

Earth out of Balance

If we remove the influence of Platonic dualism from our worldviews, we will find it difficult to view human beings as being *over* all other parts of creation. Instead of a relationship where nature is below us, we should be stewarding with, or co-sustaining, all creation.

Each area of creation is working with the Creator to maintain earth's balance. The rain and snow, oceans and sun all sustain life on earth. Animals regulate each other within their various natural cycles. Plants provide oxygen, food, and shelter for all of creation to coexist together. As human beings, we are co-sustainers with the rest of creation to ensure the abundant life for all creation the Creator intended. And God said that is good.

When considering our relationship to the earth, Christians will recognize that Jesus is earth's creator and sustainer (John 1, Colossians 1, Hebrews 1), and we simply cooperate with him in these tasks. Our job, as humans and as Christians, is to maintain the natural balance God set forth through Christ.

Unfortunately, things are out of balance. By allowing past and current exploitation of the earth and earth's resources, we are now reaping the consequences via the current climate catastrophes. Earth's topsoil is disappearing; coral reefs are dying; glaciers are melting; aquifers are not being recharged; animal, bird, fish, and plant species are dying at exponential rates. We are experiencing a steadily increasing amount of severe weather patterns through hurricanes, flooding, tornadoes, forest fires, landslides, droughts, and snowstorms—and the costs of these disasters continue to rise progressively each year, into the hundreds of billions of dollars. Earth is out of balance, and as a result all God's creation is in peril.

The Road to Restoration

Christians have evaded the responsibility of earth-care, due largely to the adoption and influence of a worldly philosophy. By ignoring the earth's problems, are we not responsible for dismissing the things important to Jesus in favor of our own selfish interests?

Indigenous Peoples have historically been condemned because we view our relationship with the earth to be very sacred. Like Jesus, Indigenous Peoples understand their relationship with creation as paramount to the abundant life God intends for all humanity. In other words, to be human is to care for creation. If we want to live our lives together in abundance and harmony, and if we want future generations to live their lives together this way, we must realize we are all on a journey together with Christ to heal our world. Earth healing will take cooperation from all of us to solve the problems.

The single conceptual integration of land, history, religion, and culture may be difficult for many Western minds to embrace. For Indigenous Peoples, this integration is often explained as a visceral "knowing," or as somehow embedded in our DNA.

This feeling we have of ourselves as a people, including our history and cultures, being connected to the land is perhaps the single most glaring difference between an Indigenous Native North American worldview and a Euro-Western worldview. But if we are all to survive the 21st century, things must change so that our Euro-Western friends can sense a similar connection. How does such a paradigm shift happen?

A Worldview both Indigenous and Biblical

Christians cannot merely leave such matters in the hands of well-meaning secular environmentalists. Although everyone should be deeply indebted to those on the frontlines of the environmental movement, many current initiatives are only helpful in the short run, because they focus on preserving earth and water for a particular use.

Unless there are guiding values that become rooted in a familial love of creation, these short-term initiatives simply may represent a more sanitized version of utilitarianism: using the earth without deeply loving the earth as sacred creation. Utilitarianism (using the earth out of self-interest, for good or bad) has been, in part, the problem.

This is where Indigenous people can be helpful. Many Indigenous Peoples understand:

- **Creation exists** because of a Creator.
- **Life is intrinsically valuable** *because* it is a gift from the Creator and, therefore, it is sacred, meaning that sacred purpose is crucial to our existence.
- **The role of human beings is unique,** and humans relate to the rest of creation uniquely. This includes restoring harmony through gratitude, reciprocity, and ceremony between the Creator, humans, and all other parts of creation.
- **Creation does not exist to be ignored** in isolation, but creation is the Creator's first discourse in which humanity has a seat of learning and in which the discourse is continuous.
- **Harmony is not simply understood as a philosophical idea;** it is about how life operates and the only way that abundant life can continue, if life is to be lived as the Creator intends.

We are now at a point in human history when we must realize that the Industrial Age has written a check to our world that has insufficient funds. Only a worldview encompassing the interconnectedness between Creator, human beings, and the rest of creation as one family will sustain abundant life.

Such a worldview is fundamentally both Indigenous and biblical. If we are wise, we will protect Christ's creation, for this creation is central to God's investment in us.

The Rights of Nature

There are a number of obstacles that the Western world and worldview will need to clear in order to rebalance and preserve creation, but there is one great and relatively timely action that could move us quickly down the road to restoration: We can pass laws to protect Christ's creation—not just because of the current climate crisis but because we love what God loves and we want to understand the world more like Jesus, earth's creator and sustainer.

Following the lead of Indigenous people's movements around the world, we can enact laws and constitutional amendments to protect the earth, as did Ecuador and Bolivia. More than three dozen U.S. municipalities have adopted similar "rights of nature" laws and regulations, including Pittsburgh, the largest U.S. city to do so.

Bolivia's "Rights of Mother Earth," as it is sometimes called, grew out of the World People's Conference on Climate Change held in Cochabamba, Bolivia, in April 2010. At that conference, more than 35,000 people from 140 nations adopted the Universal Declaration of the Rights of Mother Earth. (You can find more on the rights of nature movement at TheRightsofNature.org.)

Bolivia is one of many countries struggling to deal with the climate crisis and its weather anomalies, such as rising temperatures, melting glaciers, numerous floods, droughts, and mudslides. Bolivia, like many other nations, is a battleground country between the rights of Indigenous peoples, especially landless peoples, and a corrupt corporate state, similar to the situation in the U.S., where corporations are legally protected "persons" but the earth that supports them has no real voice or rights.

To remind us of our intimate connection with creation and to break dualistic thinking, "action" must become an important word in Western people's vocabulary. Euro-Western people might also consider developing new ways of expressing their thanks through outdoor, earth-honoring ceremony. Through expressing gratitude in ceremony, Indigenous Peoples reveal to others and themselves the connection between Creator, human beings, the earth, and all the rest of creation.

A foundation of Native American ceremony is gratitude for the relationships that exist. Euro-Western people can rediscover what their Indigenous ancestors once knew and, in so many ways, reclaim some of their Indigeneity once again. To move ahead—perhaps simply to survive—we must all be connected to Christ's creation in harmony.

Throughout the gospels Jesus gave creation a voice. We should do the same. Would you ask your spouse to remain silent or ask them to not make their needs known? We are in a relationship with the earth and all of earth's creatures. We must make the earth's voice known and protect it by recognizing the earth's rights. Unfortunately, we have waited until this late hour to realize the sacredness of this relationship. Let's not delay until it is too late. Jesus is waiting.

Randy Woodley (Keetoowah Cherokee) is a professor, author, activist, farmer and wisdom-keeper who shares his deep desire for a world that reflects the Creator's design and his Indigenous worldview. Randy and his wife, Edith (Eastern Shoshone), co-sustain Eloheh Indigenous Center for Earth Justice/Eloheh Farm & Seeds in Yamhill, Oregon. A version of this article first appeared in the May 2019 edition of "Sojourners Magazine" and can be found at: https://sojo.net/magazine/may-2019/fullness-thereof. It is reprinted here with permission from "Sojourners," (800) 714-7474, www.sojo.net.

When Religion Becomes Idolatry
By Suzie Lahoud

"For now we see in a mirror dimly, but then face
to face. Now I know in part; then I shall know
fully, even as I have been fully known."
1 Cor. 13:12 (ESV)

Like Jacob, I have often wrestled with God over the politics of
my own identity. From a young age I had attained what many
around me attested to be profound maturity in my Christian
faith. I could quote Bible verses in the proper context with
sound interpretation appropriate for any circumstance. I had
a solid theological answer for every question of faith, and even
for those questions I had not yet thought to ask, I could always
conjure an immediate response using finely tuned spiritual reasoning. I was wise in the eyes of others, and admittedly in my
own eyes as well. Again, this was called maturity.

Then war broke out in Syria and my faith was shattered.
I had been residing in Lebanon for over a year at the time.
This was not the shaken faith of, "If God is good, then why do
bad things happen?" nor the simple, yet gut-wrenching "God,
why?" It felt more complex than that. Somehow all of my biblical reasoning seemed to be in turmoil. My theological platitudes fell short. I found that I did not have all the answers, and
I was lost; drowning in a sea of blood, and destruction, and
despair. In the place of words of comfort, all I could offer was
tears. In the place of fervent prayers, tears. And then came what
I feel we seldom talk about – the silence after the tears. The

silence that is not sated, it is empty. I resented those who could rest at night, assured that "this was the will of God." I resented those who could pray, and weep, and find comfort.

Yet somehow, in the midst of this pain and suffering, God was still at work. I remember one Saturday at a food aid distribution for Syrian refugees, a mother presented me with her infant with a brain tumor so massive that it had rendered the previous curvature of her head unrecognizable. The infant's eyes stared up at me unblinking. Her mother lamented that her baby had long ago ceased to even cry from the pain. And the UN, they would not pay for her surgery. Reading over the dirty, crumpled prognosis, I didn't have the heart to tell the mother that it was because there was no hope for this child. They would not waste their limited resources on certain death. And all I could do was weep with her, standing there shivering in the cold. I called my friend over and we laid hands on the baby and prayed for her together. I didn't have the strength to do it alone. That night I couldn't sleep. I tossed and turned and prayed for that child. I was heartbroken and angry.

Two weeks later I learned that the UN had, against their standard policy, agreed to pay for the child's surgery to remove the tumor. The doctor expected a full recovery. Life from death. That's what God can do in the midst of suffering. But I still don't understand how, or when, or why.

What I have learned is that I am so small, and God is bigger than I ever imagined.

The concept of Christian worldview has received considerable attention over the past few decades. Yet, I must confess that I have found an unexpected theological kinship with post-structuralist thinkers like Levinas and Derrida. These fathers of post-modernism warned against the dangers of totalitarian systems of thought. Though I may not agree with all of their premises, for example, Derrida's perpetually absent Messiah, I do agree with doing away with neatly packaged discourses that conveniently order the world. And here's why: any system of thought, no matter how complex, that has a humanly obtainable answer for everything is essentially atheist, or at the very least, agnostic. Oftentimes, we've taken God out of the equation by making it about the equation. But while God is a God of order, He's not an equation; He's a Person. Or rather, a Being of triune existence. And He is by definition, Other. He is by definition, beyond comprehension.

When we attempt to make sense of the world by ordering the mind of God, we are fashioning Him in our own image, because the human mind is never free of prejudice. This is idolatry.

I often ponder Gandhi's confession, "I like your Christ, I do not like your Christians." Yet its historical significance did not fully dawn on me until recently. I was reading Thomas Merton's *The Seven Storey Mountain*, when the following description of the then tragically misled solidarity of the Church of England pierced me to the heart:

> It is a class religion, the cult of a special society and group, not even of the whole nation, but of the ruling minority in a nation. That is the principal basis for its rather strong coherence up to now ... The thing that holds them together is the powerful attraction of their own social tradition, and the stubborn tenacity with which they cling to certain social standards and customs, more or less for their own sake. The Church of England depends, for its existence, almost entirely on the solidarity and conservatism of the English ruling class. Its strength is not in anything supernatural, but in the strong social and racial instincts which bind the members of this caste together; and the English cling to their Church the way they cling to their King and to their schools: because of a big, vague, sweet complex of subjective dispositions ...[150]

This religious cohesion was the very force that drove colonialism. It shaped the worldview that sought to "tame the Orient" and "convert the heathen." It produced the privileged social class that E.M. Forster and Tagore decried, and against which Gandhi so famously protested.

Mournfully, I cannot help but reflect: does the predominant worldview of white evangelical Christians like me create more problems than it solves? Not for us mind you, but for the world? Does it serve to perpetuate our own comfort and peace of mind at the expense of the Other? Does it oppress and even destroy? Does it try to absolve us of our bloodguilt, when a truly righteous view of the world would bring us to our knees?

The idolatry of remaking God in our own image leads to such evil in the world. It perpetuates systems of oppression, racism, and hate. Its fruits are genocide, apartheid, and rape. Tell me that the Church's hands are clean from the blood of even the past century, and I will tell you that you are complicit in upholding the kind of bloodguilt the Church lives with every single day.

Yes, I am talking about white supremacy, but the kind comfortably ensconced in a leather chair smoking a cigar. I am talking about xenophobia, but the kind safely domesticated behind a white picket fence. I am talking about homophobia, the kind that scapegoats before an audience of well-dressed parishioners. I am talking about Islamophobia, the kind that tenderly tucks in its babies at night, never questioning the drones that take the life of another's child. I am talking about churches that offer enough of the antidote to our middle-class angst to keep us focused on how to solve our own problems, rather than opening our eyes to see the suffering of the Other and moreover, the ways that we are complicit. I am talking about answers that help us sleep at night, when we should be awake praying.

As it pertains to the current epoch, I am talking about the Trump administration and the hatred and bigotry that it normalizes, thrives upon, and propagates. I am referring to the distorted lenses that allow the Church to be not merely apathetic, but enabling. This administration has exposed the dark underbelly of the white American evangelical church and laid bare the banality of the evil that lurks in our pews. We have seen the enemy. It is us.

It is in times like these that what is required is not triumphalism but lament; not complacency but dissent. It may be that the prophets of the age are not the ones shouting from the pulpit, but the voices crying out through bullhorns in the streets. Perhaps, the words of the prophets are indeed written on the subway walls ...

Several years ago, I read an article exposing numerous facets of the politically expedient re-fashioning of God in America. The candid reflection of the author – as an academic, woman of color, and woman of faith – really stuck with me:

> I often ask myself whether I really do worship the same God of white religious conservatives. On this Holy Week, when I reflect on the Christian story of Christ crucified, it is a story to me of a man who came, radically served his community, challenged the unjust show of state power, embraced children, working-class men and promiscuous women and sexual minorities (eunuchs). Of the many things Jesus preached about, he never found time to even mention gay people, let alone condemn them. His message of radical inclusivity was so threatening that the state lynched him for fear that he was fomenting a cultural and political rebellion. They viewed such acts as criminal acts and they treated Jesus as a criminal. And all who followed him were marked for death.

This is why I identify with the story of Jesus. And frankly, it is the only story there really is. This white, blond-haired, blue-eyed, gun-toting, Bible-quoting Jesus of the religious right is a god of their own making.[151]

As theologian Walter Brueggemann reflects in his seminal work, *The Prophetic Imagination*,

"... for those who regulate and benefit from the order of the day a truly free God is not necessary, desirable, or perhaps even possible."[152] If we have managed to successfully put God into a box and chain him to our bandwagon, then He is surely not God. He must be an idol.

Now going back to the politics of my own identity. My identity as mature. My identity as wise. My identity as Christian. I cannot help but begin to question the pat answers I knew oh-so-well, the sound reasoning that let me sleep at night. And I cannot help but ask: Was my identity truly in Christ? Was this truly evidence of a well-rounded biblical worldview? Or was it all backwards? Did I have the answers because of intimate knowledge of the Holy, or because of an intimate knowledge of Self? Was my certainty a sign of solid faith or a symptom of my cultural conditioning and socialization?

My identity is in Christ. But who is Christ? And who am I? And who is my neighbor? These are the questions that I will grapple with the rest of my life. And the moment I think I've found all the answers, I have bowed to a familiar idol that bears no image other than my own. The first Other we do violence against is always God.

Suzie Lahoud holds two master's degrees in Middle Eastern Studies; from the Arab Baptist Theological Seminary in Beirut and Harvard University. She earned her bachelor's degree magna cum laude from Duke University with a double-major in Russian and Middle Eastern Studies. During her time at Harvard, she was selected, as a grant recipient through the Ramez and Tiziana Sousou Fund, to join a group of 13 students from across Harvard's graduate schools to travel to Jordan and embark on an assessment of the dilemmas facing humanitarian actors responding to the war in Syria. She was also the recipient of the best thesis prize for her department. Suzie is a published author and has over a decade of experience living and working overseas, most recently having spent five years in Lebanon managing relief and development projects for refugee and internally displaced populations in Lebanon, Syria, and Iraq. A version of this article first appeared on the IMES Blog of the Arab Baptist Theological Seminary.[153] It is reprinted here with permission.

On Foreign Policy

Kingdom Accountability

By MJ Bryant

Although I was only fifteen years old at the time, I clearly remember a feeling of excitement while I watched the live footage of American bombs falling on Baghdad in 2003. The conservative, evangelical worldview of my childhood led me to believe that something wonderful was happening when God used America's military power to annihilate terrorists. My love for America was one of the reasons that I chose to become an officer in the U.S. Army. Despite being a devout Christian, I had subconsciously believed that America was the savior the world needed, and that the American military was the hand of God to enforce his righteousness among the nations. However, as my faith in Jesus Christ deepened, my blind faith in America's righteousness naturally came under scrutiny. I began noticing glaring contradictions between my worldview and the life and teachings of Jesus. I now believe that Jesus is the undisputed savior of the world, and that the U.S. military is not the hand of God.

Having learned from the Bible about God's love for all nations and his promise to bless the nations through Jesus,[154] I was eager to make friends from other parts of the world, especially the parts that I had despised as a young man. Among them were Muslims and Christians from every corner of the Arab World, Iranians covering a broad range of religious and spiritual beliefs, and many others from Southeast Asia, South Asia, Central Asia, Africa, and elsewhere. Although I was initially driven only by a theological desire to see the blessing of Jesus take root among all nations, I found myself spending much time with my new friends because I genuinely loved them, and I could see the fingerprints of God in their lives.

For the past eight years, I had the unique perspective of serving as an officer in the U.S. military while simultaneously learning about the impact of U.S. foreign policy from many Middle Eastern friends. What I learned challenged my perception of America's purity and led me on a journey of discovering the history of American involvement in the Middle East. Most importantly, I learned to do something in recent years that my former self would have thought unpatriotic – I began using biblical principles of justice and righteousness to evaluate and critique American policies. As I engaged in this process, I noticed one aspect of our democracy that inevitably creates injustice.

Democratic systems are built on the simple principle that elected officials work for their constituents; not vice-versa. This is accomplished by an accountability loop (see Figure 1), whereby citizens choose whether an elected official is allowed

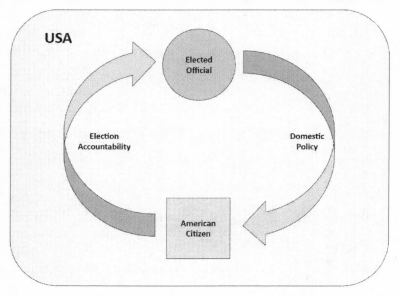

Figure 1: Domestic Accountability Loop

to stay in office. Elected officials pay close attention to how their policies affect their constituents because their career depends on it. When such an accountability loop functions as it should, it leads to policies that benefit the people rather than the few individuals in power.

The same cannot be said about policies that affect non-Americans, who are outside of the accountability loop. In such cases, those who are impacted by our policies have no means of voicing their grievance and holding officials accountable (see Figure 2). This is more of a problem with the United States' foreign policy than most other countries because the U.S. exerts disproportionate power globally, and there is no country in the world that can effectively pressure the United States into changing its policies. Even the United Nations has very limited ability to check American power. The U.S. has historically used this unrestrained power to accomplish its

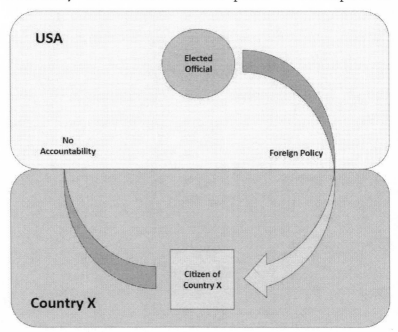

Figure 2: Foreign Policy = No Accountability Loop

purposes and protect its interests, oftentimes without regard for other nations. Unfortunately, the weak and vulnerable in other countries often become the primary losers in this arrangement.

While American presidents and diplomats have claimed to use this power to promote democracy and human rights, to eliminate terrorists, and to remove despotic regimes, an elementary reading of the history of America's involvement in the Middle East tells a much different story. The U.S. has often hindered progress toward democracy, supported some of the most inhumane and despotic regimes in the region, driven tens of thousands into the ranks of terrorist organizations, brought some historic Middle Eastern churches to the brink of extinction, and made non-Christians far more suspicious of the message that evangelicals proclaim. Those who uphold a biblical commitment to the holistic mission of God in the world must recognize that the United States is pushing the Middle East region in the wrong direction. So American evangelicals need to care deeply about U.S. foreign policy in the Middle East.

President Trump's approach to foreign policy is concerning for a number of reasons. He makes significant and far-reaching decisions erratically and often without consulting his advisors. His own cabinet members and military generals have been surprised by the president's decisions when they first hear about them on Twitter. Some of the most experienced and knowledgeable members of his cabinet, like former Secretary of Defense Jim Mattis and former National Security Advisor H.R. McMaster, agreed to work for him thinking that they could be a voice of reason within the administration. However, being reasonable got them both fired. The qualifications President Trump looks for in his advisors and cabinet members are unconditional loyalty to him personally, rather than loyalty to the country, and he expects them to never question his decisions. President Trump spent his first term purging his cabinet of the experts who were willing to stand up to him, and he has surrounded himself instead with those who are loyal to him, despite their lack of expertise or experience. This reason alone could make a second term far more chaotic than his first.[155]

Also, his policies are often driven by a nationalistic ideology that is captured in the motto, "America First." This motto means many things, and not all of them are negative in my opinion. I'm grateful that President Trump doesn't pursue the violent interventionist policies of previous neoconservative administrations. Despite this, there remain significant problems in his policies toward the Middle East. What "America First" means to President Trump is essentially that America should not care about those who suffer outside of our borders, even if American policies are the cause of their suffering. It's simply not our problem.

The Middle East rivalry between Iran and Saudi Arabia has been intensifying for decades and has spilled over into various civil wars and conflicts throughout the region. Both sides are guilty of escalating tensions and committing grave injustices. President Obama attempted to take a more balanced approach, not directly taking either side in this Middle Eastern proxy war. President Trump, however, has taken a strong stance in favor of Saudi Arabia and against Iran. Many in the Middle East see nothing but hypocrisy from President Trump for ordering the assassination of Iranian General Qassem Suleimani for engaging in terrorism, but turning a blind eye to Saudi Arabia, which is widely known as the primary exporter of terrorism in the world. Saudi prince Muhammad Bin Salman ordered the gruesome murder of journalist Jamal Khashoggi, and President Trump exonerated him in order to preserve the special U.S.-Saudi relationship.

Concerning the civil war in Yemen, President Trump brokered large weapons sales to Saudi Arabia,[156] who then used those weapons to kill civilians indiscriminately in Yemen. Substantial proof exists that Saudi airstrikes are hitting civilian targets and killing thousands of innocent people. One such airstrike hit a school bus and instantly killed twenty-six children.[157] I'll never forget being on a Zoom call with a friend who lives in Yemen, when our call was interrupted by the deafening roar of a Saudi F-16 in the skies above him. My friend knows entire families who were killed by these same F-16s. Despite public knowledge of these egregious crimes, President Trump continues brokering arms deals to Saudi Arabia, and he has boasted of the number of American jobs created through these weapons sales.[158] The message sent to the rest of the world is crystal clear – we are willing to sacrifice Yemeni children on the altar of the American economy. This is, after all, exactly what "America First" means.

I'm also deeply troubled by President Trump's policies toward the Israeli-Palestinian conflict. Despite the fact that he claims to be working toward peace in the region, he has given Israel exactly what it wants, such as moving the American embassy to Jerusalem, recognizing Israel's control of the Golan Heights, cutting off funds for Palestinian refugees,[159] and brokering a peace deal between Israel and the UAE that is regarded by many as a stab in the back to Palestinians.[160] Palestinian Christian Munther Isaac, who is the academic dean of Bethlehem Bible College and the pastor of Evangelical Christmas Lutheran Church in Bethlehem, recently lamented, "Let us be clear: implementing the [Trump peace plan] would bring catastrophic consequences for the prospects of a political solution between Israelis and Palestinians, and particularly for the fulfillment of the rights of the Palestinian people, including Palestinian Christians."[161] On top of this, President Trump has sought to block the International Criminal Court from investigating war crimes[162] that Israel almost certainly committed when it fired 50,000 artillery shells into densely packed neighborhoods of the Gaza Strip in 2014.[163]

President Trump admits that many of these policies in favor of Israel are intended to appease his Christian constituents.[164] In other words, the president is pursuing unjust policies not for the sake of national interest, which is actually quite common and expected, but for his own popularity among a certain demographic of loyal supporters. To put it another way, Palestinians are suffering. Aren't Christians supposed to be the ones who pursue justice for the oppressed?

I have known many refugees over the past decade and the majority of them have been Muslims. Refugees are among the most destitute and victimized people in the world. Between 9/11 and 2016, the U.S. admitted 784,000 refugees from many countries. Not one of them has ever been involved in a terrorist incident.[165] The path to being resettled as a refugee is the most heavily vetted path of entry into the United States, and it usually took (before Trump) up to three years to be approved by all the necessary government agencies, which is part of the reason why the 9/11 hijackers didn't come to America as refugees.[166] Concerning Syrian refugees, most of those being resettled in the U.S. during Obama's presidency were women and children.[167] The refugee resettlement program was easily one of the most noble and Christ-like programs operated by the U.S. government. It has long been supported by evangelical Christians who firmly believe in the biblical mandate to welcome the foreigner, especially those who are destitute.

President Trump, however, frequently slandered Muslim refugees and immigrants on the 2016 campaign trail. He made promises to implement a ban on Muslims entering the country, and successfully implemented a travel ban on several Muslim-majority countries. He consistently lied about the activities of Muslim Americans, the dangers of refugee resettlement, and came to power riding a wave of American xenophobia and Islamophobia. Once in office, he systematically dismantled the refugee resettlement program citing security concerns but, in doing so, did not actually make the country safer. During his presidency, American xenophobes have felt empowered and anti-Muslim hate crimes have skyrocketed.[168] Stephen Miller, one of President Trump's advisers on immigration, once said to another White House official, "I would be happy if not a single refugee foot ever again touched American soil."[169] If President Trump really cared about practicing biblical ethics, and not just using the Bible as a photo prop, he would not hire such men to advise him. The most weak, vulnerable, victimized, and destitute men, women, and children in the world became his scapegoat while his Christian voters cheered him on.

Christians should not pursue an "America First" agenda because God doesn't. When we consider those who suffer under American policies, we should remember passages like Psalm 10:17-18: "You, Lord, hear the desire of the afflicted; you encourage them, and you listen to their cry, defending the fatherless and the oppressed, so that mere earthly mortals will never again strike terror (NIV)." When I'm tempted to despair, I remember that God cares and that he is incensed at the suffering of the weak and the vulnerable.

While it's clear that God cares about these injustices, what should Christians do about them? The lack of an accountability loop in foreign policies creates many scenarios where the vulnerable cry out for justice and no one hears them. Proverbs 31:8-9 exhorts us to "Speak up for those who cannot speak for themselves, for the rights of all who are destitute. Speak up and judge fairly; defend the rights of the poor and needy" (NIV). Those who suffer under American policies might have no official voice in the U.S. government, but American Christians can step in and voice their grievances.

American Christians should be involved in the world, and relationally engaged with people from various nations. When we discover that an American policy adversely affects those outside the accountability loop, we have a responsibility to use our voting rights for their sake. I call this "The Kingdom Accountability Loop" (see Figure 3), because it is a tangible outflow of citizens of God's Kingdom using their privileges for the sake of others, just as Jesus did and instructed us to do (Philippians 2:1-8). I dream of the day when American

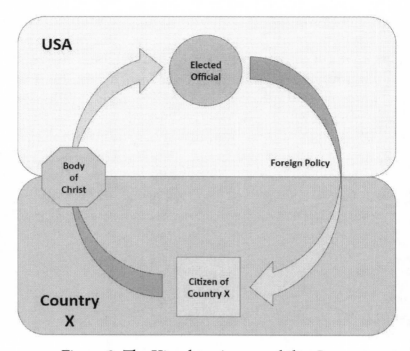

Figure 3: The Kingdom Accountability Loop

presidents steer clear of unjust policies because they fear the strength and resolve of American evangelicals.

While I don't feel excited about Joe Biden, and I won't agree with all of his policies, I expect that almost anyone would be better suited for the presidency than Donald Trump. I'm currently undecided whether I will vote for Joe Biden or for a 3rd party candidate. However, this election is more important than merely determining who will be our president for the next four years. This election is an opportunity to restore the reputation of the Church and to send a clear message to the world about what is important to Christians. President Trump despises, slanders, and tramples the weak and the vulnerable for the sake of his own popularity. It's time for Christian voters to demonstrate biblical ethics in the way we vote and to remove President Trump from office.

MJ Bryant served as an officer in the US Army and has spent the past decade welcoming Middle Eastern international students and refugees to the United States. He is currently writing his master's thesis on U.S. foreign policy in the Middle East, and he eagerly desires to see God's Kingdom come and His will be done on earth as it is in heaven. He is happily married with three daughters and currently lives in Chicago.

On the Moral Superiority of the United States of America
By Wissam al-Saliby

On January 3, 2020, the United States assassinated Iranian general Qassem Suleimani, on the orders of U.S. President Donald Trump.

As the world grappled with the consequences of U.S. action and the threat of an Iranian response, the World Evangelical Alliance (WEA) issued a statement on January 10, 2020.[170] It stated that the WEA "deeply grieves the recent acts of aggression and violence between the United States of America and the Islamic Republic of Iran, in Iraq," it appealed for de-escalation, and added that the WEA encourages "dialogue that prevents further crises and leads to the removal of sanctions which disproportionally impact civilians."

In drafting this statement, WEA leadership sought input from a large number of evangelical leaders. I took part in drafting the statement.

The statement ended with a call "for prayer for the political and military leaders of Iran, Iraq and the United States and all leaders and peoples of the region that they might seek and possess peaceable wisdom from above, leading to the path of peace," and with the prayer that "this discernment might include de-escalation of conflict, dialogue and the re-establishment of trust, and an end to the cycles of violence and death that beset the Middle East."

One day later, on January 11, 2020, the Christian Broadcasting Network (CBN) published a surprising article entitled, "Iran Statement From Evangelical Group Draws Fire Over Question of Moral Equivalency."[171]

The article quotes Rev. Johnnie Moore, the President of The Congress of Christian Leaders, who is also a commissioner of the United States Committee for International Religious Freedom, and "evangelical advisor to the Trump administration."[172] "Like many Christians around the world, I pray for peace in the Middle East and support all reasonable and moral efforts at de-escalation, whenever possible, including with Iran ..." Rev. Moore states. "However, the World Evangelical Alliance is wrong to even infer a moral equivalency between the United States of America and the Islamic Republic of Iran in their call for peace." Moore then adds that Iran is "a nation known to be one of the world's foremost violators of human rights and religious freedom; a nation where anti-Semitism is its national policy," that the Iranian regime recruits and deploys child soldiers as young as 12 years-old to armed combat, and that "Christian theology teaches that all people are born bearing the image of God, but the WEA is wrong to not acknowledge that some people choose to desecrate that image by deploying their own free will in pursuit of evil." He concludes by saying, "[the WEA] have promoted in their statement an uncritical Christian theology which is only a few steps removed from anti-Semitic Christianity that enabled the rise of Hitler and the Nazi's holocaust."

The rejection of "moral equivalence" is not new. It was part of the political debate during the Cold War. In 1986, former U.S. Ambassador to the United Nations, Jeane Kirkpatrick published an article entitled "The Myth of Moral Equivalence"[173] in which she argued against the "misleading" concept of superpower rivalry which "is the first premise in a syllogism in which moral equivalence is the conclusion." She added that "there is a contest between the imperialistic power [Soviet Union and others] and all other countries who desire to preserve their independence" whereas the United States seeks "to foster a world of independent nations."

Very recently, on July 16, 2020, at the presentation of the report of the Commission on Unalienable Rights, Secretary of State Mike Pompeo made a speech that also rejected equating the U.S. with other nations. Mr. Pompeo said, "we must reject moral equivalency ... There is indeed every reason not only to believe but to know that our exceptional nation secures infinitely more freedom for its citizens than the [China Communist Party] will ever permit."

On January 8, 2020, in the Church Politics Podcast, Justin Giboney and Michael Wear reviewed the news of the U.S. killing of General Suleimani.[174] "Iran is an oppressive regime. Oppressive to minorities; Oppressive to women,"[175] Giboney explains, as he goes on to compare the lack of freedom in Iran with the presence of freedom in the United States. He adds, "General Suleimani was a vicious man ... Some have said that the United States is killing brown people. Suleimani and Iran have no problem killing brown people. It is possible that what happened prevented people from getting killed."[176]

Giboney then states that while his preference is to avoid war, "war can be justified if the true objective is to save lives and end suffering ... Killing is wrong. To override that, you need to make a case for just war."

I am not an American. I don't vote in American elections. However, like most people on planet earth, I'm impacted by American foreign policy. As an Arab evangelical and a Lebanese who witnessed multiple wars in my country, I cannot help but express my regret that many voices of American evangelicalism legitimize US military actions abroad, and align themselves with American foreign policy in the Middle East. While I generally appreciate Giboney's perspective - and I am grateful for his and Wear's voices speaking into American politics - I would like to challenge his stance on war with Iran, which I find disappointing.

The responsibility of American brothers and sisters within the Body of Christ is commensurate to the economic and military strength of their nation. And while U.S. administrations are free to justify their actions however they please, evangelical Christians, including in government, are bound by truth, justice, peacemaking, and their membership in the Body of Christ.

In *Exclusion and Embrace*, Miroslav Volf writes:

> The question is not whether from a Christian perspective God's justice is universal, whether God can infallibly judge between cultures irrespective of their differences. The question is whether Christians who want to uphold God's universal justice can judge between cultures with divine infallibility. The answer is that they cannot. For one, Christians stand inside a culture, inside a tradition, inside an interest group. Unlike God's knowledge, their knowledge is limited and distorted. Their judgment about what is just in concrete situations are inescapably particular.[177]

I agree with Volf's statement. Not because of any profound theological exploration, but because I grew up in Lebanon. There, politics is a facet of daily life, and I learned firsthand the extent to which the United States is a bubble where "information" and "truth" in Washington, DC are different from those in Lebanon, in the Occupied Palestinian Territories, and in the Middle East.

The "culture," "tradition," and "interest group" that Volf talks about are incredibly powerful in the United States, where lobbies, think tanks, and the media — whether Christian[178] or secular, skew the reality that exists outside the U.S. and push American foreign policy, especially in the Middle East, toward a discourse and toward actions I see as incompatible with biblical justice.

I appreciate the work of Rev. Johnnie Moore for religious freedom, in his capacity as Commissioner of the United States Committee for International Religious Freedom. However, Moore's mention of Iran using child soldiers as young as 12 years-old (which is not true)[179] reminds me of how, in 2001, as the drum beats rolled to pave the way for the war in Afghanistan, the U.S. media "discovered" the oppression of Afghan women by the Taliban, only to forget about them once the objectives of U.S. foreign policy were met. Accusations of the use of child soldiers or human shields, the oppression of women, Iraq's possession of weapons of mass destruction, etc. are assertions that, more often than not, are of questionable veracity, and all serve as a cover for violence, not as genuine care for the oppressed.

Furthermore, the aforementioned moral stance on Iranian "evil" or "evildoing" is highly questionable in light of Saudi Arabia's war on Yemen. This is not a whataboutism. Christian evangelicals who genuinely care for life and dignity shouldn't attempt to justify U.S. policies toward Iran while the U.S. is providing the weapons and political backing to Saudi Arabia in its war on Yemen. While Moore was falsely claiming that Iran recruited child soldiers as young as 12 years-old, the Saudi-Emirati-led coalition was responsible for the death or injury of 222 children in Yemen in 2019.[180]

This brings me to my next point. If the U.S. were to apply a just war theory framework as Giboney suggests, then the U.S. could only wage war for a just cause. However, do the decision-making processes of the U.S. government factor in morality, truth, and justice?

To answer this question, I will reflect on one case study: the war on Yemen. The United States is an essential partner in that war through the provision of the weapons used by the Saudi-led coalition. This coalition has conducted scores of indiscriminate and disproportionate airstrikes killing thousands of civilians and hitting civilian objects in violation of the laws of war, using munitions sold by the United States.[181] U.S. State Department officials have even raised alarms about the legal risk in aiding airstrikes that kill civilians.[182] Rather than applying a just war theory lens to their decision-making —the Trump administration, Republicans,[183] as well as some Democrats[184]—have approached their partnership in the war on Yemen from the utilitarian and immoral stance of "economic benefit to the U.S."

Think tanks and lobbyists[185] skew the decision-making processes in Washington, DC. They cater to the private interest of the wealthy, in and outside of the U.S., rather than acting for the common good (or for American national interest in my opinion). William Hartung, director of the Arms and Security Project at the Center for International Policy, said in a recent interview, "[The Saudis] employ more than two dozen lobbying firms. They spent $15 million in 2018 on those firms. They had 2000 contacts either with the media, with members of Congress [sic]. They contacted virtually every Senate office. [They contacted] 200 house offices [and], in a number of cases, right after the lobbyist met to pitch arm sales to Saudi Arabia, they gave a contribution to that member's campaign." [186]

But if my American brothers and sisters were to look for opinions and truth from the Middle East, they would find many Christian and evangelical voices that speak up. Christ at the Checkpoint conference at Bethlehem Bible College in Bethlehem and the Institute of Middle East Studies of the Arab Baptist Theological Seminary in Lebanon are such platforms.

During the first week of Israel's war on Lebanon in 2006, Martin Accad, the then academic dean of the Arab Baptist Theological Seminary, wrote an essay in *Christianity Today* entitled, "Evangelical Blindness on Lebanon" in which he stated: "When did the US ever use anything other than its veto power at the United Nations, precisely in order to *prevent* policies and resolutions that might potentially have been helpful to my people?"[187]

Many Arab Christians are denied an audience in the U.S., and are sometimes vilified. To give one high profile example, in 2012, when *60 Minutes* planned to air a story on Christians in the Holy Land, Israeli ambassador Michael Oren sought to prevent its airing.[188]

As a Lebanese with vested interest in reforming the governance system in Lebanon, I am particularly attentive to how U.S. foreign policy's priority for Lebanon – undermining Hezbollah – is at odds with Lebanese efforts to combat corruption and effectively build a nation. Nadim Houry, a fellow Lebanese and the executive director of the Arab Reform Initiative, recently stated – and I agree with him – that "at this stage ... the priority is to get rid of mobsters. You can't defeat the mobsters and Hezbollah at the same time. So to me, that is the only possibly hopeful scenario."[189] Houry acknowledged that not all Lebanese agree with him, and called for a dialogue (@Nadimhoury, August 9, 2020). However, the United States and its current hawkish administration have undermined Houry's approach and call for an internal Lebanese dialogue. In September 2020, the Trump administration sanctioned two former Lebanese ministers who are allies of Hezbollah,[190] effectively attempting to tip the balance within the sectarian kleptocracy against Hezbollah, rather than helping to reform the whole system and uproot corruption, which is the popular Lebanese demand.[191]

As for Moore's warning against anti-semitism and the theology that enabled Hitler's rise, the words of Johannes Reimer, WEA Director of the Department of Public Engagement and professor of Mission Studies and Intercultural Theology at the Ewersbach University of Applied Arts come to mind. Reimer writes that evangelicals:

> saw in Adolf Hitler a man of order and a power figure able to protect them from persecution and destruction as had happened before their eyes in the

Soviet Union ... There will be no Christian world-wide praising Hitler of a 'divine' calling any longer ... It is strange, however, that on the other hand, Christians seem to hallow similar authoritarian regimes, who promise to end chaos and moral decay, introduce law and order by using force and make their nations great again.[192]

The Trump administration only exacerbated the political disconnect with the rest of the world, a nationalistic self-centeredness, which has further undermined a truthful understanding of world politics and of the other. For Christian leaders who are called to speak up in political spheres, averting the mistakes of brothers and sisters in Nazi Germany, and developing an understanding of the world that Washington, DC can never offer, requires neither moral equivalence nor moral superiority but, – and I quote Miroslav Volf – that:

We open our ears to hear how others perceive themselves as well as how they perceive us. We use imagination to see why their perspective about themselves, about us, and about our common history, can be so plausible to them whereas it is implausible, profoundly strange, or even offensive to us ...

We compare and contrast the view "from there" and the view "from here." (...) The only thing we must do as we take others into our world is let their perspective stand next to ours and reflect on whether one or the other is right, or whether both are partly right and partly wrong.[193]

Wissam is the Advocacy Officer of the World Evangelical Alliance (WEA) since January 2018. Based in Geneva, he advocates with the United Nations on behalf of national evangelical alliances in over 130 countries for freedom of religion, rule of law, and human rights. Prior to joining the WEA, al-Saliby was the Development and Partner Relations Manager of the Arab Baptist Theological Seminary, and a regional trainer on international humanitarian law with Geneva Call. He received his undergraduate degree in law from the Lebanese University Law School, and his master's degree in international law, with an emphasis on protection and human security, from Aix-Marseille University Faculty of Law, France.

Bad Theology Kills:
How We Justify Killing Arabs
By Jesse Steven Wheeler

For many, the subject of "theology" evokes the image of old white men with impressive beards and antiquated ideas sitting alone in ivory seminary towers writing really big books that nobody reads. Yet, within everything we think, say, or do can be found a variety of implicit theologies. For theology--alongside its secularized twin, ideology--encompasses our core beliefs as to how the universe functions and how we function within it. It gives shape to our identity and drives our sense of purpose, providing us with the interpretive lenses through which we make sense of and find meaning in our daily lives.[194] And, to put it bluntly, some theologies are good. Others are bad.

Hermeneutical Fruit
In an era of "deconstructed absolutes" and "Orwellian doublespeak," when it seems the very concept of truth itself is on trial and public speech has been emptied of substantive content,[195] how is it possible for one to distinguish good theology from bad? Amidst a cacophonous tumult of competing claims to truth and ethical demands, how do we determine what is true from what is false? For the follower of Jesus, the answer is surprisingly simple: fruit. In his Sermon on the Mount, Jesus cautions,

> Watch out for false prophets. They come to you in sheep's clothing, but inwardly they are ferocious wolves. By their fruit you will recognize them. Do people pick grapes from thorn bushes, or figs from thistles? Likewise, every good tree bears good fruit, but a bad tree bears bad fruit and a bad tree cannot bear good fruit. Every tree that does not bear good fruit is cut down and thrown into the fire. Thus, by their fruit you will recognize them (Matt. 7:15-20, NIV).

To distinguish between the true and false prophet, or anyone claiming to represent the will of God, Jesus does not implement a doctrinal litmus test, as important as sound doctrine is. Instead, he tells us this: "By their fruit you will recognize them."

Likewise, to distinguish between a true and false theo-ethical, ideological or political-economic system, one must examine the fruit of that system and ask:

> Does the fruit of this system, as expressed within the "laboratory of history,"[196] lead us to love God, neighbor and enemy as ourselves (Matt. 22:35-40)? Or, does it result in self-aggrandizement, or separationist and supremacist attitudes?

> Does it seek to make God's Kingdom come and His will be done on earth as it is in heaven (Matt. 6:10)? Or, does it seek to promote the dominion of some other lord, pharaoh, führer, flag, or financial system?

> Does it stand with the poor, the orphan, the widow, and the refugee (Zech. 7:10)? Or, does it harm them?

Ultimately, are we led as best as possible "to do for others as we would have others do for us" (Matt. 7:12), empathically imagining ourselves in the place and circumstances of another and responding in kind?[197]

Too often we find walking the halls of power those false prophets who provide ideological cover for authority and its abuses, violent and destructive wars, and the neglect, exploitation, and sacrifice of our world's most vulnerable upon the altars of profit and politics.[198] Unfortunately, we also too often find ourselves marching along in dutiful compliance, captive to the false allure of destructive ideological systems and their apologists. But, as a popular saying goes, "If your theology doesn't lead you to love people more, you should question your theology."[199] Because distinguishing good theology from bad theology comes down to this: Good theology brings life. Bad theology kills.

Rotten Fruit and Killing Arabs

I wish therefore to highlight three interrelated theologies which have been particularly destructive in the Middle Eastern and North African (MENA)[200] context:

First, Colonialist Paternalism

The tragic history of western imperial intervention in the Middle East is rife with examples of theological and ideological systems which have sought to promote, justify, downplay, and excuse that which in reality has been little more than violent conquest, theft and exploitation, or cold geo-strategic calculus. From the "white man's burden" and *mission civilisatrice* of the 19th century[201] through the patronizing post-WWI Mandate System of the early 20th, which under the guise of enlightened mentorship saw the victors merely carve up the spoils of war between themselves, to the modern American desire to export freedom by force of arms[202] in the early 21st century, such justifications have a deep history.[203] Often with absolute sincerity, yet degrading paternalism, we colonialists (and America is very much a colonial power[204]) have justified our aggression by convincing ourselves that we have been acting for the betterment of the colonized peoples, often on behalf of God. To be defined as "colonial," explains Brian McLaren, a particular theological system would have the following characteristics:

> It would explain--historically or theologically--why the colonizers deserve to be in power--sustained in the position of hegemony [or dominance]. It would similarly explain why the colonized deserve to be dominated--maintained in the subaltern or subservient position. It would provide ethical justification for the phases and functions of colonization [...] It would bolster the sense of entitlement and motivation among the colonizers. It would embed the sense of submission and docility among the colonized. It would facilitate alliances with political and economic systems that were supportive of or inherent to colonialism. [And] it would camouflage or cosmetically enhance its ugly aspects and preempt attempts to expose them.[205]

It must also be said that well-meaning missionaries, development practitioners, human rights activists and non-native feminist movements[206] alike have too often been incapable of disentangling themselves from their own cultural presumptions or the imperial interests of their countries of origin. While many have undertaken great work,[207] others have been responsible for great violence. Likewise, western governments have long leveraged economic and military aid under the guise of national development, economic growth, or global security for their own geo-strategic ends, with little to no concern for the often devastating impact on local communities.[208] Not only does bad theology kill, but it has justified the deaths of countless Arabs.

Second, "Henotheistic" Crusaderism

Henotheism, in its most basic form, declares: "My God can beat up your God!" It is the "warrior tribe" theology which pits one's own god against those of its neighbors. Of this, Joseph Cumming asks:

> If the Christian faith is primarily a tribal identity, where does that take us? It takes us to the belief that, "We must fight to defend the survival of Christian civilization. If necessary, we must kill the enemies of our civilization before they kill us. We must pray that our God gives us victory over their Allah-God" [...] If when thinking of Muslims, we think of Christian faith as a tribal identity we might ask: How do we avoid being killed by them? How do we prevent terrorist attacks on our homeland? How do we stop their encroachment in our countries?"[209]

This mentality can be found throughout the history of human warfare, even among monotheists who ostensibly believe God "sends rain on the just and the unjust alike" (Matt. 5:45, NLT). In this way of thinking, one's own tribe, clan, or nation becomes the chosen of God fighting an epic struggle against "the forces of darkness and their sub-human minions."[210] We see this in the crusades. We see this throughout the Cold War, which would profoundly impact the MENA region,[211] wherein American political leaders "crafted a new kind of civil religion that was nothing less than a 'diplomatic theology of containment.'"[212] We see this in the religiously tinged language of the War on Terror, about which Cumming reports:

> Recently, a U.S. army general was speaking to a large evangelical Christian church, describing a battle with a [Muslim] warlord from northern Africa, and he said "I knew that I need not fear, because my God was the true God, and his God was a demon!" That is henotheism![213]

This is the theology of "God and country" whereby the God of the universe is reduced to a territorial idol, transforming the refugee into an infiltrator and the immigrant into an invader, and it represents a wholesale rejection of our call to costly discipleship and self-sacrificial love of others.

We evangelicals see this way of thinking given expression within the popular apocalyptic fantasies of the end-times preachers.[214] Like a bad movie played out on the international stage, Arabs get swooped up into this apocalyptic drama to become--in the imaginations of others--the foot soldiers of evil committed to the destruction of God's elect, however defined. It is a form of bigotry that literally demonizes our Middle Eastern brothers and sisters.[215] Once demonized, death comes easily.

Third, "Manifest Destiny"

Referencing the origins of the term manifest destiny, evangelical activist Jim Wallis writes, "[t]he United States of America was established as a white society, founded upon the near genocide of another race and then the enslavement of yet another."[216] As historian John Fea explains:

> Manifest Destiny was deeply informed by the long-standing evangelical idea that white Protestant "civilization" must advance Westward. God gave

the continent to Christians and it was their "destiny" to conquer and tame it. This entire project was drenched in the unholy mix of evangelical Protestantism and white supremacy.[217]

It is a mistake, however, to limit theologies of manifest destiny to the North American context, for such ideas held sway in settler-colonial societies from Australia to Argentina.[218] Likewise, the Afrikaner Calvinists of South Africa understood their settler-colonial project as a direct calling from God, "not unlike the people of Israel in the Bible."[219] In its most basic form, manifest destiny seeks--in the name of God and progress--to conquer, cleanse and colonize.

In the MENA context, French colonization of Algeria was overwhelmingly destructive for the native Algerians. From conquest to independence, Algeria was subject to a level of violence that would permanently alter the region's social make-up,[220] making it next to impossible to speak of either immigration or terrorism in France without reference to the bloody Algerian Revolution.[221] Finally, the colonial Zionist project has been absolutely catastrophic to the lives, property, and psyche of the native Palestinians, sending shock waves throughout the entire MENA region which reverberate to this day.[222] "Christian Zionism," a default position within western evangelicalism until recently, has provided theological justification, financial capital, and political cover for decades of land confiscation, ethnic cleansing, settlement activity, and apartheid-equivalent practices.[223] As Colin Chapman asserts, "Our very understanding of God, our witness to the gospel, and the credibility of the Christian church" are at stake when it comes to our theology of Israel-Palestine.[224] Speaking as a western evangelical, there is far too much blood on our hands-- precisely because bad theology kills.

Idolatry, Power and the Crucified King

That which ultimately undergirds and allows for the lethal emergence of the above theological distortions is no less than the sin of idolatry, offering to another the trust and allegiance rightfully belonging to God alone.[225] In the run up to the 2016 Presidential election, then-candidate Donald Trump delivered a speech in the chapel of a small Christian college in Iowa. Following his now infamous declaration that he could shoot someone in the middle of Fifth Avenue and not lose any voters, Trump made the following statement: "Christianity will have power. If I'm there, you're going to have plenty of power; you don't need anybody else."[226] To me, the idolatrous nature of such a Faustian bargain is blatant; however, millions of American Christians took notice and have since become his most ardent supporters. So, it should come as no surprise when four years later Vice President Mike Pence, altering Hebrews 12 during his address at the 2020 Republican National Convention, implored us to "run the race marked out for us and fix our eyes on 'Old Glory' [and] this land of heroes,"[227] flagrantly replacing the Lord Jesus with symbols of American imperial power and thereby inverting the authentic message of the passage.[228] With the help of his ethical, philosophical, and partisan political enablers and in his unabashed glorification of violence and cruel self-interest, Donald Trump represents a clear and present danger to both the spiritual health of the church in America and international peace. The idolatrous fruit is rotten.

In no uncertain terms, the Trump administration must be rejected come November. It would be a mistake, however, to then become cheerleaders for Joe Biden and the Democratic Party, chaplains to a rejuvenated neo-liberal status quo.[229] Though I support their general willingness to work within the international system and respect for international law, we must not repeat the relative prophetic silence of the Obama era.[230] Because if our task is to examine fruit and avoid falling prey to seductive rhetoric, it is crucial to note that from the vantage point of the Middle East, Republican drones don't look or act much differently than Democrat drones. Biden's record on the Iraq War or Israel-Palestine, while not as appalling or destructive as that of the Republicans, is nevertheless quite bad. He is the only viable choice put before us on election day; yet we must remain vigilant in holding a potential Biden administration to account in the weeks, months and years that follow.

Ultimately, the historic difficulty of the visible Church to divest itself from imperial power--left, right and center--has resulted in a situation whereby the mission and message of Christ has become distorted beyond all recognition. For such unholy alliances represent a betrayal of the crucified messiah, who models for us the narrow path of self-sacrificial love in his rejection of imperial compromise. As Joseph Cumming reflects:

> I believe that Satan's greatest masterpiece was the crusades. Why? Is it because the Crusades were the worst atrocity that ever happened in history? I think Hitler was worse. Pol Pot was worse. What is horrible about the crusades is that it was done under the symbol of the cross, that Satan succeeded in distorting the very heart of the Christian faith.
>
> The cross is at the heart of the entire Christian faith, and for the Muslims and Jews of the world, what does the symbol of the cross now signify? The cross now signifies, "Christians hate you enough to kill you." What is the cross supposed to signify? It is supposed to signify, "God loves you enough to lay down his life for you, and I would love you enough that I would lay down my life for you." Satan succeeded in taking the very heart of the Christian faith and turning it around to mean not just something different, but to mean the exact opposite of what it's supposed to mean.[231]

But, the reality is that with the death and resurrection of Christ Jesus, an instrument of imperial domination becomes, in biblical imagination, the ultimate symbol of divine love and the power-reversing means by which God reigns. To follow Jesus, to take the narrow path, is to therefore surrender any claim to political, territorial, financial or "religious" domination. Instead, let us each carry our cross in everlasting service to a broken world in desperate need of God's love, justice, and deliverance. Like our true king, let us spend ourselves in self-sacrificial love as we trust in the resurrection and the ultimate Lordship of Jesus Christ.

Jesse Steven Wheeler holds an MDiv with an emphasis in Islamic Studies from Fuller Theological Seminary; a BA in History specializing in international and Middle Eastern history with a minor in Political Economics from the University of California, Berkeley; and a Post-Graduate Certificate in Baptistic Histories and Theologies from the University of Manchester, UK. Before returning to the US, Jesse served as Projects Manager and Support Instructor for MENA History, Politics and Economics at the Institute of Middle East Studies (IMES) at the Arab Baptist Theology Seminary (ABTS) in Beirut, Lebanon. Among his responsibilities, he administered the Master of Religion in Middle Eastern and North African Studies program and directed the annual Middle East Consultation. A version of this article first appeared on the IMES Blog of the Arab Baptist Theological Seminary. [232] It is reprinted here with permission.

From Excluded to Embraced

Anonymous

For Christian Palestinian-Americans, our lived experience is one of decades filled with hope deferred and lament. Our hearts are sick. The grief of our diaspora, for ourselves and our families, back in Palestine or spread elsewhere, often leaves us feeling like strangers and aliens who lack comforters; often rejected within the walls of too many American churches. We are people who ache for Jerusalem, and long literally, metaphorically, spiritually for the Promised Land. A great number of my relatives were made refugees in 1948. An even greater number of their children were born displaced in diaspora as stateless child refugees, including me. Just like Jesus' family was forced to flee the Holy Land under violent threats, so too were 750,000 Palestinians. Unlike Jesus and his family, we are denied the basic right of return to our homeland, including over 400 Palestinian villages. We are well practiced in lament. Grief is the only response to the continued injustice, excessive use of force and violence against our people, and daily public humiliations through the abuse of power. Moreover, innocent people have been killed, maimed, and unjustly incarcerated. Our women wail in the streets, pleading with God for justice. I believe God hears us and sees us; what greater hope do we have than knowing El Roi (Gen. 16:13), the God who sees.

As a Christian Palestinian-American, the Trump administration is just another in a series of presidential administrations seeking to sell peace agreements that ring hollow in addressing issues of truth, justice, reconciliation, and lasting peace. Palestinians are all too familiar with White House attempts at peace talks that refuse to give us full and equal rights. These peace talk efforts refuse to begin and end with granting Palestinians full and equal rights. One would think full and equal rights are basic starting points for negotiations when inequities in rights are the basis for justifying the violent forced migration of Palestinians by the newly created state of Israel.

Neglect of Palestinian refugee rights as defined in International and Humanitarian Law have been the norm for American presidents and presidential candidates. In 2008, presidential candidate Mike Huckabee actively touted a position that could only lead to the further mass expulsion of Palestinians, and even went so far as to deny their existence.[233] This candidate shamelessly espoused such positions on national television as part of his foreign policy platform. Later that year, in 2008 or early 2009, during Israel's 22 straight days of heavy missile strikes on Gaza, I heard the pastor of a mega-church I attended for several years interview an Israeli General on a very popular and widely listened to Christian radio station. This influential pastor advocated for much more extensive military use of force at a time when Israel's military was criticized by the international community for excessive and disproportionate use of force. I remember the pastor saying, "General, if I was you, I would hit them back 100 times for every 1 of theirs ..." I had stopped listening to American Christian Radio back in July 2006 when Israel invaded Lebanon because the constant display of partiality throughout the reports triggered PTSD I had developed years earlier as a result of numerous stints in Israeli detention. While traveling alone as a teenager through Ben-Gurion airport in Israel, I was repeatedly detained. For five hours upon every arrival and departure, uniformed Israeli agents interrogated and strip-searched me aggressively. Clearly, they meant to psychologically traumatize me. They succeeded.

The repeated isolation, detention, interrogation, and searches conveyed one message: "you don't belong here, we don't want you here, don't return ever again." This pattern of detention, interrogation, and searches continued into my adulthood. I have had all my pieces of luggage searched as if I had criminal intent. On my last trip an entire full piece of luggage was confiscated. A complete list of packed items included: several kilograms worth of locally made cheese and fresh, roasted nuts -both from the West Bank, as well as a DVD aptly titled "Under the Guise of Security" and several pieces of written materials produced by an Israeli human rights organization called B'Tselem (B'Tselem means "in the image of [God]"). These items were confiscated indefinitely in Israel upon my departure and were only returned to my home in the United States days later. During one of these episodes, my new, expensive camera was destroyed along with nine rolls of film. When I returned to the United States and shared my story with church leaders, I was met with a silence that seemed to say, "What did you expect? You are Palestinian. You're not The Chosen." I was so pained by the reception and lack of empathy, but I hid my hurt. To continue going to church meant I had to learn to navigate these injustices within my faith community. Sometimes that meant burying my pain and confusion alongside other buried hopes. Once, when I asked for prayer for revival in Palestine in a prayer circle in 1992, I was met with, "God doesn't want revival in that part of the world, there are some vessels made for honor, and some made for dishonor."

When I shared my traumatic experiences with other believers I expected to be met with empathy and care. Instead I was met with cold words and silence. My heart broke for the evil that would not meet my tragic suffering with the hands and feet of Jesus. In the same way that Palestinians long to be met with full and equal rights, many Palestinian Christians both in the United States and abroad, long to be embraced by the church as co-heirs of God's promises. How is this bias against Palestinian believers acceptable within Christ's body the church? Multiple American administrations of both parties have refused to grant full and equal political rights to the Palestinian people. The reason is a false, underlying theology that God is hostile toward Palestinians. Romans 8:1 says, "Therefore, there is now no condemnation for those who are in Christ Jesus ..." (NIV). We know from Scripture that Christian Palestinians are not under condemnation, yet the failure of inclusion on all levels is clear. From silencing us in the American church, to ensuring inequities in the White House's negotiations, to keeping our narrative and voices off the pages of newspapers, particularly when it comes to issues like the illegal confiscation of Palestinian land for Israeli settlements.

As I write this, the United States is in a state of great turmoil and division, politically, socially, spiritually. Clarence Jordan, co-founder of Koinonia Farm, wrote, "The Good News of the resurrection is ... that he is risen and comes home with us, bringing all his hungry, naked thirsty, sick, prisoner brothers with him."[234] This kind of radical inclusion is how God ministers to us in his Holy Spirit, in Jesus dying for us, in the Father pursuing us and caring for us. God's perfect, complete, lavish love and inclusion enables us, a sin-weary people, to live out Christ's call to follow him to be blessed peacemakers. Faith calls us to be moved with the same compassion of Christ. Our faith in Christ enables us to see the world through the eyes of Christ's humility, compassion, and care. Therefore, we are to reach people where they are; and in and through Christ's love for all of us. Peter in the book of Acts declares, "God does not show favoritism but accepts from every nation the one who fears him and does what is right" (Acts 10:34b-35, NIV). The church must choose: do we continue operating under the status quo of division, or do we seek reconciliation with God, with each other, within our communities, and beyond to distant communities where our words, beliefs, and actions have a profound impact? Jesus is clear; peacemakers are the children of God. Do we trust Jesus enough to follow Him? Do we trust

Jesus enough to follow Him all the way to the cross? Will we die to ourselves and to our rights?

Over the last several years Trump has failed to bring the country together, and our nation is more divided than ever. I will not vote for a reckless candidate who has disparaged women and immigrants. I will not vote for a candidate whose cabinet and staff are fired and hired based on loyalty to Trump's reputation and ego. For me, as someone who has engaged in various activist circles locally and abroad, this means I will choose to vote for an imperfect candidate from an imperfect party; Biden. Incredibly imperfect. It pains me to think of how Palestine will be sold out again in a new administration. I know I will be tempted by my proclivity for anger and self-righteousness at the lack of care and foresight of so much of American foreign policy. In those times I will need to be gently reminded that God is in control; the arc of history is long, but He bends it toward justice. Thankfully one of the prayer and Scripture reading apps I use reminds me to regularly pray for our leaders. I will pray for Biden as I have prayed for Trump and others. Part of my self-reflection is realizing my own tendency to be prideful. I must remember who God is, His great love for me, from before Creation to His coming humbly to earth, and His death on the Cross. If my activism is to be fruitful, I must continue to look to the Father, Jesus, and Holy Spirit for my identity and strength. I must remember: I am not a mistake, I am not the evil and hurtful things that people spew out of their hate and ignorance, I am not what people say or think about me. I am a child of God; loved, embraced, eternally. Nothing can come between Christ and me. I am united to Christ, and I have done nothing to earn this, so I can do nothing to lose this Holy love.

Looking forward, I am more convinced than ever that reconciliation is the only process that makes any restorative sense right now, and yet I know truth-telling needs to happen before any reconciliation can be realized. Truth alone would be cruel and unhelpful without space and time for grief and lament. Grief and lament require that we listen to and bear each other's burdens. Reconciliation is in God's will for us. We know God desires that we be reconciled to Him and to each other. The question is, what are we waiting for? There is much work to be done, not just in Israel-Palestine, but also in the U.S. and in the church. I hope and pray you will join me and that God blesses you with wisdom, discernment, and every spiritual blessing as we rest in His finished work and love for us. May His love and life encourage us to also love and live for Him. Let's show up as the hands and feet of Jesus, not just as we vote but also in social media, in our churches, communities, friendships, and families. May God help us and bless us in His Way.

On Race & Cultural Conflict

My Hope for America
By Jeanelle Austin

When I was a little girl, my teacher asked me, "What do you want to be when you grow up?" My response to her: I can be anything I want to be. Years later, on September 1, 2020, Seitu Jones, a distinguished Black artist based in the Twin Cities, looked at me and said, "You are a public theologian." I never aspired to become a public theologian, but the uprising of the people in response to unjust killings of Black lives by the state brought me to the intersection of race, democracy, faith, and protest. It forced me to wrestle with power, politics, and prophetic action in the streets.

George Floyd was killed at the hands of the Minneapolis Police Department on May 25, 2020 less than a quarter mile from my childhood home where my mother still lived. This was not the first time a Black person was unjustly killed by law enforcement; nor would it be the last. However, the proximity of this incident to home turned my world upside down.

I was living in Austin, Texas when George Floyd was lynched publicly on Memorial Day. The following Tuesday morning, my brother-in-law posted the link to the video of his death on my family group chat with the note "this is right by your house." Before the day ended, the streets of Minneapolis swelled with protesters that included my mother, siblings, nieces and nephews; and I watched my hometown go up in flames from afar. Wednesday, I texted my family a list of information that they would need to prepare for what was about to happen. I knew a curfew would be ordered. I knew the National Guard would be called. I knew there would be tear gas and rubber bullets. I also knew that there were ways the churches could respond. Thursday, my family reached out to me and asked me to return home to help. They knew that my vocation was racial justice work and requested that I come to work in my hometown. I pushed back. There would be plenty of community organizers and people on the ground equipped to do the very same work I do. I was certain that my return home would not be welcomed and would be unnecessary. However, my family insisted. So, I booked my flight to return home that Friday, packing only a carry-on with a week's worth of clothes and a suitcase full of supplies to support peaceful protesters. I arrived the same day the National Guard was called and a curfew was ordered. I could smell the smoke in the air. Police officers with rifles greeted airport passengers in baggage claim. It was a different Minneapolis.

By Monday, June 1, I was traumatized from the weekend of protesting. At 6 AM that day, I decided that I would tend to the memorial that mourners built for George Floyd to do something for the movement that would help me heal. I walked around and picked up trash. Day after day I continued this routine. Then, my work expanded to other memorial offerings such as tending to flowers and protest signs. I noticed others who were doing the same work. We connected and more people joined us. Eventually, someone called us "caretakers." The name stuck. To date, I lead a team of 19 caretakers who operate in three units: outdoor, conservation, and administration. All of us are community volunteers lending our strengths to live into our two guiding principles: 1) Everything is somebody's offering, therefore nothing is thrown away. 2) The people are more sacred than the memorial.

It is a privilege to lead this team of amazing caretakers who give selflessly for the betterment of our community. Our service to the movement is a priesthood of sorts. We tend to that which is considered sacred, while walking the thin line that exists between preservation and protest.

I realize that people expect a protest to look like marches to City Hall, blocked off streets or highways, or maybe even peaceful protests eventually disrupted by people filled with justified rage or young (often white) teens with destructive intentions. Such is not our reality at the intersection of East 38th Street and Chicago Avenue South (38th & Chicago). Our reality is a protest that holds sacred space and builds authentic community as we push for racial justice in political spaces.

When you come to 38th & Chicago, you will see large art installations, community gardens springing from the street, and a kind of organized beauty. People who live in the houses close to the intersection of 38th & Chicago tend to the memorial with no expectation of removing it without first seeing justice. And as caretakers, we are only one part of what immediate community members call "George Floyd Square."

There are others. They are protesting through providing security, volunteering their time as medics, doctors, and nurses, cooking food from the gardens, brewing coffee, providing cold beverages, serving youth educational needs, building benches for visitor seating, purchasing tents for shade, offering free hand sanitizer and masks, making art, and so much more. Together, we hold space at 38th & Chicago, asking the City of Minneapolis not to ignore the injustices bestowed upon this community and to respond to Justice Resolution 001[235] and its addendum because we believe that the people are more sacred than streets, than property, than the memorial itself.

We are over 100 days deep into this protest and experience opposition on a regular basis. On September 10, a Minneapolis Police Department vehicle followed me for five miles. I dropped my brother off at a rental car store downtown. Due to freeway construction, I planned to take side streets home, about 2.5 miles away. I noticed the cop car behind me at 3rd Avenue S and E Franklin Avenue. Because I am a visible participant in this local movement, I immediately decided that it would not be safe to return home. I checked my gas tank and verified that I had plenty of gas to drive around town, approximately 250 miles worth of gas. I then made a decision to drive South on Portland Avenue, knowing that once I reached Richfield, the cops could not follow me into the next city. I drove the speed limit at 30 miles per hour for five miles to leave South Minneapolis. I was nervous. I went down my check lists: I own my car. The tags are not expired. I legally have Texas plates still. I have car insurance. I am driving the speed limit. I have signaled every turn in advance. I have stopped at every red light. They have no reason to follow me, except that they have seen my car at or near the intersection of 38th and Chicago—a place in active protest against the actions of the police. I was extremely nervous but kept my resolve. The cops ran two red lights without turning on their sirens or lights in order to keep following me from a safe distance. I successfully drove to Richfield and forced them to turn off at 60th St and Portland Avenue. They did not pull me over.

In South Minneapolis, we are disrupting systems through our unwavering commitment to the people in our community and to justice. Not everyone is going to like what we are doing, but pursuing racial justice is not about being liked. It is about loving the people that our political systems repeatedly refuse to acknowledge and support.

All of this is happening in the context of an election year. Though the work that we do is extremely local, it is not lost on us that the death of George Floyd sparked an international uprising. Race is at the forefront of the presidential debates. Much is at stake.

I believe we have a moral obligation to vote. We must vote for people with character and resolve to do justice, love mercy, and walk with humility. How we choose to vote, if we get to vote, and if our votes will be counted will all be indicators of the state of race and democracy in the United States.

And let me be clear: the political binary that exists between the Republican and Democratic parties are not a direct correlation to the artificial black-white racial binary. These dominant political parties emerged out of constructs of whiteness and have oppressed Black people, indigenous people, and other people of color for generations. So for Black liberation—which liberates everyone—we cannot afford to vote along party lines. And as people of faith, we must cast our votes with a love ethic for the oppressed and marginalized.

Furthermore, we can no longer afford to be one-issue voters. We must wake up to the reality that uneducated voting is literally costing lives. We also must wake up to the reality that hyper-focusing on the national presidential candidates and ignoring local and state elections is costing lives too. There are people in office across the nation who sustain racist systems with no regard for human life, especially if we are racially categorized as Black, brown, or indigenous. Every day, my community wakes up to publicly protest unjust systems that are run by elected officials by holding space at 38th and Chicago. The elected city officials complain that they do not have enough money to do justice and point to the county and state officials. The state officials complain that they do not have enough money to do justice and point to the national government. The national officials complain about money and spend more time fighting over the distribution of our tax dollars rather than caring about the wellbeing of their constituents.

Our political systems perpetually fail to honor the sacredness of life. And I implore every reader of this essay—of this book—to follow the instruction provided to us in James 2:1, "As believers in our glorious Lord, Jesus Christ, do not show favoritism" (NIV). The people of God in the United States of America have an obligation to lead our nation. And if through our votes we consent to further oppress Black people, indigenous people, immigrants, the unhoused, the imprisoned, the poor, the underemployed, the unemployed, and anyone who falls into the category of marginalized and oppressed; we fail in our divine call to center the oppressed and root them into our community as our equals. We favor ourselves over our brothers and sisters who are equally sacred.

At the intersection of 38th and Chicago, our protest is grounded in community. We advocate for homeowners, renters, the unhoused, store owners, gang members, children, parents, adults, youth, people with and without disabilities, artists, accountants, school teachers, security team members, gardeners, people of any faith tradition or none, and whoever else lives in the geographical community, as we choose to center the movement of justice for Black lives. The work of living in community is extremely difficult, but when embraced as a way of life in the direction of justice, it is extremely rewarding. How we choose to live in community today will influence our vote, and our vote will reflect how we want to live in community tomorrow.

So, how will we vote? As I have come to accept that I am a public theologian, I believe that I have a moral obligation to speak up and tell anyone who is willing to listen to not vote for Donald Trump. Again, as a no-party-preference voter, this is not about the Republican Party against the Democratic Party. It is not about conservatives against moderates against liberals. This is about a man who has demonstrated a disregard for the sanctity of life. He claims to believe in our sacred scriptures within the Judeo-Christian faith, yet he uses his power to favor the wealthy, the powerful, and himself. More importantly, his practice of favoritism perpetuates racial oppression across the lines of class and gender.

His very campaign slogan to "Make America Great Again" is an offense to Black and indigenous people who have historically been oppressed and disenfranchised in the kind of America he idolizes. The call to "Make America Great Again" is a violent call against Black bodies. It is a call to oppress us through the ideology of whiteness. Under the banner of making America great again, we can expect more excessive use of force by law enforcement, more prisons, more racial profiling, more racial harassment, more racialized violence of all kinds followed by inequitable treatment in a court of law. Donald Trump openly empowers the systems of racial oppression that I wake up every morning to fight against for true liberty and justice.

Let me put this in simple evangelical terms. If you vote for and believe in the United States presidency of Donald Trump, you do not truly believe in the ministry of racial reconciliation of the church. The results of the two are opposites. And until you give your life to be shaped by racially diverse community in the United States, it will always be difficult to understand this statement.

My hope for all of us is that we find the courage to be active participants in racially diverse community and educated voters in a kind of way that is rooted in the love and justice of God. Your community may not look like the protest community we have built at 38th and Chicago in Minneapolis. That is expect-ed. What is important is that your life is intersecting with the lives of people who are different from you, and that you allow their experiences to expand your understanding of how your vote impacts their livelihood. If, as the people of God, we are committed to ending racial oppression, building diverse com-munity, and voting mindfully, we must vote to establish lead-ership in our nation who will walk in the way of justice, mercy, and humility. Donald Trump has repeatedly demonstrated that he is not that leader.

Jeanelle Austin, creator of Racial Agency Initiative, coaches people to leverage their agency for racial justice. A resident of Minneapolis, she is the lead caretaker of the George Floyd Memorial, guiding a team of volunteers to stand in the unique space of preservation and protest. Jeanelle earned an MDiv and an MA in Intercultural Studies from Fuller Theological Seminary. She speaks nationwide on topics as they intersect with race in America.

The Promise & Perils
of Critical Race Theory
By Rasool Berry

We live in a time of great racial tension. Cries for justice flood
the streets and dominate our national discourse. The killings
of George Floyd, Breonna Taylor, Ahmaud Arbery, and many
others sparked hashtags that read BLACK LIVES MATTER
in what some consider the largest protest movement in our
nation's history.[236] *But are these cries the results of real, structural
injustices or simply the result of an insidious ideology manufac-
turing rage to indoctrinate us to a new social order? Is the fight
for racial justice a legitimate roadmap to peace, or is it a road to
nowhere fabricated by proponents of Critical Race Theory (CRT)?*
Christians are often made to choose between the two extremes
of wholeheartedly embracing CRT or rejecting all it has to say
about race and justice. But is such a dichotomy necessary or
even the right way to think about this issue? A quick look at
how Christians engage other secular social theories gives us
great clarity regarding how to move forward.

In a recent post[237] analyzing our society's competing theories of justice, Dr. Tim Keller observed the virtues and vices
of a couple such theories. Keller noted, for example, that what
he called the "liberalism theory of justice" upholds individual
rights while maintaining that we don't need a consensus on morality. He pointed out the internal inconsistency of that view
because, without morality, what are "rights" and why should
we uphold them? In responding to this theory, Keller aptly observed that in spite of the "contradictions and fatal flaws in

Liberalism's approach ... Christians can agree with much in this justice theory."

Similarly, Christian Philosopher J.P. Moreland argues that common grace enables us to learn from all people. Common grace is the doctrine that God allows everyone including those who don't believe in him to understand truths about reality. As a result of common grace, we can learn from philosophers, scholars and activists regardless of their personal beliefs. In fact, as Moreland notes, several biblical authors leverage the value of common grace, such as Paul and Jude. Paul favorably quotes the pagan prophet Epimenedes in Acts 17:28 and Jude quotes the noncanonical *Assumption of Moses* in Jude 3 to support one of his arguments. So the Bible clearly endorses the usefulness of common grace as a means to learn about the world. In spite of these truths, many Christians deny that Critical Race theorists have anything to teach us.

Over the last 20 years, however, Christians have gained insights from postmodern theorists that have helped them fill out their own theological maps with more detail.

Millard Erickson, a leading evangelical systematic theology scholar, wrote a book called *Truth or Consequences: The Promise & Perils of Postmodernism*[238]. In it he noted that the Christian reaction to postmodernism tended to only focus on its perils, while very few ever sought to explore the promise of insights in this worldview. Erickson recognized that in spite of its flaws, the postmodern worldview had many penetrating insights: "Postmodern theory can help us understand the relationship between knowledge and power, the importance of narratives, the role of communities, and the value of suspicion." Erickson does this while still describing the perils of postmodernist theory. Biola University Professor Tim Muehlhoff, who writes on philosophy, communications and apologetics, also acknowledged "I have found the writings of postmodern thinkers to be useful in understanding issues of gender, race, and identity," even while he offers strong critiques of that worldview.[239]

Critical theorists and Christians often disagree on the answers to key philosophical questions such as the existence of truth or the moral grounding of social justice, BUT we do agree that questions surrounding these issues are crucial. Both Critical Race theorists and Christians who uphold the Scriptures agree that human liberation from tyrannical oppression is good, and that our justice system should treat everyone fairly regardless of their economic status, race, ethnicity or gender. We, no doubt, disagree on some aspects of what "human liberation" or "justice" look like. But we all agree that racial discrimination is wrong. C. S. Lewis wrote "The man who agrees with us that some question, little regarded by others, is of great importance can be our friend. He need not agree with us about some answer." [240]

But it's not just in philosophy or postmodernism where we see Christians apply what Moreland refers to as "conceptual integration" of biblical truths with ideas discovered in secular arenas. We see it in the field of psychology as well.

For most evangelical Christians it is not controversial to describe someone as suffering from something like narcissism or to urge them to get therapy. We approve of these in spite of the fact that "narcissism" and "psychotherapy" were both the innovations of Sigmund Freud, the 20th century neurologist and founder of psychoanalysis. Freud regarded religion as an "illusion" that should be shaken off by reason and science. His worldview and convictions would be considered "anti-Christian" and yet we freely use his concepts.

We do conceptual integration when we celebrate the statement: "We hold these truths to be self-evident, that all men are created equal, that they are endowed by their Creator with certain unalienable Rights." It's well established that the author of the Declaration of Independence, Thomas Jefferson, was not an orthodox Christian, but a Deist. Because he believed that miracles were myths, he cut out mention of them in his Bible. He also rejected the historicity of the resurrection, the doctrine of the atonement, and the idea that God could be known or called by name. He owned slaves because he didn't believe that Black people were made in the image of God.[241] Even though Jefferson's words and personal life did not reflect Christian orthodoxy, we find his "roadmap" of our representative democracy helpful and consistent with Christian teaching.

Why is it that when it comes to theories of justice, postmodern theory, psychology or the Declaration of Independence we can use conceptual integration, but when it comes to CRT, or the Black Lives Matter movement, the reaction from many Christians is to reject them wholesale and denounce anything or anyone associated with them? Why can't many Christians see that common grace belongs to theorists who critique racial injustice? Ironically, many Christians seem to believe that when it comes to critiquing power, leftists have a monopoly.

But the Scriptures clearly offer a Critical Theory of the world that shines a light on oppression. Ecclesiastes 4:1 (NIV) reads:

> *Again I looked and saw all the oppression that was*
> *taking place under the sun:*
> *I saw the tears of the oppressed—*
> *and they have no comforter;*
> *power was on the side of their oppressors ...*

But before we get to the Bible's critique of power, we must understand what Critical Theory is.

The first word in the approach reveals its intention: the idea of being "critical" was inspired by philosopher Immanuel Kant.[242] To Kant, "critique" meant examining and questioning the validity of universally accepted theories of his time. Similar to how Kant, and later Karl Marx critiqued prevalent theories in their disciplines, Max Horkheimer sought to build on those previous critical approaches with a focus on social theory. The assumption of Kant, Marx, Horkheimer and others was that traditional theories were uncritical of power and injustice, and therefore unable to affect human liberation. Horkheimer and his colleagues were trying to understand why capitalism and authoritarian Marxism failed to provide human freedom. So, they tried to make a map that could lead people to freedom.

What Are Critical theorists critical of? To put it simply, Critical theorists offer critiques on what they see as oppressive abuses of power. The abuses of power Critical theorists challenge can be the result of wealth, ideological dominance (hegemony), or the power to shape language and/ or physical domination via state sanctioned violence, to name a few. Critical theorists seek to critique and undermine traditional theories because they see these narratives as part of the establishment's abusive power.

The concept of human emancipation from violence and oppression is noble and can be good if we have the right definition of "emancipation." This is where CT's cohesion and premise break down.

There's a sophisticated slight-of-hand maneuver inherent in Critical Theory's philosophy. In order to undermine traditional theories, Critical theorists often reject all narratives that seek to explain the world, with the notable exception of their own, because clearly Critical Theory is a narrative that seeks to explain the world. The CRT narrative is that the problem with the world is powerful people who create narratives that they say we must all believe in. The way we experience human liberation is to reject their narratives. Some have readily recognized this inherent inconsistency.[243]

So that's Critical Theory, but what about Critical Race Theory (CRT)? We have to fast-forward, about 40 years after Horkheimer's writings to the 1970s.

At that time, the Civil Rights Movement of the 50s and 60s had failed to bring about the changes hoped for and expected. Years had passed since the Civil Rights Act of 1964 and other sweeping legislation (such as the Voting Rights Act, the

Fair Housing Act, etc.) passed with the promise of justice, and yet racial inequalities still existed and in some cases worsened. For example, many studies show that schools are more segregated now than they were 50 years ago).[244] There seemed to be a need for another map.

Critical Race Theory sprang up in the mid-1970s, as a number of lawyers, activists, and legal scholars across the country realized that the heady advances of the civil rights era of the 1960s had stalled, and, in many respects, were being rolled back by newer, subtler forms of racism. A group of Critical Race theorists held CRT's first conference at a convention outside Madison, Wisconsin in the summer of 1989.[245] This theoretical movement within American law schools was a reworking of critical legal studies that also sought human liberation, but with the emphasis on addressing issues of race.[246] It was relatively unknown by those outside the legal studies and activist communities until recently. **Contrary to what some Christians assume, while every Critical Race theorist sees systemic racism as a problem to confront, not everyone who sees systemic racism as a problem to confront is a Critical Race theorist.**

One important thing critics of CRT often overlook is that theorists are not monolithic, nor ideologically aligned. They are unified more by what they are against (what they see as racist abuses of power) than by a common worldview. For example, law professor, Vinay Harplani, is a friend I met in college. He also was the last person awarded a Derrick Bell Fellowship to work with the late Professor Derrick Bell in his legal studies class. Vinay told me that, after countless hours of listening to Professor Bell share his philosophy, one thing became clear. Bell *was* inspired by a radical revolutionary, but it wasn't Karl Marx; it was Jesus Christ. Vinay, who is not religious himself, pointed to Bell's own writing as proof of his faith orientation. Bell wrote a book titled, *Gospel Choirs: Psalms of Survival in an Alien Land Called Home*. And even Bell's unique contribution to legal studies pedagogy was the use of parables and stories to educate. But the most meaningful evidence was the way Bell shared with Vinay how his faith and worldview were central to his activism. His faith was the source of his legal work and theory. While Bell, the person widely considered the founder of CRT, pointed to Jesus' teachings and not Marx as his motivation, there are others whose point of reference would be the reverse. And that's actually the point. Because CRT is more of a methodology than a philosophy, those who leverage it for their work will have a wide range of worldviews.

Some Christians argue that recent Black Lives Matter (BLM) protests and activism should be rejected by Christians because the BLM organization may be influenced by Critical Race Theory. They conflate the spontaneous movements of outrage against racialized violence with the young organization, even though the movement includes millions of people from all over the world unaffiliated with the BLM organization. To these observers, the entire movement to end racism is considered guilty by association of being somehow Marxist and therefore evil. This is a well-worn argument used with great effectiveness many times before.[247] Southern segregationists accused Rev. Dr. Martin Luther King Jr., of being a Marxist to thwart his agenda in ad hominem attacks though he denied it repeatedly. .[248]

According to many Christians, the conceptual "maps" that point out racism end in division, violence, or the end of America as we know it. There are legitimate concerns and critiques to be leveled against any organization, including BLM, when that organization's version of human liberation contradicts the Bible. However, the structural inequality and race-based oppression CRT and BLM decry are historical truths that are part of our nation's past and present. That is a fact. The oppression of the poor by the rich, the foreigner by the secure citizen, and the racial minority by the ethnic majority are all particularly egregious to the Lord (Micah 6:10–13). And yet, the problem of sin as described in the Bible is actually much worse than a power play of the elite over the poor. Christianity's analysis of sin says that the problem is within each of us as well (Romans 3:10–19). Those with less power can sin against each other.

There are legitimate criticisms of the story CRT tells, but much like with the postmodernism that informs it, the church focuses only on seeing the faults of CRT. But why is it so hard for some Christians to see the value of CRT's critique of racism?

Christian author Andy Crouch helps us answer that question. He wrote in his book *Playing God: Redeeming the Gift of Power*,[249] "The powerful have a hard time seeing their own power. Unmapped power is a perilous thing."

When people map out power by pointing out racial or gender privilege, it can cause our defenses to go up. I know that defensive reflex first hand because when my male privilege needs to be called out, my guard goes up. According to Crouch's analysis of mapping, if there is such a thing as "white privilege," the last people to realize it would be white people because such power would be "unmapped."

What are the implications if I acknowledge that lighter skin is "unmapped power" in our culture? What does it mean to recognize the history of white supremacy in our nation? It doesn't mean that all white people are racists. But it does mean that more racism and bias exists than people think because they are unaware that they are recipients of power.

Christians should be aware our sin often blinds us and makes us susceptible to using culture and power for self-justification. Culture often blinds us to what the Bible is saying. Power allows us to insist that our blinded version of reality MUST BE TRUE. Look at Peter — an apostle! — he let his Jewish upbringing keep him from eating with Gentile fellow believers (Galatians 2:11–13). His culture blinded him to his wrongdoing and his power as an apostle permitted the status quo that kept the Gentiles as second-class citizens in the church; that was until Paul used his power as an apostle to pub-licly critique Peter's abuse of power (Galatians 2:14). This is what CRT is helpful to do. It maps racial power that Christians fail to see. But CRT only echoes what Christians have been saying for centuries.

For example, anti-racism author, Ibram X. Kendi, notes in his book, *Stamped from the Beginning: The Definitive History of Racist Ideas in America*, that on April 18, 1688, a group from the Mennonite Church in Philadelphia made an appeal to end slavery. "They wrote: 'In Europe there are many oppressed" for their religion, and "here those are oppressed" for their "black colour." Both oppressions were wrong. Actually, as an oppres-sor, America "surpassed Holland and Germany."[250] In what was the first known written argument that slavery was morally wrong, the Mennonites made an argument that America was systemically racist. African American Christians would make the same arguments themselves.

In 1787, Richard Allen and Absalom Jones left the Methodist Church, which used its power to marginalize them so they started the first Black church, the African Methodist Episcopal Church. They had to fight all the way to the Supreme Court in order to be allowed to worship independently. Allen recognized systemic racism in the American church that neces-sitated the founding of the Black Church and used the legal system to challenge it.

From Nat Turner, to Sojourner Truth, Harriet Tubman, and Frederick Douglass, Black Christians critiqued the pre-vailing theories that dehumanized and marginalized them; and called out racial injustice. A helpful map to guide them to lib-eration was the Bible.

Herman Bavinck, the Dutch Reformed theologian noted systemic racism when he traveled to the U.S.A. in 1908. Upon reflecting on his observations and readings of W.E.B. DuBois, Bavinck wrote, "In the future, there truly lurks a danger, and in the future a struggle will doubtless be fought between black and white, a heated struggle, fanned into flame by the strong antipathy on both sides."[251] Bavinck essentially predicted the social unrest we're experiencing today over 100 years ago.

And writing over 50 years ago, Dr. Martin Luther King Jr. appealed to traditional theories of justice when he wrote: "The God we worship is a God of justice and he has ordered human beings toward justice and [America's] systemic racism dishonors God and violates human nature."[252] In other words, Christians got a very long head start on CRT . Before anyone conceptualized CRT, the need for Black liberation was clear. But CRT has been helpful, for instance, to point out the particular ways that white supremacy has mutated from legalized *de jure* institutional racism (explicit laws like "separate but equal") to *de facto* institutional racism (implicit ways discrimination continues illegally). but attempts to use CRT to discredit anti-racism work is ahistorical and inaccurate.

Criticism of racial injustice is not the same as Critical Race Theory. Those of us Christians who have experienced the oppressive force of institutional racism have gained insights from CRT and rejected the aspects that contradict a biblical worldview.

The Black Church has always stood in opposition to injustice, abuse of power and oppression; the same is true with BLM. The hashtag #BLM predates the organization and is much, much broader in its scope and impact. There are only 16 BLM chapters, according to their website. But of the millions who have come out and protested both in America and throughout the world, very few are actively involved in the inner workings of the organization's chapters. And based on BLM's philosophy of organizing, the only ideological requirement to participate in BLM is that you care about Black life.[253] Unlike the previous Civil Rights Movement of the 1960s, BLM is not based in the Black church and as a result includes ideologies and perspectives that the church finds offensive, false, and even problematic. But isn't it strange that we can agree with

Keller's observation that there is some value in secular theories of justice, Moreland's value of aspects of postmodernism, embrace Freud's concepts of narcissism and psychotherapy, and even embrace the Deist rhetoric of Thomas Jefferson, and yet find CRT or uttering "Black Lives Matter" contemptible? Why is this held to such a different standard? Could it be that we are afraid of where that map will take us? Could the Apostle Paul's observation about us in Romans 2:1–5 be true: that we who pass judgment are without excuse because we baptize our blind spots in Christian platitudes of being "color blind" while rejecting any insights from about wrongdoing and injustice because they utilize a Critical Race theorist's lens?

We must remember that critique of institutional racism and structural inequalities predates CRT by centuries. Our nation was built on the racist institutions of slavery, segregation and the false narrative of racial difference that justified them. While this is all true, it's also important to identify the shortcomings of CRT. Within CRT, there often persists a Machiavellian suspicion and vision of power, as well as a postmodern rejection of absolute truth that undermines historic Christian doctrine.

But we don't need to simply critique CRT; we need to understand it and explore the directions that this map can point us.

We need to discover how theories that seek to understand and overcome racial injustice help us find roads that we may have missed along the way. Systemic racism has always been a problem in America, and the need for CRT emerged because the Church failed to see that the Bible in James 2:1–9 pronounced that the wealthy and powerful were prone to the sin of partiality and tended to oppress the poor. As Jemar Tisby noted in *The Color of Compromise: The Truth about the American Church's Complicity in Racism,* "Complicit Christianity forfeits its moral authority by devaluing the image of God in people of color."[254]

The American church was complicit in supporting racism because it exchanged God's truth that the *Imago Dei* (the doctrine that all of us are made in the image of God) was equally reflected in the ebony and mahogany skin tones of its darkest citizens for the lie that God's image was mostly reflected in the culture and people who were lighter skinned. As a result, the dominant, Eurocentricity of American culture corrupted the church – a church that failed to announce that the gospel of Jesus Christ is one that pronounces freedom to the captives. This freedom is both for those burdened by personal sins, and, through the ushering of the kingdom of God, those oppressed by corporate ones.

The gospel reveals not only a personal pietistic plan of salvation, but a plan of restoration that redeems and restores. Jesus critiques unjust political, economic and social systems as well as personal sins. CRT is on the lookout for systemic, institutionalized racism and injustice. Because of its philosophical assumptions, CRT will not accurately analyze all it seeks to critique. But because of common grace it will see things we should see. And because of our sin we know we don't always read the Bible rightly and we need to listen to other voices. The gospel gives us insight to respond and subversively fulfill CRT with something greater, Critical Grace Theory.

> Critical Grace Theory is what Paul does when he writes:
> *[We] have divine power to demolish strongholds. We demolish arguments and every pretension that sets itself up against the knowledge of God, and we take captive every thought to make it obedient to Christ.* (2 Cor. 10:5–6, NIV)

The same Paul that spoke of taking every thought captive is the same one who quoted pagan scholars through his knowledge of the gospel. That is applying common grace while at the same time being critical. That is what we do in affirming the statement Black Lives Matter while critiquing racial nihilism and the rejection of absolute truth or moral order that is sometimes associated with it.[255] It's proclaiming the good news that God cares about injustice and Jesus empowers us to do justice, love mercy, and walk humbly before our God. That is how we avoid the perils of CRT while fulfilling the promise of our call to challenge the world.

Rasool Berry serves as teaching pastor at The Bridge Church in Brooklyn, New York. He graduated from UPenn with a BA in Africana Studies and Sociology. He is currently seeking his MA in Biblical Studies at Reformed Theological Seminary. He is committed to helping people live out a biblical framework for social justice. He hosts the "Where Ya From?" podcast which uses stories to highlight people applying their faith for social change. This essay is based on a blog post by the author.

Loving God and Neighbor
During an Election
By David Osborn

My first pastoral ministry was in Mississippi during 1963-1970. My experience there formed the values I now follow in elections. I was a white pastor from the North serving a white church that was committed to segregation. I was committed to work for integration of the church and the schools.

Segregation was always going to be a highly emotional issue. People all over the country sided with either the bigots or Black people, or were disinterested because "it does not affect me." This disheartened me because people did not engage with those with whom they disagreed, which is the only way differences can be understood and resolved. Their overriding goal was to win rather than to understand. But winning did not and does not change people. People, unfortunately, do not say, "All right, since you defeated me, I will join your side." Rather, they are like a two-year-old boy who stood in a pew at the beginning of a church service. His father told him to sit down, but he refused. When his dad forced him to sit down, he looked up and said, "I may be sitting down on the outside, but I'm standing up on the inside."

I am all for good laws; laws that protect minorities. However, laws cannot make people sit down on the inside. Laws do not compel people to willingly change. But when we love people, we can persuade them to do what is right. If we depend only upon passing legislation, many will look for ways to subvert the law. This is what happened in Mississippi, the South, and across the country.

In the South, private schools and clubs grew up in order to maintain segregation. Yet my experience taught me that people are open to change when they know that they are loved. Loving was my approach. I wanted everyone I met to know that they were important to me and that I cared. The main way I did that (and continue that practice today) was to speak to people everywhere—before a meeting, in a line at the bank, or at a store, or buying a ticket, or in any place that puts people together briefly. I particularly focused upon people who were a minority or were poor, but I included everyone. My actions told them that I saw them, and that they were important to me. That provided opportunities to learn good things from them that I could share with people different from them. I sought to humanize everyone to others—to be a honeybee, spreading the pollen of good to everyone, including those in my church. I have often thought of the difference it would make if every evangelical would engage in such brief conversations rather than ignoring those who are different.

On one occasion in a drug store I spoke to a man standing in the aisle. He told me that evolution was true but only of Black people. I listened. Then, without telling him that he was wrong (so he would not need to defend himself), I told him I had problems with that and explained what my problems were. I was surprised when he said to me, "You need to be telling others about that." I said, "I do and will."

In a group luncheon with men from various churches, a pastor about ten feet from me began speaking loudly about how Sickle Cell Anemia was a disease of only "the mulatto," proving that Blacks and whites were not meant to marry. I noticed that many heads were nodding in agreement. Then he looked at me and asked. "Don't you agree?" I said I had a problem with that and then explained my problem. As I spoke, I noticed that many of the heads that were nodding for him were now nodding for me. They only needed to hear another perspective.

Everyone can be loved. The Scriptures say, "Love covers over a multitude of sins" (1 Pet. 4:8, NIV). Love does not overlook sin. Rather, it loves people as they are while seeking to help them change. Of course, it changes the lover also. Sometimes people would explain in a way that changed my thinking. Every person I meet knows something good that I do not know, so I choose to learn from others.

In Mississippi I chose to love both the downtrodden and the downtrodders because God loves them all as they are, however they may think or act. I wanted to make a difference for both groups so that I could help them come together and become better people. At my first church board meeting in Mississippi I asked what our position on Black people attending was. I was told, "If a Black attends we will show him the door." I said, "OK." There was work to be done.

Though it was clear to me where they stood, that did not tell me why they were that way. The problem was in their thinking, which led to their actions. As I learned their thinking and their emotional baggage, I was able to promote change through relevant teaching. I was also their honeybee to share thought pollen from others for them to consider. Time did the rest. There was no magic bullet. Simply disagreeing at the beginning would not have accomplished what understanding and example did. In the end, our segregated congregation committed to an integration policy. Black people lived across the city from us, so they did not attend before I moved to Florida. But one prominent member said to me, "Though I would have to deal with my emotions on it, I now believe that there is nothing wrong with a Black marrying a white," something that had been illegal in Mississippi. People had changed.

The perspective I developed from all of this and the experiences I had led me to be very disheartened during the 2016 election. I could not vote for division. Trump's approach was to divide and conquer. Mine is to unite for all to win. I had witnessed too much divisiveness in Mississippi. Since 2016, divisions in our country and Trump's tweets have both grown. What is worse is his claim to be supporting the church, even holding a Bible for pictures as others were teargassed to move them out of the way. But I seek to follow the approach below which I believe is God's way.

Respected Old Testament scholar and friend, Knut Heim, once said to me, "With very few exceptions, God gets angry about only two things in the Old Testament: idolatry and social injustice." This is consistent with the two greatest commandments: to love God (which idolatry prevents), and to love neighbor (which social injustice prevents). The two greatest commandments, coupled with an awareness of what angers God, guide me in how I interact with others as I prepare to vote.

First, if we love God, we will trust God rather than leaders and laws. Politics and political power must not be our idols. However, rather than trusting God, we often believe that electing the people we think will make the *right* laws will save us— as if God could not help us regardless of the circumstances. Certainly, electing the right people is important, and good laws can effect important change. However, God is at work and can help us even with bad leaders and bad laws in place. We must not think God has abandoned us when bad things happen. The cross was the worst sin that was ever committed. Yet God transformed it into the best thing that ever happened. God used sin to defeat sin. Therefore, God can use anything for good that we give to him (Rom. 8:28).

And God is against social injustice. That means we must work against injustice out of our love for God and our love for our suffering neighbors. In the new heaven and the new earth there will be no more death, or mourning, or crying, or pain (Rev. 21:4). That clearly means that those things are inconsistent with God's will. Therefore, we must now work against the things that God will eradicate.

Second, our neighbor includes our enemy. To be like God, we must love our enemies and pray for them (Matt. 5:43-48). That kind of love exemplifies the perfection to which we are called (Matt. 5:48). We see that type of love in action through Jesus on the cross where the Lamb of God proclaims, "Father, forgive them, for they do not know what they are doing" (Luke 23:34, NIV). We see it again when Stephen, as he is being stoned, pleads with God saying, "Lord, do not hold this sin against them" (Acts 7:60, NIV). And yet again, when Paul, referring to the Jews who want to kill him, wrote, "For I could wish that I myself were cursed and cut off from Christ for the sake of my people, those of my own race" (Rom. 9:3, NIV). He loved them.

Martin Luther King Jr., in his book, *Strength to Love*, recalls Abraham Lincoln once saying to a woman who wondered how he could speak a kind word toward the South during the Civil War: "Madam, do I not destroy my enemies when I make them my friends?"[256] King also viewed loving our enemies as a practical tool for individual and collective transformation. "Returning hate for hate multiplies hate, adding deeper darkness to a night already devoid of stars. Darkness cannot drive out darkness; only light can do that. Hate cannot drive out hate; only love can do that."[257]

King provides yet another compelling reason to love our enemies. "We must recognize that the evil deed of the enemy-neighbor, the thing that hurts, never quite expresses all that he is. An element of goodness may be found even in our worst enemy."[258] We must love those whom Jesus loves, including our enemies; and we must see them as Jesus sees them.

When it comes to elections then, we must support what seems right and best, and seek good outcomes for everyone. But we must not hate those who disagree with us. We must not assign motives to what they say or how they vote. No one has ever seen a motive.

For example, a policeman was driving down the road. As he passed a woman she shouted, "Pig!" Angrily he shouted back, "Sow!" Then he drove around the curve and hit the biggest pig he ever saw. In reality, he did not hear her call him a pig. He only heard her shout, "Pig!" He added to it the motive that she hated him and was calling him a pig. But she was not. She was trying to protect him.

Often, we don't see things as they are. We see things as we are. We each have particular experiences and knowledge. That is all we have to work with in order to understand. When we see others act, or hear what they say, we process what we perceive through our own backgrounds.

That problem of misunderstanding is why we need to ask questions. In asking, we are not assuming that the person is right, but we are acknowledging that they may see things differently. Why they see things differently can only be learned by asking them. We will always learn something by asking. At the very least, we will learn why they think the way they do. We might still see things differently, but we cannot answer what we do not understand. We may also realize that there is a way of viewing the subject at hand that we had not considered. This might cause us to adjust our thinking. It made a difference in Mississippi.

David Osborn is Senior Professor of Christian Leadership at Denver Seminary. He served as director of the DMin program for seventeen years, bringing his experience as a pastor, church leader, and conciliator. In Tupelo, Mississippi in the 1960s, he helped assist in the peaceful integration of the school system. In the 1970s, he served as president of the state and regional conventions in Florida.

The Silenced Minority
By Andrew Y. Lee

Racial politics is alive and well in the United States as evidenced by President Donald Trump's ascent to power. The president's campaign slogan when he ran for office in 2016 was "Make America Great Again" (MAGA). While this catch phrase means different things to different people, as a Chinese American person of color, I interpreted it as coded language for "Make America White again. Minorities belong in the shadows of mainstream America."

Whereas the president has stated that he is relying on an anonymous "silent majority" to help re-elect him this year,[259] there exists a silenced minority on the receiving end of racial targeting. One study showed that when white Americans were told in 2016 that they would become a minority group themselves by the year 2042, they responded by increasing their support for Trump and his anti-immigration policies.[260]

In this present election, the president hasn't introduced a new platform as is customary political practice. Instead he continues to rely on the "Make America Great Again" ethos to rally his troops to action. He persists in preying on those who belong to the dominant culture in America who are fearful of relinquishing control to minorities. Racial politics remains a fixture as minorities continue to be marginalized.

The Common Origin of Humanity
Yet when we turn to the very first book of the Bible, the creation of humanity in Genesis teaches our common origin. The

human race descended from one couple. Adam and Eve are the progenitors of humanity. This highlights not only our kinship but also our equality. One race cannot be superior to any other if all can ultimately trace their origins to a primal family.

In Ephesians 3:14-15 (ESV), the apostle Paul makes this declaration. "For this reason I bow my knees before the Father, from whom every family in heaven and on earth is named." We have a common heritage through our creator God as every family in heaven and on earth is included.

We also share a common spiritual bond through Jesus Christ who has demolished the walls of separation. "For as many of you as were baptized into Christ have put on Christ. There is neither Jew nor Greek, there is neither slave nor free, there is no male and female, for you are all one in Christ Jesus" (Gal. 3:27-28). Categories including ethnicity, socio-economic status, and gender are eradicated when God's people are intent on obeying the commandment to love our neighbor as ourselves.

Despite awareness of these well-known passages from the Bible, barriers to full inclusion of all peoples remain in place. "All men" are not treated equally even if this is a supposed "self-evident" truth. There is preferential treatment for the majority. Moreover, inequities for the minority have been exacerbated during the tenure of President Trump.

The Historical Heritage of Chinese Americans

This should not be surprising for Chinese Americans. However, their inclusion in America as a "model minority" has obscured their tragic history and minimized their current plight. The enticement of the California Gold Rush brought the Chinese to America in the 19th century. While few found success through gold mining, the lure of employment opportunities drew many to these shores. Political and economic turmoil in southern China were powerful factors that drove immigrants to America. An estimated 300,000 Chinese came to the United States between the beginning of the California Gold Rush and

1882, when they were legally barred from entry. They faced discrimination wherever they went, whether prospecting in mines, constructing railroads or laboring on farms and plantations.[261]

Anti-Chinese sentiment gained momentum as greater numbers of Chinese arrived and found employment doing menial labor. Much as immigrants today are blamed for taking low wage jobs that should belong to whites, the same argument was launched against the Chinese more than a century ago. The irony was that the white employers and owners of factories, railroads and farms established the pay scale. Yet it was the Chinese who were victimized by those in control.[262]

Within this climate and with little legal protection in place, white Americans burned Chinese homes and businesses and drove the Chinese out of towns, attacking and murdering them with impunity. Although European immigrants initially faced discrimination in America as well, with the acquisition of English they eventually blended into the general populace. The distinctive physical characteristics of Asians prevented this from happening. Not having whiteness, they were considered an inferior race as were African Americans and Native Americans. One Californian made this assessment: "One white man is worth two Chinamen; that one Chinaman is worth two negroes, and that one negro is worth two tramps."[263]

The Chinese Exclusion Act of 1882 banned one specific race as an act of xenophobia. America's borders were closed in this landmark legislation, denying naturalization to the Chinese.[264] Discrimination against other Asian Americans, including Japanese, Filipinos, Koreans and South Asians, continued into the 20th century.[265] Some pushed for the exclusion of all Asians from America. What resulted was the Immigration Act of 1917, also known as the Barred Zone Act. Prohibited from entry were "inhabitants of most of China, all of India, Burma (Myanmar), Siam (Thailand), and the Malay states, part of Russia, all of Arabia and Afghanistan, most of the Polynesian

Islands, and all of the East Indian islands."[266] The warm reception given to Lothrop Stoddard's book, *The Rising Tide of Color Against White World Supremacy*, is representative of the anti-Asian sentiment at the time as it warned about the "yellow peril" from Asia.[267]

The Model Minority

It was decades later after passage of the Immigration and Nationality Act of 1965 that it became permissible for large numbers of Asians to gain entry into the United States. Since that time, Asian Americans have come to be celebrated for their career success. The blueprint for their accomplishments supposedly rests on their strong work ethic, and family emphasis on study and education. Amy Chua's bestseller, *Battle Hymn of the Tiger Mother,* served to reinforce this formula. She imposed discipline, strict rules and tough love upon her children, values presumed to be typical of Chinese Americans.[268]

It was actually the Japanese who were first lauded in 1966 as the model minority by sociologist William Petersen.[269] While acknowledging the obstacles immigrants faced, Petersen pointed to the diligence, frugality and achievement orientation of the Japanese as the basis for their ability to overcome discrimination. Later publications concurred with Petersen's assessment, associating the model minority with all Asian Americans.[270] While mainstream society commonly accepts this myth as truth, it is not reflective of reality.

Asian Americans are not a monolithic group as they come with varied backgrounds and life circumstances. Some immigrants are highly educated multilingual professionals, welcomed into America for their knowledge, expertise and skills. On the other extreme are the laborers with limited or no ability to speak English. They scrounge for work, toiling long hours at low wages to eke out a meager livelihood.

"For every dollar the average white man makes in the United States, an Asian Indian woman makes $1.21 and a

Taiwanese woman makes $1.16. A Samoan woman makes $0.62. A Burmese woman makes 50 cents. The experiences of these groups are not the same."[271]

Nonetheless Asian American students in general have internalized their status as the model minority. Largely unaware of how Asian Americans were historically treated, they subconsciously subscribe to their portrayal as the model minority. Many diligently pursue their studies believing that hard work and good grades will gain them entry into prestigious universities.[272] At one Silicon Valley high school, students joke about the Asian grade scale. A is Average, B is Bad, C is Catastrophic, D is Disowned and, an F means Forever forgotten.[273]

Asian American students believe in the concept of meritocracy. Success is the product of diligent studies; hard work will ultimately lead to financially rewarding careers. Thus they immerse themselves in academics to achieve the American dream.[274]

However, they are unaware that the model minority script is actually an exercise in white privilege and used as a wedge to divide people of color. This stereotype originated during the era of "Black Power" and the call for civil rights. One implication of Petersen's study was that if the Japanese could be successful apart from strident demands for equality, then so could Black people. What was needed was not more public and vocal demonstrations but rather following the path of Asian Americans who succeeded without the benefit of social programs.[275]

This argument shifted the focus from race and ethnicity to culture. One succeeds, not because of one's color (therefore one cannot be called racially privileged), but due to one's cultural and personal values. If white people are successful, it is because of their values. If Chinese and other Asians are able to climb the corporate ladder, it is because of their values. Conversely if Blacks and other people of color are unable to point to similar achievements, it is due to their philosophy of life. It is not color that defines the pecking order in society but rather cultural convictions.

As whites represent the majority of those in power, they perch at the top of the social pyramid. Beneath them are the model minority—yellow Asians. Brown and Black form the base of the triangle. Furthermore, "racial triangulation" occurs as Asians are pitted against other minorities and presented as the role model to follow.[276]

On the one hand, Asian Americans are valorized. They are commended for their many achievements and financial accomplishments. Other people of color are to emulate them. On the other hand, they never attain complete assimilation into American society. They are still a minority group that continues to be ostracized, put in their place when the occasion calls for it. They occupy a liminal space in society, subjugated by the demands of those in power.[277]

President Trump's Rhetoric and Actions

President Trump's comments and actions target Asian Americans. He persists in identifying COVID-19 with the Chinese by employing the terms "Chinese Flu," "Wuhan Virus," "China Virus" and "Kung Flu." The World Health Organization maintains that the virus is neither defined by national borders nor by ethnicity. Yet Trump continues to use these terms and denies that they are racist in nature. He also rebuffed the idea that his language endangers Asian Americans.[278]

In reality, data reveals that racist attacks escalated greatly in the aftermath of the president's remarks. Unable to differentiate between Chinese Americans and other Asian Americans, all Asian Americans are placed at risk. The Asian Pacific Policy and Planning Council and Chinese for Affirmative Action responded to these attacks by creating a website where verbal and physical assaults on Asian Americans could be reported. More than 2,500 incidents were logged from March 19 to August 5,

2020. These confrontations were national in scope, collected from 47 states and Washington, DC. Examples include:

- A healthcare worker on a subway car in New York City who was spat and coughed upon and subjected to racial slurs by a maskless man.
- A white woman in California who drove her SUV onto a sidewalk in an attempt to run over an Asian family.
- An Asian woman in Georgia who was sprayed with Lysol. Her attacker shouted, "You're the infection. Go home. We don't want you here!"[279]

In New York City, the Police Department created an Asian Hate Crime Task Force in response to reports of victimization of those of Asian descent.[280] Residents in Manhattan's Chinatown took matters into their own hands by forming a neighborhood watch to patrol their streets.[281]

The vilification of Asian Americans in a presumed era of tolerance is a reminder that the model minority are not woven into the fabric of mainstream society. Just as Japanese Americans were dispatched to internment camps during World War II, the scapegoating of Asian minorities continues today. The strain of COVID-19 that viciously attacked New York City making it an early epicenter of the disease was primarily transmitted from Western Europe, not China.[282] Yet Trump insists on profiling only the Chinese as he appeals to his base of supporters.

In the wake of nationwide protests against the deaths of George Floyd, Breonna Taylor, Ahmaud Arbery, Jacob Blake, and other Black victims, white Americans are the least engaged with reform efforts according to a recent poll. Only 30% of whites have personally taken actions recently to better understand racial issues in America as opposed to 51% of Hispanics, 49% of Asians and 41% of blacks.[283]

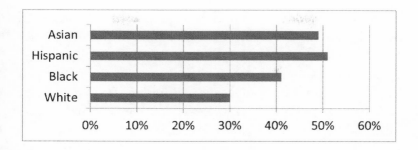

To the question "Have you or a close friend or family member attended a rally or protest since George Floyd's death in May, or not," whites again lagged behind at 21%. Both Asians and Hispanics were at 35% while Blacks registered 55%.[284]

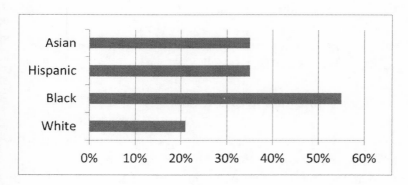

In refusing to support the movement to protect Black lives, a neuropsychologist from Georgia stated that it was divisive, a rationale also offered by President Trump and other conservatives. "What about the Hispanics? What about the Indians? What about us? The Caucasians?" she asked. "So no, I have a big problem with how the movement is being portrayed and encouraged."[285]

This woman's response reflects the attitude of white privilege. It ignores the systemic racism faced by people of color especially among those in the African American community who encounter Black disprivilege.[286] Former Democratic Party presidential candidate Andrew Yang, a member of the model minority, thought that his achievements had secured a place for him in society until he encountered racism yet again in the wake of Trump's comments. "It had been years since I felt that way. I grew up with semi-regular visitations of that sense of racially tinged self-consciousness. It didn't help that I was an awkward kid. But after adulthood, marriage, a career, parenthood, positions of leadership and even a presidential run, that feeling had disappeared — I thought."[287]

But Yang's call for Asian Americans to step up to display their patriotism even more at this time, to prove that they are worthy of being counted as American, is ill founded. It only serves to underscore that Asian Americans have not fully assimilated into American society and that they remain a perpetual foreigner even as the so-called model minority.[288] No minority group has yet to achieve complete acceptance and full equality. The establishment will not permit them to "outwhite Whites."[289]

In conjunction with his xenophobic speech, under this president, legal immigration is projected to decline dramatically by 49% by fiscal year 2021.[290] The loss of immigrants will adversely affect economic health. "Average annual labor force growth, a key component of the nation's economic growth, will be approximately 59% lower as a result of the administration's immigration policies, if the policies continue," concludes an analysis from the National Foundation for American Policy. [291] The contributions of immigrants in combating COVID-19 are downplayed while the current crisis is weaponized "to scapegoat immigrants and further curtail immigration."[292]

The pro-life, pro-religion, pro-Israel policies of President Trump and his appointment of conservative judges appeal to many in the evangelical camp. They turn a blind eye to his foibles and make excuses for his documented moral failures in return for policy decisions that align with their beliefs.[293] They endorse a President who uses his position of authority and power to continually marginalize and malign the oppressed. He builds walls of separation rather than tear down "the dividing wall of hostility" (Eph. 2:14). He promotes division, not unity.

The president's actions have been compared to throwing gasoline on the fire of civil unrest spreading through our nation with tweets such as "When the looting starts, the shooting starts."[294] A recent poll found that the majority of Americans agree with this assessment concluding that Trump's rhetoric about the protests has actually worsened the situation. Furthermore, comparing Trump to Biden, the latter "would do more to unite Americans rather than divide them" (64% to 33%) and "would do a better job handling racial discrimination" (64% to 34%).[295]

Trump's former personal lawyer, Michael Cohen, has noted the president's disdain for minorities who are "not my people." He also pronounced Hispanics and Blacks as being "too stupid" to vote for him.[296]

Trump disregarded the circumstances of minorities when he recently directed the Office of Management and Budget to desist from sensitivity training sessions. He considers bringing awareness about racism and white privilege "divisive."[297] In an interview with Bob Woodward, he expressed the opinion that those who believe in the narrative of white privilege have "drank the Kool-Aid."[298]

A *New York Times* article made the assessment that Trump has made himself the candidate of White America. "After a summer when hundreds of thousands of people took to the streets protesting racial injustice against Black Americans, president Trump has made it clear over the last few days that, in his view, the country's real race problem is bias against white Americans."[299]

The voice of the dominant culture is once again denying its role in ignoring and overlooking the plight of the minority. The situation has become grave over the course of Trump's first term. Re-election to a second term will only embolden him to further advance white privilege at the expense of national unity and full equality for people of color, the silenced minority.

Andrew Y. Lee holds a PhD in Religion and is Associate Director of the Global Diaspora Institute at the Wheaton College Billy Graham Center. He has served on staff at the largest Chinese churches in New York City and Chicago. He has also taught for Southern Baptist Theological Seminary, Gordon-Conwell Theological Seminary, and New Brunswick Theological Seminary. His writings are in both the academic and ministry worlds.

A Grief Unobserved
By Tamice Spencer

When they flipped his body over, the bright canary yellow blanket fell on the grass. His hoodie was damp because he'd been laying there a while and it had been raining that night. He was wearing jeans and fresh Fusion Force 20s. The red black and white ones with the red strap and the patterned flap. I recognized the Jordan's because my brother has a pair. His fade was cut the same and his skin was a darkened caramel color too. That could have been my brother under that sheet. His 7-Eleven lighter was strewn on the lawn along with the Skittles he'd bought his own little brother and they found the AriZona iced tea a little bit later. I didn't sleep that night. I kept thinking about the shoes.

That Sunday when I went to church, we sang happy songs about God's goodness and glorious reign and no one talked about Trayvon, not even the pastor. We sang songs about joy and gladness the week the 9-1-1 tapes came out, and we prayed for revival during the rallies in Sanford.

In November of the same year Trayvon died, Jordan Davis was shot to death because a white man thought his music too loud, and Rekia Boyd was shot in the head while leaving a pool party because the officer who approached her group thought her cell phone was a gun. At church they talked about how sad it was that the guy from Glee died. I remember because it was the same day the jury acquitted Trayvon's killer. They didn't know anything about that. They didn't even know his name.

I began to feel a deep and nauseous sadness that became more and more unbearable. I told my friends about this, but they didn't understand why I would be so upset about some thug in Florida being in the wrong place at the wrong time or why I was concerned about how many white people were on the jury of that other trial I'd been telling them about—the one where the boy stole the Snickers and died.

His name was Trayvon and he didn't steal, I told them. I didn't tell them about my brother and I didn't tell them about his shoes. They didn't deserve to know.

A year later in the middle of the night, Renisha McBride was shot in the face with a 12-gauge pistol grip Mossberg shotgun. She was shot through a screen door on the porch of one of her neighbors because she was knocking too loudly. A year later in New York, Eric Garner was choked to death in broad daylight for selling Newport Kings, the kind Rigby, my auntie, used to smoke. She called them "loosies." Eric told the officer he could not breathe, but it didn't matter. In Ohio one month later, John Crawford was shot inside a Walmart for picking up a gun they sold in the store while his girlfriend gathered ingredients to make s'mores. Michael Brown was shot six times and left lying face down in Ferguson, MO, in August in the middle of the road. The officer let his body fry on the asphalt of his neighborhood for four hours in front of his mother's house. Two days after that, Ezell Ford was shot in the back at close range for walking in the street. So was Laquan McDonald, only he was shot sixteen times in thirteen seconds.

The next month, a twelve-year-old boy was shot in the torso for playing with a toy gun in the park; he died the next day. His name was Tamir Rice. In April of the same year, Freddie Gray's spinal cord was snapped in half while he was being transported by police for possessing what they referred to as an illegal switchblade; they didn't buckle him in when they drove him away. In November, Jamar Clark was shot in the head while handcuffed and Akai Gurley was shot to death while walking down the stairs. Walter Scott was shot dead by an officer who lied in his report. And just across the town border only two months later, nine black men and women were massacred in their own church during Bible study. Alton Sterling was selling CDs out of his trunk at a corner store in Baton Rouge when he was pinned to the ground and shot five times, in the chest, at close range. And the very next day, the entire world watched live as Philando Castile bled to death in front of his four-year-old daughter and his girlfriend. He was shot seven times while sitting in the passenger seat. He was wearing his seatbelt.

But still the pastor didn't talk about it.

Numb is not the right word because it was sharper than that. Angry won't suffice either because it was deeper. It was as if the world was spinning, and I could not find my balance. With every hashtag, the crack in the toxic foundations of my faith grew wider. Where do you run when all you've been given is White Jesus to turn to? I could not breathe. I could not sing another damn song about joy. I didn't know it then, but I was fellowshipping with the 81% and there was leaven in the bread.

How could they be so oblivious to the issue at hand? How could they not see it? Why did they argue with me so much about it? Why did I have to calm down?

They were convinced all those who had been killed had done something wrong; something to deserve being gunned down like beasts with no family, no future, and no dignity. Why were all the pictures of the slain so dark and thuggish? Why were all the murderers shown in uniforms and family photos? The anguish was unbearable. It was the culmination of so many things that I'd ignored for so many years. How many black bodies have to drop before they cared? Didn't Jesus care? Why didn't they know any of their names? And why did all the GoFundMe money go toward George's bail instead of Trayvon's burial. Deep inside I knew something was happening to me, and I knew it was the beginning of the end. Of what?

I didn't know, I hoped it wasn't my faith, but I honestly didn't care.

I couldn't see Jesus past the pile of dead black bodies anyway. I spent the next two years in mourning.

It felt like there was trauma in my bones. Like I was carrying the pain and the weight of the entire struggle for freedom and dignity and I couldn't decide if I wanted to be free. The pain at once made me feel connected to a narrative I'd only just begun to know, and removed from a community I'd come to know too well. I chose the new narrative because in an odd way, being united with my ancestors was better than the enmeshment of the 81%. This pain gave me a sort of strength and it began to lift me. Right as I began to pick myself up, Donald J. Trump was coming down an escalator to announce his run for the presidency.

And I began seeing red.

Suddenly all those who'd encouraged me to be careful not to lose my integrity and to try and be more respectful on social media platforms didn't apply that ethic to the leaked audio of their pundit's boastful remarks on sexually assaulting women; "it's locker room talk" they said. The colleagues who'd gone on and on about facts when it came to police shootings, dismissed facts when it came to unfavorable media reports, "it's fake news" they said. The leaders who told me that anger was unbecoming railed against the young teens who were peacefully protesting the installation of the Dakota Access Pipeline and the availability of military grade assault weapons to civilians. With every news story dripping with corruption and misogyny, bigotry, and greed, xenophobia and deceit—the 81% has continued to stand unrelentingly still. I knew it was only the beginning.

But I wasn't ready.

I raged and I cried.

I argued and I lamented.

I mourned and I groaned.

The uninformed opinions of the 81% cannot and do not weigh more than a lifeless black body. So, two years and one Charlottesville later, I let it go. For there is nothing hidden that will not be exposed, and wisdom is justified by her children.

The Trump administration has been a gauntlet for the faith of this weary black soul, but I supposed the hysteria taught me to take my place and to stay there.

I am approaching this election less naive and more faithful. As I watch the leaders fumble, the idols topple, and all the statues come down, I am approaching the election with hope. A hope rested not upon the outcome of the election, but in the inevitability of the Justice of God and the vindication of the righteous.

I've realized that standing our ground is all we can really do. I find a terrible irony that I am right back where I started seeing as how "stand your ground" is the phrase that sparked the journey toward this beautiful and arduous amelioration of faith and orthodoxy.

In a way I am thankful. The experience of seeing the contrasting realities, the deceit and the idolatry that the 2016 election exposed breathed life when I'd thought my bones could no longer live. The breath of God transformed my trauma into a tempest, the tempest pulled up every root, and the journey planted them down deep into the soil of an ardent hope. When people ask me about my story, I tell them about Trayvon. I like saying his name; I owe it to him. And if I sense that they are hearing me, I say *all* their names.

There are people who have more tragic stories to tell than me, but mine is worth telling. It is a story about how the evangelicalism that served as the foundation of my faith was almost the cause of its demise. It is a story about what it feels like to be hanging on to belief by a tiny thread and the fear of disclosing it to anyone. It's a story about loss and failure and disillusionment; a broken heart and a broken will. It's also a story about survival and it began with Trayvon Martin, and his shoes.

Tamice Namae Spencer has over 15 years of experience in full-time, young adult ministry. In 2018, she established the faith-based nonprofit Sub:Culture Inc. Sub:Culture Inc. provides Black students with the resources and guidance needed to successfully incorporate their religious beliefs into their academic, professional, and personal lives, and to become pillars within their respective communities.

Meet the Editors

Jonathan Walton is the author of *Twelve Lies that Hold America Captive and the Truth that Sets Us Free*. He is also an Area Director for InterVarsity NY/NJ focusing on Spiritual Formation and Experiential Discipleship. Recognized as one of *Christianity Today*'s 33 Under 33 and one of New York's New Abolitionists, Jonathan was also the recipi-  ent of a Young Christian Leaders World Changer award. He has been featured in media outlets such as *New York Daily News*, the *Christian Post*, and *King Kulture* for his work combatting human trafficking. Jonathan earned his bachelor's degree in Creative Writing from Columbia University and holds a master's degree in the Study of the Americas from City College. He is from Southern Virginia and lives in New York City where he attends New Life Fellowship Church. You can follow him on Patreon.com/IVED, Instagram @JonathanWalton655, and Twitter @foreverfocused.

Suzie Lahoud holds two master's degrees in Middle Eastern Studies; from the Arab Baptist Theological Seminary in Beirut and Harvard University. She earned her bachelor's degree *magna cum laude* from Duke University with a double-major in Russian and Middle Eastern Studies. During her time at Harvard, she was  selected, as a grant recipient through the Ramez and Tiziana Sousou Fund, to join a group of 13 students from across Harvard's graduate schools to travel to Jordan and embark on an assessment of the dilemmas facing humanitarian actors responding to the war in Syria. She was also the recipient of the best thesis prize for her department. Suzie is a published author and has over a decade of experience living and working overseas, most recently having spent five years in Lebanon managing relief and development projects for refugee and internally displaced populations in Lebanon, Syria, and Iraq.

Sy Hoekstra is a public defender in the child welfare system in New York City. He previously was a Staff Attorney at the United States Court of Appeals for the Second Circuit. Sy graduated *cum laude* from New York University School of Law in 2014. During law school, he worked in the fields of criminal justice and disability rights. In 2010, he earned his bachelor's degree in History and German literature from Columbia University. After graduating from Columbia, he spent a year organizing college students for political advocacy in Washington, DC with International Justice Mission. Sy was born in North Dakota, grew up in the Midwest and Northeast, lived for several years as a teenager in Zurich, Switzerland, and now lives in New York City with his wife. He is a member at Trinity Grace Church where he has attended for 10 years.

Endnotes

1   Michael Lipka and Gregory A. Smith, "White evangelical approval of Trump slips, but eight-in-ten say they would vote for him," *Pew Research*, July 1, 2020, https://www.pewresearch.org/fact-tank/2020/07/01/white-evangelical-approval-of-trump-slips-but-eight-in-ten-say-they-would-vote-for-him/.

2   These are Franklin Graham and Eric Metaxas, respectively, in an interview of Graham on Metaxas's show; available on *YouTube* as "Franklin Graham claims 'demonic power' behind attacks on Trump," uploaded by *The Washington Examiner*, November 21, 2019, https://www.youtube.com/watch?v=FpU9dHv9_Bs.

3   Gabby Orr, "'Using the Lord's name in vain': Evangelicals chafe at Trump's blasphemy," *Politico*, August 12, 2019, https://www.politico.com/story/2019/08/12/trump-evangelicals-blasphemy-profanity-1456178.

4   John Piper, "Do Not Take God's Name in Vain: The Weight and Wonder of the Third Commandment," *Desiring God*, March 8, 2020, https://www.desiringgod.org/messages/do-not-take-gods-name-in-vain.

5   See Andy Rowell's account of the event and corresponding social media links: "List of worship leaders gathering at the White House on Friday, Dec 6, 2019," *AndyRowell.net*, December 11, 2019, https://www.andyrowell.net/andy_rowell/2019/12/list-of-worship-leaders-gathering-at-the-white-house-on-friday-dec-6-2019.html.

6   Fox News. "Jerry Falwell Jr.: Moderate Republicans make my blood boil," April 30, 2017, https://video.foxnews.com/v/5416587832001?playlist_id=937116552001#sp=show-clips.

7   Dave Barnhart, *Facebook*, June 25, 2018, https://www.facebook.com/553606030/posts/10156549406811031.

8   The Barna Group, 'Survey Reveals Challenges Faced by Young People," *Barna.com*, September 10, 2007, *https://www.barna.com/research/survey-reveals-challenges-faced-by-young-people/*.

9   See: David Kinnaman and Gabe Lyons, *unChristian: What a New Generation Really Thinks about Christianity...and Why It Matters* (Grand Rapids: Baker Books, 2007).

10   Jon Huang, Samuel Jacoby, Michael Strickland and K.K. Rebecca Lai, "Election 2016: Exit Polls," *New York Times*, Nov. 6, 2016, https://www.nytimes.com/interactive/2016/11/08/us/politics/election-exit-polls.html.

11   CNN, "Watch Brett Kavanaugh's Full Opening Statement," filmed September 28, 2018, video, https://www.cnn.com/videos/politics/2018/09/27/brett-kavanaugh-opening-statement-senate-hearing-vpx.cnn.

12   Ambrosino, Brandon, "'Someone's Gotta Tell the Freaking' Truth': Jerry Falwell's Aides Break Their Silence," *Politico Magazine*, September 9, 2019, https://www.politico.com/magazine/story/2019/09/09/jerry-falwell-liberty-university-loans-227914.

13   Ambrosino, Brandon, "My Weekend at the Falwells' South Beach Flophouse," *Politico Magazine*, August 25, 2017, https://www.politico.com/magazine/story/2017/08/25/jerry-falwell-miami-hostel-liberty-university-trey-falwell-215528.

14   Eusebius, *Church History, Documenta Catholica Omnia*, ~340AD, https://www.documentacatholicaomnia.eu/03d/0265-0339,_Eusebius_Caesariensis,_Church_History,_EN.pdf.

15   Eusebius, *The Life of the Blessed Emperor Constantine, Internet Medieval Sourcebook,* Fordham University Center for Medieval Studies, May 1997, https://sourcebooks.fordham.edu/basis/vita-constantine.asp.

16   Steve Newcomb, "Five Hundred Years of Injustice: The Legacy of Fifteenth Century Religious Prejudice," *Shaman's Drum*. Fall 1992, p. 18-20, http://ili.nativeweb.org/sdrm_art.html.

17   John Winthrop, "City Upon a Hill," 1630, https://www.gilderlehrman.org/sites/default/files/inline-pdfs/Winthrop%27s%20City%20upon%20a%20Hill.pdf.

18   John Winthrop, "John Winthrop Dreams of a City on a Hill," The American Yawp Reader, 1630, https://www.americanyawp.com/reader/colliding-cultures/john-winthrop-dreams-of-a-city-on-a-hill-1630/.

19   History.com Editors, "Congress Issues a 'Declaration on the Causes and Necessity of Taking Up Arms,'" *History,* October 15, 2010, https://www.history.com/this-day-in-history/congress-issues-a-declaration-on-the-causes-and-necessity-of-taking-up-arms.

20   Blakemore, Erin, "Why Thomas Jefferson Rewrote the Bible Without Jesus' Miracles and Resurrection," *History*, July 31, 2019, https://www.history.com/news/thomas-jefferson-bible-religious-beliefs.

21   Michael O. Emerson and Christian Smith, *Divided by Faith: Evangelical Religion and the Problem of Race in America* (New York: Oxford University Press, 2001).

22   Clifford Geertz and Robert Darnton. *The Interpretation of Cultures: Selected Essays.* (New York: Basic Books, 2017), 90.

23   William Cummings, "'Battle for the Soul of the Nation': Before They Were Running Mates, Joe Biden and Kamala Harris Both Used Slogan," *USA TODAY*, August 13, 2020, https://www.usatoday.com/story/news/politics/elections/2020/08/13/biden-and-harris-both-see-election-fight-soul-nation/3355971001/.

24   Colin Campbell, "Donald Trump Trademarked a Ronald Reagan Slogan and Would like to Stop Other Republicans from Using It," Business Insider, May 12, 2015, https://www.businessinsider.com/donald-trump-trademarked-make-america-great-again-2015-5.

25   Danny Halhbohm, *You are not alone Mr. President*, 2020, Paint, 2020, http://www.inspired-art.com/gallery_13/Mr._President.html.

26   Jon McNaughton, *Legacy of Hope*, 2020, Paint, 2020, https://jonmcnaughton.com/legacy-of-hope/.

27   Oscar Wilde, *The Decay of Lying* in *Intentions* (1891)

28   Ayesha Rascoe and Tamara Keith, "Trump Defends 'Law And Order' Symbolism Of Photo-Op At St. John's Church," NPR.org, June 3, 2020, https://www.npr.org/2020/06/03/868779265/trump-defends-symbolism-of-photo-op-at-st-johns-church.

29   Stephan Schultze, "The Trump Prophecy," *Vudu.Com*, October 2, 2018, https://www.vudu.com/content/movies/details/The-Trump-Prophecy/1050752.

30   Donald   Trump,   "https://www.youtube.Com/watch?V=-JK6K-SWTAtM," www.youtube.com, July 15, 2020, https://www.youtube.com/watch?v=JK6K-sWTAtM.

31   Donald Trump, "Statement by the President," *White House Remarks*, June 1, 2020, https://www.whitehouse.gov/briefings-statements/statement-by-the-president-39/.

32   Sarah Pulliam Bailey, "White evangelicals voted overwhelmingly for Donald Trump, exit polls show," *The Washington Post*, November 9, 2016, https://www.washingtonpost.com/news/acts-of-faith/wp/2016/11/09/exit-polls-show-white-evangelicals-voted-overwhelmingly-for-donald-trump/

33   Brandon Andress, Reimagined Beatitudes posted in a private Facebook group, and reprinted with permission.

34   Stephen Backhouse, "Followers of the Way III," *Tent Theology,* Podcast audio, July 13, 2020, https://tent-talks.simplecast.com/episodes/followers-on-the-way-iii.

35   Adrienne LaFrance, "The Prophecies of Q," *The Atlantic,* June 2020, https://www.theatlantic.com/magazine/archive/2020/06/qanon-nothing-can-stop-what-is-coming/610567/;

Abby Ohlheiser, "Evangelicals are looking for answers online. They're finding QAnon instead:

How the growing pro-Trump movement is preying on churchgoers to spread its conspiracy theories," *MIT Technology Review*, August 26, 2020, https://www.technologyreview.com/2020/08/26/1007611/how-qanon-is-targeting-evangelicals/.

36   Anna Merlin, "United States of Conspiracy," interview by Bob Garfield, *On the Media* WNYC, July 1, 2020, https://www.wnycstudios.org/podcasts/otm/episodes/united-states-conspiracy-on-the-media-1.

37   Walter Brueggemann and Davis Hankins, *The Prophetic Imagination* (Minneapolis: Fortress Press, 2018).

38   Hal Lindsey and Carole C. Carlson, *The Late Great Planet Earth* (Grand Rapids: Zondervan, 1970).

39   Ohlheiser, https://www.technologyreview.com/2020/08/26/1007611/how-qanon-is-targeting-evangelicals/.

40   Tenpas, Katherine Dunn, "Tracking turnover in the Trump administration," *Brookings,* September 2020, https://www.brookings.edu/research/tracking-turnover-in-the-trump-administration/.

41   Michael Lipka and Gregory A. Smith. "White Evangelical Approval of Trump Slips, but Eight-in-Ten Say They Would Vote for Him." *Pew Research Center*, July 29, 2020, https://www.pewresearch.org/fact-tank/2020/07/01/white-evangelical-approval-of-trump-slips-but-eight-in-ten-say-they-would-vote-for-him/.

42   Terence McArdle. "The 'Law and Order' Campaign That Won Richard Nixon the White House 50 Years Ago," *The Washington Post,* November 5, 2018, https://www.washingtonpost.com/history/2018/11/05/law-order-campaign-that-won-richard-nixon-white-house-years-ago/.

43   James Limburg, "Commentary on Isaiah 1:10-18 by James Limburg," *Luther Seminary,* October 31, 2010, https://www.workingpreacher.org/preaching.aspx?commentary_id=734.

44   John Goldingay, "Faithfulness in the Exercise of Power," in *The Theology of the Book of Isaiah (*Downers Grove, IL: IVP Academic, 2014), 19–21.

45   Martin Luther King. "Letter from a Birmingham Jail [King, Jr.]," University of Pennsylvania, accessed August 29, 2020, https://www.africa.upenn.edu/Articles_Gen/Letter_Birmingham.html.

46   Jemar Tisby, Essay In *The Color of Compromise: the Truth about the American Church's Complicity in Racism*, (Grand Rapids: Zondervan, 2019), 142.

47   Kevin Michael Kruse. "Which Side Are You On?", In *One Nation Under God: How Corporate America Invented Christian America* (New York, NY: Basic Books, 2016), 243.

48   Donald Trump, "'I Will Be President for All Americans' - Transcript of Donald Trump's Election Night Victory Speech," *Los Angeles Times*, November 9, 2016, https://www.latimes.com/politics/la-na-pol-trump-election-night-speech-20161108-story.html.

49   Pew Research Center, Global Attitudes and Trends, "Emerging and Developing Economies are Much More Optimistic than Rich Countries about the Future," October 9, 2014, https://www.pewresearch.org/global/2014/10/09/emerging-and-developing-economies-much-more-optimistic-than-rich-countries-about-the-future/; George Gao, "How do Americans Stand Out from the Rest of the World?" *Pew Research Center, Facttank*, March 12, 2015, https://www.pewresearch.org/fact-tank/2015/03/12/how-do-americans-stand-out-from-the-rest-of-the-world/; Nicki Lisa Cole, "Four Things That Set Americans Apart and Why They Matter," *ThoughtCo*, Feb. 11, 2020, thoughtco.com/what-makes-americans-unique-4048010.

50   Jack Alexander, *The God Impulse: The Power of Mercy in an Unmerciful World* (Grand Rapids: Baker Books, 2018) Ebook edition, location 536.

51   Lael Arrington, "Trump is Mistaken: Hitting Back 'Twice as Hard' Really Isn't the Way to Win," *The Stream*, April 24, 2016, https://stream.org/trump-mistaken-hitting-back-twice-hard-not-way-to-win/.

52   Bishop Robert Barron, *Catholicism*, Word on Fire, 2011, Episode 2: "Happy Are We: The Teachings of Jesus," Scene 4: "The Path of Non-violence," 26:58-28:53. Videocassette (VHS).

53   Oral History Interview with John Lewis, *Documenting the American South*, November 20, 1973, https://docsouth.unc.edu/sohp/A-0073/excerpts/excerpt_7341.html; Erin Blakemore, "John Lewis' Arrest Records Are Finally Uncovered," *SmithsonianMag.com*, December 1, 2016, https://www.smithsonianmag.com/smart-news/john-lewis-arrest-records-are-finally-uncovered-180961255/; Renee Graham, "John Lewis—the 'Conscience of Congress,' the Conscience of America," *Microsoft News*, July 18, 2020. https://www.msn.com/en-us/news/us/john-lewis-e2-80-94-the-e2-80-98conscience-of-congress-e2-80-99-the-con-science-of-america/ar-BB16UbXg.

54   *On Being with Krista Tippett,* "John Lewis: Love in Action," March 28, 2013, https://onbeing.org/programs/john-lewis-love-in-action/#transcript.

55   F. Michael Wuthrich and Melvyn Ingleby, "The Pushback Against Populism: Running on 'Radical Love' in Turkey," *Journal of Democracy*, April 2020, https://www.journalofdemocracy.org/articles/the-pushback-against-populism-running-on-radical-love-in-turkey/.

56   Leo Tolstoy, *A Letter to a Hindu* (1908), III, https://en.wikisource.org/wiki/A_Letter_to_a_Hindu.

57   Dr. Cornel West, *Facebook*, October 28, 2010. West often repeats this in public addresses and private conversations.

58   Kasprak, Alex, "Abortion Rates Fall During Democratic Administrations and Rise During Republican Ones," *Snopes*, November 11, 2016, https://www.snopes.com/fact-check/abortion-rates-presidencies/.

59   Glen H. Stassen and David P. Gushee, *Kingdom Ethics: Following Jesus in Contemporary Context* (Downers Grove: IVP Academic, 2003), 467-483.

60   Elizabeth Dias, "Christianity will Have Power," *New York Times,* August 9, 2020, https://www.nytimes.com/2020/08/09/us/evangelicals-trump-christianity.html?campaign_id=9&emc=edit_nn_20200810&instance_id=21130&nl=the-morning&regi_id=93344751&segment_id=35682&te=1&user_id=b19c16e3ca-8c1e367d0b25121ef2306a.

61   In "For the Health of the Nation: An Evangelical Call to Civic Engagement," *the National Association of Evangelicals* commends: 1. Protecting religious freedom and liberty of conscience, 2. Safeguarding the nature and sanctity of human life, 3. Strengthening marriages, families and children, 4. Seeking justice and compassion for the poor and vulnerable, 5. Preserving human rights, 6. Pursuing racial justice and reconciliation, 7. Promoting just peace and restraining violence, 8. Caring for God's creation.

National Association of Evangelicals, "For the Health of the Nation: An Evangelical Call to Civic Responsibility," accessed September 14, 2020, https://www.nae.net/for-the-health-of-the-nation/.

62   Tom Murse, "Why Donald Trump's Companies Went Bankrupt: Details About the 6 Trump Corporate Bankruptcies," *ThoughtCo.,* October 16, 2019, https://www.thoughtco.com/donald-trump-business-bankruptcies-4152019.

63   Peter Baker, "Trump Is Fighting So Many Legal Battles, It's Hard to Keep Track," *The New York Times*, November 6, 2019, https://www.nytimes.com/2019/11/06/us/politics/donald-trump-lawsuits-investigations.html.

64   Peter Nicholas, "John Kelly Finally Lets Loose on Trump," *The Atlantic,* February 13, 2020, https://www.theatlantic.com/politics/archive/2020/02/john-kelly-alexander-vindman-north-korea-and-trump/606496/.

65   Amanda Macias, "Read Former Defense Secretary Mattis' Statement on Trump's handling of nationwide protests," *CNBC*, June 3, 2020, https://www.cnbc.com/2020/06/03/read-mattis-statement-on-trumps-handling-of-nationwide-protests.html.

66   Mark Bowden, "Top Military Officers Unload on Trump," *The Atlantic*, November 2019, https://www.theatlantic.com/magazine/archive/2019/11/military-officers-trump/598360/.

67   World Relief, "World Relief Strongly Condemns the Trump Administration for its Reported Plan to Abandon Persecuted Christians and Other Refugees," July 19, 2019, https://worldrelief.org/world-relief-strongly-condemns-the-trump-administration-for-its-reported-plan-to-abandon-persecuted-christians-and-other-refugees/;

Arnold Isaacs, "Trump's Cruel Refugee Policies Are Somehow Getting Worse," October 22, 2019, https://www.thenation.com/article/archive/trump-public-charge-local-option/

68   Kathleen Newland, "The U.S. Record Shows Refugees Are Not a Threat," *Migration Policy Institute,* October 2015, https://www.migrationpolicy.org/news/us-record-shows-refugees-are-not-threat?gclid=EAIaIQobChMIrvP25KyR6wIVkxh9Ch0WYAMOEAAYAiAAEgLwDPD_BwE.

69   Michelle Alexander, *The New Jim Crow: Mass Incarceration in the Age of Colorblindness* (New York: The New Press, 2012).

70   William J. Stuntz, *The Collapse of American Criminal Justice* (Cambridge: Belknap Press, 2011).

71 For an accessible Christian understanding of systemic evil, see: Tim Keller, "Racism and Corporate Evil: A White Guy's Perspective," *Desiring God,* YouTube, August 26, 2017, https://www.youtube.com/watch?v=EhJJcTKTVGo&feature=youtu.be.

72 Jeremy Bowen, "Trump's Middle East peace plan: 'Deal of the Century' is huge gamble," *BBC,* January 29, 2020, https://www.bbc.com/news/world-middle-east-51263815.

73 Ron Sider has written a helpful overview asking if abortion "trumps" all other issues in the 2020 presidential election. He deals with the sanctity of life from conception to natural death. Ron Sider, "Does Abortion Trump Everything Else," *Ron Sider Blog*, August 17, 2020, https://ronsiderblog.substack.com/p/does-abortion-trump-everything-else.

74 Editors' note: the author wrote this essay prior to the death of Justice Ruth Bader Ginsburg on September 18, 2020.

75 Tetsunao Yamamori and C. René Padilla, eds., *The Local Church, Agent of Transformation: An Ecclesiology for Integral Mission* (Buenos Aires, Kairos Ediciones, 2004), 9.

76 Robert Chao Romero, *Brown Church: Five Centuries of Latina/o Social Justice, Theology, and Identity* (Downers Grove: IVP Academic, 2020), 208-209.

77 For a detailed discussion of the family of Herod, see, N.T. Wright, *Jesus and the Victory of God* (Minneapolis: Fortress Press, 377, 482, 304, 284-286).

78 Jack Jenkins and Emily McFarlan Miller, "Citing Scripture, Pence switches out Jesus for the American flag in convention speech," *Religion News Service*, August 27, 2020, https://religionnews.com/2020/08/27/citing-scripture-pence-switches-out-jesus-for-the-american-flag-in-convention-speech/.

79 Katie Reilly, "Here Are All the Times Donald Trump Insulted Mexico," *Time*, August 31, 2016, https://time.com/4473972/donald-trump-&/

80 For more on Manifest Destiny, see Robert Chao Romero, *Brown Church: Five Centuries of Latina/o Social Justice, Theology, and Identity,* (Downers Grove: IVP Academic: 2020), 101-104.

81 Associated Press, "Children Fleeing Danger Come to the U.S. for Refuge and are Expelled," August 6, 2020, https://www.latimes.com/world-nation/story/2020-08-06/seeking-refuge-in-us-children-fleeing-danger-are-expelled.

82 Jens Manuel Krogstad, "Key Facts about Refugees to the U.S." *Pew Research Center,* October 7, 2019, https://www.pewresearch.org/fact-tank/2019/10/07/key-facts-about-refugees-to-the-u-s/.

83 "Universal Declaration of Human Rights," United Nations, accessed August, 24, 2020, https://www.un.org/en/universal-declaration-human-rights/.

84 Nadwa Mossad, "Annual Flow Report: Refugees and Asylees 2017," Department of Homeland Security, March 2019,

https://www.dhs.gov/sites/default/files/publications/Refugees_Asylees_2017.pdf.

85 Human Rights Watch, "El Salvador: Events of 2018," *World Report 2018,* https://www.hrw.org/world-report/2019/country-chapters/el-salvador. While there has been some improvement in the past two years in the homicide rates for the Northern Triangle countries, analysts note that organized crime remains in control of the same amount of territory but that apparent agreements between the governments and the gang leaders have contributed to a drop in the total number of homicides. See also: Alex Papadovassilakis, "Are El Salvador's Gangs Behind Historic Murder Drop?" InSight Crime, January 20, 2020, https://www.insightcrime.org/news/analysis/gang-truce-behind-el-salvador-historic-murder-drop/). The continued domination by gangs means that individuals who are personally targeted as a result of their religious commitment (for example) still merit asylum as their government cannot protect them from persecution.

86 "The 1951 Convention relating to the Status of Refugees and its 1967 Protocol," UNHCR The UN Refugee Agency, September 2011, https://www.unhcr.org/en-us/about-us/background/4ec262df9/1951-convention-relating-status-refugees-its-1967-protocol.html.

87 Rebecca Rainey, "Wolf and Cooch," *Politico*, November 14, 2019, https://www.politico.com/newsletters/morning-shift/2019/11/14/wolf-and-cooch-782366.

88   All scriptural references in this article use *The Holy Bible, New International Version.* (Grand Rapids: Zondervan Publishing House, 2011).

89   Rev. Alexia Salvatierra and Dr. Peter Heltzel, *Faith-Rooted Organizing: Mobilizing the Church in Service to the World* (Downers Grove: InterVarsity Press, 2014).

90   Adam Gabbatt, "Donald Trump's Tirade on Mexico's 'Drugs and Rapists' Outrages US Latinos," June 16, 2015, *The Guardian,* https://www.theguardian.com/us-news/2015/jun/16/donald-trump-mexico-presidential-speech-latino-hispanic.

91   "MS-13 Gang: The Story behind One of the World's Most Brutal Street Gangs," *BBC News,* April 19, 2017, April 19, 2017, https://www.bbc.com/news/world-us-canada-39645640.

92   Natalia Kohn Rivera, Noemi Vega Quiñones, and Kristy Garza Robinson, *Hermanas: Deepening our Identity and Growing our Influence* (Downers Grove: InterVarsity Press, 2019), 42.

93   Alan K. Simpson, "S.1200 - 99th Congress (1985-1986): Immigration Reform and Control Act of 1986," November 6, 1986, https://www.congress.gov/bill/99th-congress/senate-bill/1200.

94   Sandra Van Opstal, "Sandra Van Opstal's Message," video, 36:08, Lecture, Racial Reconciliation Conference, New Life Fellowship Church, New York City, https://youtu.be/H-jTDVWjVSo.

95   "U.S. Abortion Rate Continues to Decline, Hits Historic Low," *Guttmacher Institute,* September 1, 2020, https://www.guttmacher.org/state-policy/explore/state-funding-abortion-under-medicaid.

96   "U.S. Abortion Rate Continues to Decline, Reaching Historic Low in 2017," *Guttmacher Institute,* September 18, 2019, https://www.guttmacher.org/news-release/2019/us-abortion-rate-continues-decline-reaching-historic-low-2017.

97   Janet Adamy, "U.S. Birthrates Fall to Record Low," *The Wall Street Journal,* May 20, 2020, https://www.wsj.com/articles/u-s-birthrates-fall-to-record-low-11589947260.

98   Elizabeth Nash and Joerg Dreweke, "The U.S. Abortion Rate Continues to Drop: Once Again, State Abortion Restrictions Are Not the

Main Driver," *Guttmacher Institute*, September 18, 2019, https://www.guttmacher.org/gpr/2019/09/us-abortion-rate-continues-drop-once-again-state-abortion-restrictions-are-not-main.

99   Tara C. Jatlaoui, MD; Lindsay Eckhaus, MPH; Michele G. Mandel; Antoinette Nguyen, MD; Titilope Oduyebo, MD; Emily Petersen, MD; Maura K. Whiteman, PhD, "Abortion Surveillance – United States, 2016," Centers for Disease Control and Prevention, Surveillance Summaries/November 29, 2019/68 (11); 1-41, https://www.cdc.gov/mmwr/volumes/68/ss/ss6811a1.htm?s_cid=ss6811a1_w%22%20\.

100   Sarah McCammon, "Planned Parenthood Withdraws from Title X Program Over Trump Abortion Rule," *All Things Considered: NPR*, August 19, 2019, https://www.npr.org/2019/08/19/752438119/planned-parenthood-out-of-title-x-over-trump-rule.

101   David French, "A Federal Judge Has Defied the Law to Protect Abortion," *National Review,* April 26, 2019, https://www.nationalreview.com/2019/04/a-federal-judge-has-defied-the-law-to-protect-abortion/.

102   Sam Dorman, "Planned Parenthood reports record-high abortions, taxpayer funding amid battles with Republicans," *Fox News*, January 7, 2020, https://www.foxnews.com/politics/planned-parenthood-record-abortions-government-funding.

103   Aaron Gregg, "Stimulus turns political as SBA tries to claw back funding from Planned Parenthood," *The Washington Post*, May 23, 2020, https://www.washingtonpost.com/business/2020/05/23/planned-parenthood-sba-ppp-loans/?arc404=true.

104   Carrie Budoff Brown, "Stop These Abortions," *Ben Smith Blog: Political News and Analysis (Politico)*, March 29, 2008, https://www.politico.com/blogs/ben-smith/2008/03/stop-these-abortions-007374.

105   Supreme Court of the United States "JUNE MEDICAL SERVICES L. L. C. ET AL. v. RUSSO, INTERIM SECRETARY, LOUISIANA DEPARTMENT OF HEALTH AND HOSPITALS," Argued March 4, 2020; Decided June 29, 2020, https://www.supremecourt.gov/opinions/19pdf/18-1323_c07d.pdf. Editors' note: the author wrote this article before the recent death of Justice Ruth Bader Ginsburg.

106   Ibid.

107   Joan Biskupic, "How Brett Kavanaugh tried to sidestep abortion and Trump financial docs cases," *CNN Politics,* July 29, 2020, https://edition.cnn.com/2020/07/29/politics/brett-kavanaugh-supreme-court-abortion-trump-documents/index.html.

108   Carrie Severino, "Why Josh Hawley's New Supreme Court Litmus Test Is False Advertising," *The Federalist,* August 5, 2020, https://thefederalist.com/2020/08/05/why-josh-hawleys-new-supreme-court-litmus-test-is-false-advertising/.

109   "An Overview of Abortion Laws," *Guttmacher Institute*, September 1, 2020, https://www.guttmacher.org/state-policy/explore/overview-abortion-laws. Editors' note: this sentence originally contained a hyperlink to the study cited here.

110   "State Funding of Abortion Under Medicaid," *Guttmacher Institute*, September 1, 2020, https://www.guttmacher.org/state-policy/explore/state-funding-abortion-under-medicaid.

111   Maggie Astor, "What is the Hyde Amendment? A Look at Its Impact as Biden Reverses His Stance," *The New York Times,* June 9, 2019, https://www.nytimes.com/2019/06/07/us/politics/what-is-the-hyde-amendment.html.

112   "Abortions by State of Residence," *Guttmacher Institute*, 2018, https://data.guttmacher.org/states/map?topics=68&dataset=data. Editors' note: this sentence originally contained a hyperlink to the source cited here.

113   Caitlin Myers, Rachel Jones, and Ushma Upadhyay, "Changes in abortion access and incidence in a post-Roe World," *Middlebury College Department of Economics,* (July 2019), http://community.middlebury.edu/~cmyers/files/postroe.pdf. Editors' note: this sentence originally contained a hyperlink to the study cited here.

114   Editors' note: the author originally published this article as a newsletter, and then as an online article.

115   Tricia C. Bruce, "How Americans Understand Abortion: a comprehensive interview study of abortion attitudes in the U.S." University of Notre Dame McGrath Institute for Church Life, (2020), https://news.nd.edu/assets/395804/how_americans_understand_abortion_final_7_15_20.pdf.

116   John McCormack,"The Hyde Amendment is in Peril," *National Review*, August 20, 2020, https://www.nationalreview.com/magazine/2020/09/07/a-biden-presidency-would-imperil-the-hyde-amendment-as-never-before/. Editors' note: this sentence originally contained a hyperlink to the source cited above.

117   Gabrielle Blair, "Men Cause 100% of Unwanted Pregnancies," Human Parts, Sept 24, 2018, https://humanparts.medium.com/men-cause-100-of-unwanted-pregnancies-eb0e8288a7e5.

118   Ariana Eunjung Cha, "Quadriplegic Man's Death from Covid-19 Spotlights Questions of Disability, Race and Family," *The Washington Post,* July 5, 2020, https://www.washingtonpost.com/health/2020/07/05/coronavirus-disability-death/.

119   Chris Kaposy,"The Ethical Case for Having a Baby with Down Syndrome," *The New York Times,* April 16, 2018, https://www.nytimes.com/2018/04/16/opinion/down-syndrome-abortion.html.

120   David French, Do" Pro-Lifers Who Reject Trump Have 'Blood on their Hands'?" August 23, 2020, https://frenchpress.thedispatch.com/p/do-pro-lifers-who-reject-trump-have. Editors' note: the article cited here by David French is reprinted in this anthology.

121   The author uses Kānaka Maoli, Kānaka, Hawaiian, and Native Hawaiian interchangeably. All refer to the original human inhabitants of Hawai'i.

122   David E. Stannard, *Before the Horror: The Population of Hawai'i on the Eve of Western Contact* (Honolulu, Hawaii: Social Science Research Institute, University of Hawaii, 1989); Liliuokalani, *Hawaii's Story By Hawaii's Queen*, 9. print (Honolulu, Hawaii: Mutual publ, 2004).

123   'Ka Baibala Hemolele' (the Hawaiian Language Bible) was translated from the original languages and not through the English language.

124   Reference is made to a mat woven from the leaves of the pandanus tree, 'hala' also means to pass and can be used poetically and metaphorically to mean death or the passing from this life or phase into the next.

125   In Hawaiian language, 'honua' means both earth and placenta.

126   Mary Kawena Pukui, ed., "'Ōlelo No'eau: Hawaiian Proverbs & Poetical Sayings," *Bernice P. Bishop Museum Special Publication,* no. 71, (Honolulu, Hawai'i: Bishop Museum Press, 1983).

127   See Note 1.

128   'Ai means "food" or "to eat" and is often used to refer to kalo (taro), one of the main staples in the traditional Hawaiian diet. 'Ōlelo means "language" or "speech."

129   The power of the spoken word is demonstrated consistently throughout the old and new testament. Some additional examples include: Gen. 1; Prov. 18:21; Matt. 8:5-13; Mark 7:20; Mark 11:20-24; Luke 7:1-10. This is by no means an exhaustive list.

130   This is not an exhaustive list, as there are many other references of Jesus' interactions with women throughout the gospel.

131   The Kumulipo, one of the Hawaiian creation chants, begins in pō (night/darkness). Similar to the biblical account presented in Genesis, the mele (song/chant) goes through each era describing the organisms, lands, and people being formed.

132   We also see biblical accounts reminding the people of Israel to remember, and to teach their children, of their own history with the Lord. "So the next generation would know them, even the children yet to be born, and they in turn would tell their children. Then they would put their trust in God and would not forget his deeds but would keep his commands. That they would not be like their ancestors- a stubborn and rebellious generation, whose hearts were not loyal to God, whose spirits were not faithful to him." (Ps. 78:6-8, NIV).

133   *"Nuclear Legacy,"* Marshallese Educational Initiative, accessed September 4, 2020, https://www.mei.ngo/nuclear.; Susanne Rust, "How the U.S. Betrayed the Marshall Islands, Kindling the next Nuclear Disaster," *Los Angeles Times,* November 10, 2019, https://www.latimes.com/projects/marshall-islands-nuclear-testing-sea-level-rise/.

134   Darlene Keju-Johnson, "For the Good of Mankind," *Seattle Journal for Social Science* 2, no. 1 (May 2003), https://digitalcommons.law.seattleu.edu/sjsj/vol2/iss1/59/.

135   Adam Jonas Horowitz, *Nuclear Savage: The Islands of Secret Project 4.1*, DVD (Primordial Soup Company and Equatorial Films, 2011).

136   Keju-Johnson, https://digitalcommons.law.seattleu.edu/sjsj/vol2/iss1/59/.

137   Donald J. Trump, "Energy And Environment," Promises Made, Promises Kept!, n.d., https://www.promiseskept.com/achievement/overview/energy-and-environment/.; Nadja Popovich, Livia Albeck-Ripka, and Kendra Pierre-Louis, "The Trump Administration Is Reversing 100 Environmental Rules. Here's the Full List.," The New York Times, July 15, 2020, https://www.nytimes.com/interactive/2020/climate/trump-environment-rollbacks.html.

138   Ashley Westerman, "'We Need Support': Pacific Islands Seek Help And Unity To Fight Climate Change," *NPR*, October 5, 2019, https://www.npr.org/2019/10/05/764570478/we-need-support-pacific-islands-seek-help-and-unity-to-fight-climate-change.

139   Mark Charles and Soong-Chan Rah, *Unsettling Truths: The Ongoing, Dehumanizing Legacy of the Doctrine of Discovery* (Downers Grove, Illinois: IVP, an imprint of InterVarsity Press, 2019).

140   Time Staff, "Here's Donald Trump's Presidential Announcement Speech," *TIME*, June 16, 2016, https://time.com/3923128/donald-trump-announcement-speech/.

141   Nick Corasaniti, "A Look at Trump's Immigration Plan, Then and Now," *The New York Times*, August 31, 2016, https://www.nytimes.com/interactive/2016/08/31/us/politics/donald-trump-immigration-changes.html.

142   Donald J. Trump, "Immigration," Promises Made, Promises Kept!, n.d., accessed September 4, 2020. https://www.promiseskept.com/achievement/overview/immigration/#.

143   Moʻo refers to a succession or series. Meheu can mean track, footprint, trail, or clue.

144   Young-Hak Hyun, "Minjung the Suffering Servant and Hope," in *Unpublished Paper Presented at Union Theological Seminary in New York*, 1982. Quoted in Andrew Park, *Racial Conflict and Healing* (New York: Orbis Books, 1996), p. 9.

145   Today "Ke Aloha o ka Haku" is commonly known as "The Queen's Prayer.".

146   Liliuokalani, *Hawaii's Story By Hawaii's Queen.*

147   Liliuokalani, *The Queen's Songbook,* (Honolulu: Hui Hānai, 1999), p. 60.

148   The metaphor of pearls was chosen intentionally to speak to the process of formation as well as the value of what was shared.

149   Reference made to Isaiah 61.

150   Thomas Merton, *The Seven Storey Mountain* (Boston: Mariner Books, 1998), 72.

151   Brittney Cooper, "The right's made-up God: How bigots invented a white supremacist Jesus," *Salon,* April 2, 2015, https://www.salon.com/2015/04/01/the_rights_made_up_god_how_bigots_invented_a_white_supremacist_jesus/.

152   Walter Brueggemann and Davis Hankins, *The Prophetic Imagination* (Minneapolis: Fortress Press, 2018), 23.

153   "When Religion Becomes Idolatry: Reflections on the Politics of Identity in the Midst of the Syrian Crisis," IMES Blog, October 22, 2015, https://abtslebanon.org/2015/10/22/when-religion-becomes-idolatry-a-reflection-on-the-politics-of-identity-in-the-midst-of-the-syrian-crisis/.

154   Genesis 12:1-3, fulfilled in Christ according to Galatians 3:14, 16, 29.

155   Peter Bergen, *Trump and His Generals: The Cost of Chaos,* (Penguin Press, 2019).

156   Michael LaForgia and Walt Bogdanich, 2020. "Why Bombs Made in America Have Been Killing Civilians in Yemen." *The New York Times,* May 16, 2020. https://www.nytimes.com/2020/05/16/us/arms-deals-raytheon-yemen.html.

157   Human Rights Watch, "World Report 2019", 2019, https://www.hrw.org/sites/default/files/world_report_download/hrw_world_report_2019.pdf

158   Mike Stone, "Defense firms say Trump's Saudi arms deal will create 500 American jobs, while Trump claimed as many as 500,000," *Business Insider*. October 30, 2018. https://www.businessinsider.com/trump-saudi-arms-deal-job-creation-2018-10.

159   *BBC News*. "US ends aid to Palestinian refugee agency Unrwa," September 1, 2018, sec. US & Canada. https://www.bbc.com/news/world-us-canada-45377336.

160   Steven A. Cook, "The Middle East Plays Hardball, and the Palestinians Always Lose", *Foreign Policy*, August 20, 2020, https://foreignpolicy.com/2020/08/20/the-middle-east-plays-hardball-and-the-palestinians-always-lose/.

161   Munther Isaac and Jamal Khader, "Donald Trump Is Complicit in a Catastrophe for Christians - Middle East News" *Haaretz.Com,* May 6, 2020. https://www.haaretz.com/middle-east-news/.premium-donald-trump-is-complicit-in-a-catastrophe-for-christians-1.8825832.

162   "Trump authorises sanctions against ICC officials," *Al Jazeera*, June 11, 2020, https://www.aljazeera.com/news/2020/06/trump-authorises-sanctions-international-court-officials-200611134349115.html.

163   Rashid Khalidi, *The Hundred Years' War on Palestine: A History of Settler Colonialism and Resistance, 1917-2017*. NY: Metropolitan Books, 2020), 223.

164   Allison Kaplan Sommer, "Trump Says Moved Embassy to Jerusalem 'For the Evangelicals'," *Haaretz*, August 19, 2020, https://www.haaretz.com/israel-news/.premium-trump-israel-moved-embassy-jerusalem-for-evangelicals-more-excited-than-jews-1.9081183.

165   V. V. B., "Why America Does Not Take in More Syrian Refugees", *The Economist*, October 18, 2015, https://www.economist.com/the-economist-explains/2015/10/18/why-america-does-not-take-in-more-syrian-refugees.

166   Margaret K Nydell, *Understanding Arabs: A Contemporary Guide to Arab Society,* 6th ed, (Boston: Intercultural Press, 2018).

167   Ibid.

168   Eric Lichtblau, "Hate Crimes Against American Muslims Most Since Post-9/11 Era." *The New York Times,* September 17, 2016. https://www.nytimes.com/2016/09/18/us/politics/hate-crimes-american-muslims-rise.html.

169   Peter Bergen, *Trump and His Generals: The Cost of Chaos,* (New York: Penguin Press, 2019).

170   World Evangelical Alliance, "A Statement by the World Evangelical Alliance on the Recent Violence in the Middle East," January 10, 2020,   https://worldea.org/en/news/a-statement-by-the-world-evangelical-alliance-on-the-recent-violence-in-the-middle-east/statement-by-the-world-evangelical-alliance-on-the-recent-violence-in-the-middle-east/.

171   CBN News, "Iran Statement From Evangelical Group Draws Fire Over Question of Moral Equivalency," January 11 2020, https://www1.cbn.com/cbnnews/world/2020/january/iran-statement-from-evangelical-group-draws-fire-over-question-of-moral-equivalency.

172   John Wesley Reid, "Evangelical Advisor to Trump Calls for Solidarity with the Vatican," *CBN News,* August 8, 2017, https://www1.cbn.com/cbnnews/us/2017/august/evangelical-advisor-to-trump-calls-for-solidarity-with-the-vatican.

173   Jeane Kirkpatrick, "The Myth of Moral Equivalence," *Imprimis* 15, No. 1 (January 1986): https://imprimis.hillsdale.edu/the-myth-of-moral-equivalence/.

174   "Debriefing Iran and 2020 as Christians," released January 8, 2020 on the podcast *Christian Politics*, hosted by Michael Wear and Justin Giboney, https://podcasts.apple.com/us/podcast/cp-debriefing-iran-and-2020-as-christians/id1289898626?i=1000461934989.

175   "Debriefing Iran," *Christian Politics.*

176   Ibid.

177   Miroslav Volf, *Exclusion and Embrace: A Theological Exploration of Identity, Otherness, and Reconciliation*, 1996, p. 198.

178   Christian media includes "end-times prophecy" industry which has promoted fictitious Middle Eastern political narratives for decades. I blogged about this here:

"From our Vantage Point: The Signs of the Times Unfolding in the Middle East Today," a blogpost by Wissam al-Saliby, displayed on *Arab Baptist Theological Seminary,* May 18, 2017, https://abtslebanon. org/2017/05/18/from-our-vantage-point-the-signs-of-the-times-unfolding-in-the-middle-east-today/.

179   Iran is not and never was listed as a violator of children rights by the United Nations. See: "In Focus," *United Nations,* https://childrenandarmedconflict.un.org/.

180   "Iran blasts UN dropping Saudi-Yemen coalition from blacklist," *Al-Jazeera,* June 17, 2020, https://www.aljazeera.com/news/2020/06/slammed-saudi-coalition-child-rights-blacklist-200616061613193.html.

181   Human Rights Watch, "Yemen: Events of 2018," World Report 2018, 2019, https://www.hrw.org/world-report/2019/country-chapters/yemen.

182   Michael Laforgia and Edward Wong, "War Crime Risk Grows for U.S. Over Saudi Strikes in Yemen," *New York Times*, September 14, 2020, https://www.nytimes.com/2020/09/14/us/politics/us-war-crimes-yemen-saudi-arabia.html.

183   Marcia Robiou, "What You Need to Know About Trump's $8 Billion Saudi Arms Deal," *PBS Frontline*, July 16, 2019, https://www.pbs.org/wgbh/frontline/article/saudi-arabia-arms-deal-trump-what-to-know/.

184   Jack Detsch, "Lawmakers Demand to See the Side Deals in Trump's Arms Sales to Saudi Arabia," *Foreign Policy*, July 7, 2020, https://foreignpolicy.com/2020/07/07/trump-saudi-arabia-arms-sales-side-deals-congress-oversight-offsets/.

185   Center for Public Integrity and Andrew Cohen, "Defense Contractors Spend Millions to Overturn Limits on Military Spending," *Time Magazine*, August 5, 2015, https://time.com/3984453/defense-contractors-lobbying/.; Ben Barbour, "How 'Defense' Contractors Lobbied for War in Yemen and Reaped the Profits from Death and Destruction," *Global Research*, March 25, 2020, https://www.globalresearch.ca/how-defense-contractors-lobbied-war-yemen-reaped-profits-death-destruction/5707484.;

There are 681 defense industry lobbyists according to calculations by the Center for Responsive Politics based on data from the Senate Office of Public Records, "Sector Profile: Defense," OpenSecrets.org: Center for Responsive Politics, accessed August 30, 2020, https://www.opensecrets.org/federal-lobbying/sectors/lobbyists?cycle=2019&id=D.

186   William Hartung, "William Hartung on Press the Button," interview by Joe Cirincione, *Press the Button Podcast*, August 20, 2019 https://www.ploughshares.org/issues-analysis/article/william-hartung-press-button.

187   Martin Accad, "Another Point of View: Evangelical Blindness on Lebanon," *Christianity Today,* July 20, 2006, https://www.christianitytoday.com/ct/2006/julyweb-only/129-42.0.html.

188   Robert Wright, "60 Minutes on the Plight of Palestinian Christians," *The Atlantic*, April 23, 2012, https://www.theatlantic.com/international/archive/2012/04/60-minutes-on-the-plight-of-palestinian-christians/256218/.; Adam Horowitz, "'60 Minutes' profiles Palestinian Christians, Michael Oren falls on his face," *Mondoweiss*, April 22, 2012, https://mondoweiss.net/2012/04/60-minutes-profiles-palestinian-christians-michael-oren-falls-on-his-face-defending-israel/.

189   Martin Chulov, "Chain reaction: disaster hastens Lebanon's moment of reckoning," *The Guardian*, August 9, 2020, https://www.theguardian.com/world/2020/aug/09/chain-reaction-disaster-hastens-lebanons-moment-of-reckoning.

190   Zeina Khodr, "US sanctions Lebanese allies of Hezbollah for first time," *Al Jazeera*, September 9, 2020, https://www.aljazeera.com/news/2020/09/sanctions-lebanese-allies-hezbollah-time-200909163935890.html.

191   A key slogan of Lebanese popular mobilization in October 2019 was "Kellon ya'ne kellon" which means "All means all." Commenting on U.S. sanctions on Hezbollah allies, Nadim Houry wrote on Twitter "I don't believe this is about anti-corruption & there is a risk that a selective approach undermines broader anti-corruption drive." Nadim Houry (@NadimHoury), September 9, 2020, https://twitter.com/nadimhoury/status/1303601726285590528.

192   Johannes Reimer, "Evangelicals and populistic politics," *Evangelical Focus Europe,* August 24, 2020, https://evangelicalfocus.com/features/7693/evangelicals-and-populistic-politics.

193   Miroslav Volf, *Exclusion and Embrace*, 252.

194   For an expanded discussion on the nature and task of theology, see: Stanley J. Grenz, *Theology for the Community of God* (Grand Rapids: William B. Eerdmans Publishing Company, 2000), 1-25.

195   See: Vinoth Ramachandra, *Gods that Fail: Modern Idolatry and Christian Mission* Revised Edition (Eugene: Wipf & Stock Publishers, 2016), 1-25. Also: Nancey Murphy, *A Philosophy of the Christian Religion* (Louisville: Westminster John Knox Press, 2018), 107-124.

196   H. Richard Niebuhr tells us, "History is the laboratory in which our faith is tested," as quoted in Glen Stassen, *Living the Sermon on the Mount: A Practical Hope for Grace and Deliverance* (San Francisco: Jossey-Bass, 2006), Kindle Location 2158.

197   The late Glen Stassen--to whom I am greatly indebted--writes: "All these teachings [of Jesus] mean that we should beware of those who claim to be Christian spokespersons but whose words tell us to give our loyalty to the ruling powers. They deceive us. We are trying to beware of those who claim to speak truth but whose words try to persuade us to serve greed, war, and ethnic division. Beware of those who put before us a corporate brand, or a national flag, or a racial loyalty, or the almighty dollar, or an image of our nation that stands for goodness against another nation that stands for evil and inflames us to make war and arouses passions to serve that image rather than serve God who is revealed in Jesus Christ and the Holy Spirit." Stassen, *Living the Sermon,* Kindle Location 2125.

198   As I write, the tragic cases of notorious court prophets Jerry Falwell Jr. and Eric Metaxes are both currently in the headlines. For instance: https://www.washingtonpost.com/education/2020/08/25/fallwell-re-signs-confirmed/; and: https://thewayofimprovement.com/2020/08/28/eric-metaxas-is-caught-on-camera-throwing-a-punch-at-an-anti-trump-protester/?fbclid=IwAR2LP0x82u9g3-IhNUdgNM4-2bToDQn_GWP-3WbvGrVgkm8_-bmPtKz15yEw

199   Source unknown.

200   Accepted nomenclature with regard to the region under discussion is undergoing a transition. In light of the colonial origins of the term "Middle East," clearly referencing a British and American vantage point, the term "West Asian" has grown in popularity. "Middle East," however, is still in regular usage even within the region. The

following is an interesting reflection on this topic: https://egyptianstreets. com/2020/08/20/middle-east-of-what-on-identity-politics-and-eurocentric-definitions/?fbclid=IwAR166BnE2JX0d_eVZXvC-JjRSRLKYc-cUQzMQ-qr5JPk0rsFre2KeZ_ykfac.

201   Paraphrasing Matthew Burrows the Wikipedia entry for *mission civilisatrice,* of which Rudyard Kipling's poem "White Man's Burden" is an example, reads: "The *mission civilisatrice* (civilising mission) is a political rationale for military intervention and for colonization purporting to facilitate the modernization and the Westernization of indigenous peoples, especially in the period from the 15th to the 20th centuries." Burrows, Mathew "'*Mission civilisatrice*': French Cultural Policy in the Middle East, 1860-1914". *The Historical Journal* 29, no. 1 (1986): 109–135. https://en.wikipedia.org/wiki/Civilizing_mission.

202   Michael Safi, "Conflicts since Start of US 'War on Terror' Have Displaced 37m People–Report, *The Guardian*, September 9, 2020, https:// www.theguardian.com/us-news/2020/sep/09/conflicts-us-war-on-terror-displaced-37-million-people-report?fbclid=IwAR2Yf404y-F8zAaDZopD7va9Uq_FgpeBHM84hsHkf09BYLcXIBYnpC05W9_A.

203   One of the absolute best resources for newcomers to the history of the modern MENA is Eugene Rogan's *The Arabs: A History* Revised and Expanded Edition (New York: Basic Books, 2017).

204   In reference to a previous era, but in many ways still applicable, historian A.G. Hopkins states, "[Many] believed that the United States had a civilising mission. The US was driven to encompass the world to fulfil a benign duty, that of liberating other peoples." However, of the tendency for Americans to dismiss or downplay the extent to which their country constitutes an empire, he adds, "An ex-colonial state that advertised anti-imperial values found it difficult to accept that it had become a colonial power itself. Consequently, the US was 'in denial' when it came to its own empire, while criticising other powers that feely admitted that they ruled over colonial subjects." A.G. Hopkins, "The Best Books on American Imperialism: Recommended by A.G. Hopkins," interview by Cal Flyn, *Five Books,* 2018, https://fivebooks.com/best-books/american-imperialism-ag-hopkins/.

205   Brain Mclaren, "Post-Colonial Theology," *Sojourners*, September 15, 2010, https://sojo.net/articles/post-colonial-theology. The consultation anticipated in the above article would produce the following

book: Kay Higuera Smith, Jayachitra Lalitha and L. Daniel Hawk, eds. *Evangelical Postcolonial Conversations: Global Awakenings in Theology and Praxis* (Downers Grove: IVP Academic, 2014).

206   See: Jayachitra Lalitha, "Postcolonial Feminism, the Bible and Native Indian Women," in Kay Higuera Smith, Jayachitra Lalitha and L. Daniel Hawk, eds. *Evangelical Postcolonial Conversations: Global Awakenings in Theology and Praxis* (Downers Grove: IVP Academic, 2014), Kindle Location 1144-1359.

207   For an important counter narrative, see: Robert D. Woodberry, "The Missionary Roots of Liberal Democracy," *American Political Science Review* 106, No. 2 (May 2012): 244-274.

208   Vinoth Ramachandra tells us: "'Development' has become a neo-colonial project through which an aggressive, expanding Corporation Culture sought to establish a bridgehead among the political and commercial elites of the Majority World. The attraction of 'development' is that it has brought substantial improvements in health care, education and general well-being to scores of people in many countries. But it has, more often than not, given legitimacy to the acquisition and control of other people's resources, inevitably increasing poverty and distress under the guise of eliminating them. In the name of 'national development' (usually identified with 'the national interest') whole generations have been induced to accept enormous sacrifices in personal freedoms, the mutilation of their cultural endowments and the destruction of their physical and moral environments." Vinoth Ramachandra, *Gods that Fail: Modern Idolatry and Christian Mission* Revised Edition (Eugene: Wipf & Stock Publishers, 2016), 113.

209   Joseph Cumming, "Toward Respectful Witness," in *From Seed to Fruit: Global Trends, Fruitful Practices and Emerging Issues among Muslims*, J. Dudley Woodberry, ed. (Pasadena: William Carey Library, 2008), 320.

210   See: Mark Juergensmeyer, *Terror in the Mind of God* Fourth Edition: *The Global Rise of Religious Violence* (Oakland: University of California Press, 2017), 182-203.

211   See: Rashid Khalidi, *Sowing Crisis: The Cold War and American Dominance in the Middle East*, (Boston: Beacon Press, 2009).

212   Joseph Kip Kosek, "Review: Faith in the Cold War," review of *Religion and American Foreign Policy, 1945–1960: The Soul of Containment*, by William Inboden, *Diplomatic History* 35, No. 1 (January 2011): 125-128.

213   Cumming, "Witness," 322.

214   Bill Musk, *The Certainty Trap: Can Christians and Muslims Afford the Luxury of Fundamentalism?* (Pasadena: William Carey Library, 2008), 29-32.

215   As an experiment, I suggest re-watching Peter Jackson's *Lord of the Rings* or *The Hobbit* trilogies with this thought in mind.

216   Jim Wallis, "The Most Controversial Sentence I Ever Wrote," *Sojourners,* October 24, 2013, https://sojo.net/articles/12-years-slave/most-controversial-sentence-i-ever-wrote.

217   As quoted in Emily McFarlan Miller and Jack Jenkins, "How Trump's Republican National Convention Speech Wove Faith into the 'Great American Story,'" *Religion News Service,* August 28, 2020, https://religionnews.com/2020/08/28/how-trumps-republican-national-convention-speech-wove-faith-into-the-great-american-story/.

218   Nicholas Ferns, "Manifest Destiny Crosses the Pacific: The Utility of American Expansion in Australia, 1850-1901," *Australian Journal of American Studies* 34, no. 2 ((December 2015), pp. 28-43. Also: Rory Carroll, "Argentinian Founding Father Recast as Genocidal Murderer," *The Guardian,* January 13, 2011, https://www.theguardian.com/world/2011/jan/13/argentinian-founding-father-genocide-row.

219   André Du Toit, "Puritans in Africa? Afrikaner "Calvinism" and Kuyperian Neo-Calvinism in Late Nineteenth-Century South Africa," *Comparative Studies in Society and History* 27, no. 2 (1985): 209–240.

220   Algerian sociologist Fanny Colonna writes, "[After 1871] a coherent colonial policy, officially assimilationist, and in fact profoundly destructive, was implemented under the influence of the settlers [...] It was then that one saw the application of a whole series of measures with converging effects: the land tenure laws [...] aimed at the breakup of 'native' property and at the collapse of the tribal structures, extension of civilian administration [subjecting natives] to the power of the settlers, increase of native taxation, abolition of traditional justice, persecution of the holy lodges, and the establishment of an 'official' clergy controlled

by the state [and] the Gallicisation of place names [...] Thus one can place between 1870 and 1880 the destruction of the economic and social base of traditional society [and] the elimination of its own culture." Fanny Colonna, "Cultural Resistance and Religious Legitimacy in Colonial Algeria, *Economy and Society* 3, no. 3, (1974): 240-241.

221   Robert Fisk, "Charlie Hebdo: Paris Attack Brothers' Campaign of Terror Can Be Traced Back to Algeria in 1954," *The Independent,* January 9, 2015, https://www.independent.co.uk/voices/comment/charlie-hebdo-paris-attack-brothers-campaign-of-terror-can-be-traced-back-to-algeria-in-1954-9969184.html.

222   Although many great and not-so-great histories exist, one of the best introductions from an evangelical perspective to the myriad historical and theological dimensions of the Palestine-Israel conflict is: Colin Chapman, *Whose Promised Land? The Continuing Conflict over Israel and Palestine* (Oxford: Lion Hudson, 2015).

223   See: Steven Sizer, *Christian Zionism: Roadmap to Armageddon?* (Downers Grove: IVP Academic, 2006).

224   Colin Chapman, "A Biblical Perspective on Israel/Palestine" in *The Land Cries Out: Theology of the Land in the Israeli/Palestinian Context*, eds. Salim J. Munayer and Lisa Loden (Eugene: Wipf and Stock Publishers, 2012), 238. For a constructive approach to thinking theologically about the conflict, written from the perspective of both a Palestinian Evangelical Christian and a Messianic Israeli Jew, see: Salim J. Munayer and Lisa Loden, *Through My Enemy's Eyes: Envisioning Reconciliation in Israel-Palestine* (Milton Keynes: Paternoster, 2014).

225   In what were perhaps the most eye-opening and personally transformative paragraphs of my seminary career (in the mid-aughts), Glen Stassen and David Gushee wrote, "Here is the problem. Christian churches across the theological and confessional spectrum [...] are often guilty of evading Jesus, the cornerstone and center of the Christian faith [...] This evasion of the concrete ethical teachings of Jesus has seriously malformed Christian moral practices, moral beliefs, and moral witness. Jesus taught that the test of our discipleship is whether we act on his teachings, whether we "put into practice" his words [...] And so it is no overstatement to claim that the evasion of the teachings of Jesus constitutes a crisis of Christian identity and raises the question of who exactly is functioning as the Lord of the church. When Jesus's way of discipleship is thinned down, marginalized, or avoided, then churches

and Christians lose their antibodies against infection by secular ideologies that manipulate Christians into serving the purposes of some other lord. We fear precisely that kind of idolatry now." Glen Stassen and David Gushee, *Kingdom Ethics: Following Jesus in Contemporary Context* (Downers Grove: Eerdmans, 2016), xi.

226   Elizabeth Dias, "'Christianity Will Have Power,'" *The New York Times,* August 8, 2020, https://www.nytimes.com/2020/08/09/us/evangelicals-trump-christianity.html?auth=linked-google&fbclid=IwAR3SjpTR5CbTkEaNYWirj7YdV89dS3WgeoGFeRNXU4IoL5ymdqCrICp-KazE.

227   Relevant Staff, "Mike Pence Swapped out 'Jesus' for 'Old Glory' in his RNC Address," *Relevant,* August 27, 2020, https://relevantmagazine.com/culture/vice-president-mike-pence-swapped-out-jesus-for-old-glory-in-his-rnc-address/.

228   "Therefore, since we are surrounded by such a huge crowd of witnesses to the life of faith, let us strip off every weight that slows us down, especially the sin that so easily trips us up. And let us run with endurance the race God has set before us. We do this by keeping our eyes on Jesus, the champion who initiates and perfects our faith. Because of the joy awaiting him, he endured the cross, disregarding its shame. Now he is seated in the place of honor beside God's throne. Think of all the hostility he endured from sinful people; then you won't become weary and give up" (Heb. 12:1-3, NLT).

229   The phrase "chaplains to the status quo" is not original. For instance: Rev. William Alberts, "Prophets of the People or Chaplains of the Status Quo?" *Counterpunch,* June 19, 2015, https://www.counterpunch.org/2015/06/19/prophets-of-the-people-or-chaplains-of-the-status-quo/.

230   As Cornel West writes, "We are witnessing the postmodern version of the full-scale gangsterization of the world. The reign of Obama did not produce the nightmare of Donald Trump – but it did contribute to it. And those Obama cheerleaders who refused to make him accountable bear some responsibility." Cornel West, "Pity the Sad Legacy of Barack Obama," *The Guardian,* January 9, 2017, https://www.theguardian.com/commentisfree/2017/jan/09/barack-obama-legacy-presidency.

231   Cumming, "Witness," 322-3.

232   Bad Theology Kills: How We Justify Killing Arabs," IMES Blog, April 17, 2014, https://abtslebanon.org/2014/04/17/bad-theology-kills-how-we-justify-killing-arabs/.

233   Luke Brinker, "Mike Huckabee: There's no such thing as the Palestinians," *Salon*, Feb 24, 2015, https://www.salon.com/2015/02/24/mike_huckabee_theres_no_such_thing_as_the_palestinians/.

234   See: Shane Claiborne, *Common Prayer: A Liturgy for Ordinary Radicals* (Grand Rapids: Zondervan, 2010), 217.

235   Jeanelle Austin, Marcia Howard, and Madi Ramirez-Tentinger, eds. "Justice Resolution with Addendum.pdf." Google Drive. Google, August 12, 2020. https://drive.google.com/file/d/1imey1mzBoCn-mhaV1JhQ5GPy1dfqeTEL8/view?usp=drivesdk. "Resolution 001" (Unpublished manuscript, August 7, 2020), Google Doc, bit.ly/george-floydsquare-a.

236   Larry Buchanan, Quoctrung Bui, and Jugal K. Patel, "Black Lives Matter May Be the Largest Movement in U.S. History," *The New York Times,* July 3, 2020, https://www.nytimes.com/interactive/2020/07/03/us/george-floyd-protests-crowd-size.html.

237   Timothy Keller, "A Biblical Critique of Secular Justice and Critical Theory," *Life in the Gospel,* August 2020, https://quarterly.gospelinlife.com/a-biblical-critique-of-secular-justice-and-critical-theory/.

238   Millard J. Erickson, *Truth or Consequences: The Promise & Perils of Postmodernism*, (Downers Grove, IVP Academic, 2001).

239   Tim Muehlhoff and Todd Lewis, *Authentic Communication: Christian Speech Engaging Culture,* (Downers Grove: IVP Academic, 2010).

240   Quoted by Tim Muehlhoff and Todd Lewis, *Authentic Communication: Christian Speech Engaging Culture,* (Downers Grove: IVP Academic, 2010).

241   "Jefferson's Religious Beliefs", *TH Jefferson Monticello*, https://www.monticello.org/site/research-and-collections/jeffersons-religious-beliefs.

242   "Immanuel Kant", *Stanford Encyclopedia of Philosophy*, July 28, 2020, https://plato.stanford.edu/entries/kant/#:~:text=The%20fundamental%20idea%20of%20Kant's,1790)%20%E2%80%93%20is%20human%20autonomy.

243   Walter Truett Anderson ed., *The Truth About the Truth: De-confusing and Re-constructing the Postmodern World*, (New York: Tarcher/Putnam, 1995), 268.

244   Valerie Strauss, "Report: Public schools more segregated now than 40 years ago", *The Washington Post*, August 29, 2013,

https://www.washingtonpost.com/news/answer-sheet/wp/2013/08/29/report-public-schools-more-segregated-now-than-40-years-ago/.

245   Richard Delgado & Jean Stefancic, *Critical Race Theory: An Introduction* (New York Press; 2001), 3.

246   Richard Delgado and Jean Stefancic, "Critical Race Theory", *New Dictionary of the History of Ideas, Encyclopedia.com, August 11, 2020*, https://www.encyclopedia.com/social-sciences-and-law/sociology-and-social-reform/sociology-general-terms-and-concepts/critical-race-theory.

247   SNCC Digital Gateway, "Red-Baiting", *SNCC Digital Gateway*, accessed September 16, 2020, https://snccdigital.org/inside-sncc/international-connections/red-baiting/.

248   Stanford: The Martin Luther King, Jr. Research and Education Institute, "Communism", The King Encyclopedia, accessed September 16, 2020, https://kinginstitute.stanford.edu/encyclopedia/communism.

249   Andy Crouch, *Playing God: Redeeming The Gift of Power,* (IVP, 2013), 126.

250   Ibram X. Kendi, *Stamped from the Beginning: The Definitive History of Racist Ideas in America,* (Bold Type Books, 2016), 52.

251   Qtd in James Eglinton, James Eglinton WordPress, June 5, 2020, https://jameseglinton.wordpress.com/2020/06/05/bavinck-on-racism-in-america/.

252   Martin Luther King Jr., Letter from a Birmingham Jail, April 16, 1963, https://www.africa.upenn.edu/Articles_Gen/Letter_Birmingham.html.

253   "We are expansive. We are a collective of liberators who believe in an inclusive and spacious movement", Qtd from Black Lives Matter, "About", *Black Lives Matter,* https://blacklivesmatter.com/about/.

254   Jemar Tisby, *The Color of Compromise: The Truth about the American Church's Complicity in Racism,* (Grand Rapids: Zondervan, 2019), 24.

255   And Campaign, *About (&),* 2020, www.andcampaign.org.

256   Qtd. In Martin Luther King Jr., *Strength to Love,* (Minneapolis: Fortress Press, 2010), 49.

257   Ibid, 47.

258   Ibid, 45.

259   Sabra Ayres, "Does Trump's 'Silent Majority' Really Exist?", Spectrum News NY1, September 3, 2020, https://www.ny1.com/nyc/all-boroughs/news/2020/09/03/trumps-silent-majority-texas.

260   Brenda Major, Alison Blodorn, and Gregory Major Blascovich, "The threat of increasing ddiversity: why many White Americans support Trump in the 2016 presidential election," *Group Processes & Intergroup Relations* 21, no. 6 (2016): pp. 931-940, https://doi.org/10.1177/1368430216677304.

261   Wikipedia, The Free Encyclopedia, s.v. "History of Chinese Americans," last modified August 27, 2020, 18:11, https://en.wikipedia.org/wiki/History_of_Chinese_Americans.

262   Erika Lee, *America for Americans: A History of Xenophobia in the United States* (New York: Basic Books, 2019), 89.

263   Claire Jean Kim, "The Racial Triangulation of Asian Americans," *Politics & Society* 27, no. 1 (1999): pp. 105-138, https://doi.org/10.1177/0032329299027001005.

264   Lee gives details about the Coolie Trade Act of 1862 and the 1875 Page Act which preceded the 1882 Chinese Exclusion act, 81-93.

265   Erika Lee, *The Making of Asian America: A History* (New York: Simon & Schuster, 2015).

266   Ibid., 171.

267   Lothrop Stoddard, *The Rising Tide of Color Against White World-Supremacy* (New York: Charles Scribner's Sons, 1920).

268   Amy Chua, *Battle Hymn of the Tiger Mother* (New York: Penguin Books, 2011).

269   William Petersen, "Success Story, Japanese-American Style," *The New York Times Magazine*, January 6, 1966, 20ff.

270   Kim, "Racial Triangulation," 119-122.

271   Sarah Soonling Blackburn, "What Is the Model Minority Myth?," Teaching Tolerance, March 31, 2019, https://www.tolerance.org/magazine/what-is-the-model-minority-myth.

272   Candace J. Chow, "Raced Curriculum: Asian American College Students' Lives," in Bic Ngo and Kevin K. Kumashiro, *Six Lenses for Anti-Oppressive Education: Partial Stories, Improbable Conversations* (New York: Peter Lang, 2014), p. 87. Even academically under achieving students have internalized the "model minority" myth and respond to this script. See also Stacey J. Lee, "Behind the Model-Minority Stereotype: Voices of High- and Low-Achieving Asian American Students," *Anthropology & Education Quarterly* 25, no. 4 (1994): pp. 413-429, https://doi.org/10.1525/aeq.1994.25.4.04x0530j.

273   Sharon Noguchi, "High grades, high stress for Asian-American students in Bay Area," *The Mercury News*, August 14, 2016, https://www.mercurynews.com/2009/01/02/high-grades-high-stress-for-asian-american-students-in-bay-area/.

274   Chow, "Raced Curriculum," 87.

275   Kim, 119.

276   Another facet of triangulation is that Asian sub-groups are also pitted against one another to see who will emerge on top.

277   Kim, 118-122.

278   Deb Riechmann, "Trump dubs COVID-19 'Chinese Virus' despite hate crime risks," *AP NEWS*, March 18, 2020, https://apnews.com/a7c233f0b3bcdb72c06cca6271ba6713.

279   "Attacks Against AAPI Community Continue to Rise During Pandemic," *Asianpacificplanningandpolicycouncil.org*, August 27, 2020, http://www.asianpacificpolicyandplanningcouncil.org/wp-content/uploads/PRESS_RELEASE_National-Report_August27_2020.pdf.

280   Taylor Romine, "NYPD Creates Asian Hate Crime Task Force after spike in Anti-Asian attacks during Covid-19 pandemic," *CNN*, August 19, 2020), https://www.cnn.com/2020/08/18/us/nypd-asian-hate-crime-task-force/index.html.

281   Nina Strochlic, "America's long history of scapegoating its Asian citizens," *National Geographic*, September 4, 2020, https://www.nationalgeographic.com/history/2020/09/asian-american-racism-covid/?cmpid=org.

282   "Mount Sinai Study Finds First Cases of COVID-19 in New York City Are Primarily from European and US Sources," June 2, 2020, https://www.mountsinai.org/about/newsroom/2020/mount-sinai-study-finds-first-cases-of-covid-19-in-new-york-city-are-primarily-from-european-and-us-sources-pr.

283   Adrian Florido and Marisa Peñaloza, "As Nation Reckons with Race, Poll Finds White Americans Least Engaged," *NPR*, August 27, 2020, https://www.npr.org/2020/08/27/906329303/as-nation-reckons-with-race-poll-finds-white-americans-least-engaged?utm_source=npr_newsletter.

284   Ibid.

285   Ibid.

286   For further explanation of Black disprivilege, see Andrew Lee, "Standing Between White Privilege and Black Disprivilege: An Asian American Perspective," *The Exchange | A Blog by Ed Stetzer*, June 18, 2020, https://www.christianitytoday.com/edstetzer/2020/june/standing-between-white-privilege-and-black-disprivilege-asi.html.

287   Andrew Yang, "Opinion | Andrew Yang: We Asian Americans are not the virus, but we can be part of the cure," *The Washington Post,* April 8, 2020, https://www.washingtonpost.com/opinions/2020/04/01/andrew-yang-coronavirus-discrimination/.

288   Ibid.

289   Kim, 126.

290   Stuart Anderson, "Immigrants and America's Comeback from the COVID-19 Crisis," NFAP Policy Brief (*National Foundation for American Policy*, July 2020), https://nfap.com/wp-content/uploads/2020/07/Immigrants-and-Americas-Comeback-From-The-Covid-19-Crisis. NFAP-Policy-Brief.July-2020.pdf.

291   Ibid.

292   Ibid., quotation from Ali Noorani, executive director of the National Immigration Forum.

293   Tom Cullen, "Evangelicals see Trump as a way to get what they want after decades of defeat," *The Guardian*, February 1, 2020, https://www.theguardian.com/us-news/2020/feb/01/evangelicals-trump-policy-defeat-us-election-2020-christians.

294   Tim Levin, "Rep. Val Demings Says President Trump Was 'walking around with a gasoline can' while 'America was on fire' during civil unrest," *Business Insider*, September 6, 2020), https://www.businessinsider.com/rep-val-demings-trump-gasoline-can-protests-2020-9.

295   Chris Jackson and Mallory Newall, "Most Americans say Trump making protests, unrest worse," *Ipsos*, September 4, 2020, https://www.ipsos.com/en-us/news-polls/abc-Trump-Biden-protest.

296   Michael Cohen, *Disloyal: A Memoir: The True Story of the Former Personal Attorney to President Donald J. Trump* (New York: Skyhorse Publishing, 2020).

297   Maggie Haberman, "Trump Moves to Cancel Contracts for Government Sensitivity Training," *The New York Times*, September 5, 2020, https://www.nytimes.com/2020/09/04/us/politics/trump-race-sensitivity-training.html.

298   CBS News, "Trump Dismisses Question on White Privilege: 'You Really Drank the Kool-Aid,'" 60 Minutes Overtime, September 10, 2020, https://www.cbsnews.com/news/trump-bob-woodward-george-floyd-black-lives-matter-60-minutes-2020-09-10/.

299   Peter Baker, "More Than Ever, Trump Casts Himself as the Defender of White America," *The New York Times*, September 6, 2020, https://www.nytimes.com/2020/09/06/us/politics/trump-race-2020-election.html?action=click.

Made in the USA
Middletown, DE
07 October 2020

21320314R00196